EYE OF THE HURRICANE

EYE OF THE HURRICANE

THE ALEX HIGGINS STORY

JOHN HENNESSEY

MAINSTREAM
PUBLISHING

EDINBURGH AND LONDON

First published in Great Britain in 2000 by

MAINSTREAM PUBLISHING COMPANY (EDINBURGH) LTD

7 Albany Street

Edinburgh EH1 3UG

ISBN 1 84018 385 3

A catalogue record for this book is available from the British Library

Typeset in ACaslon and Plantin MT

Printed and bound in Great Britain by Butler and Tanner Ltd, Frome and London

CONTENTS

	Introduction	7
1	Jam-packed Beginnings	13
2	The Learning Game	22
3	The Final Flourish	31
4	New Dawn	41
5	Back to Reality	49
6	The Long Road Back	60
7	Black and Blue all Over	71
8	Return of the Good Years	88
9	The Down Side	109
10	Born Again	116
11	Simply the Best	130
12	Simply the Worst	142
13	Pride of Ireland	150
14	The Absolute Pits	160
15	Hanging On	176
16	The End is Nigh	188
17	Last Cut is the Deepest	207
18	If Only	223

INTRODUCTION

Alex 'Hurricane' Higgins – the very nickname conjures thoughts of turmoil, high-speed fear, danger and destruction. It tells you this is no ordinary man, no ordinary sportsman. In fact, the little Irish genius, who transformed the history of snooker, almost transcended it as well. Little did his first manager, John McLaughlin, know – when he bestowed on the young, feisty Higgins that label after watching him tear round the table at breakneck speed – just how apt it was to prove over the next 30 years.

Tragically, the Belfast man walked hand in hand with trauma and triumph throughout an astonishing career which spanned four decades, yet realised nothing like the rewards – monetary or otherwise – it should have done. Even more tragically, it was his own fault to a large degree. And today, 51-year-old Higgins, who survived a throat cancer operation in 1998, has all but wasted away. Just like his once-supreme talent. He sits restlessly on the sidelines, flitting painfully between his native Belfast (where two sisters live) and his adopted Manchester, recounting the fact that arch-enemy Steve Davis and '90s legend Stephen Hendry have collected 13 world titles between them, shared more than 140 major crowns and will never have to work again if the mood so takes them.

Poor, two-times world champion Higgy can number his successes on the fingers of two hands – and his reserves probably on one digit. Potless, penniless, beset with health problems and no longer pursuing a long-standing battle for cash compensation from the World Professional Billiards and Snooker Association (WPBSA) after being ripped off by an unscrupulous manager . . . he must wonder where it all went wrong. For all his faults, for all the trouble in which he has landed because of his outspoken views and, at times, obnoxious behaviour bordering on insanity, he is the best-loved player of all.

Ann Yates was for years the most powerful woman in British sport as professional snooker's tournament director. Now retired to her native Co. Cork, she has sympathy but nothing good to say about Higgins. 'The little rat made my life a misery,' she says. 'He tormented me for ten years at every opportunity and I was forced to batten down the hatches whenever he came looking for an argument – which was pretty often.'

Higgins is way past the twilight of his halcyon days and now unable even to wield his once-golden cue to any effect. His wondrous, nay unique, talent ebbed away in the early '90s and he is never seen on TV today. Yet he still has an adoring audience, ever-willing to forgive him his trespasses. Never mind the hundreds of people he must have upset in his time, he is loved by millions in Britain and the Republic of Ireland. Put him on a kitchen table with a kiddy's set of snooker balls and a sharpened broomstick for a cue and he will still draw a bigger crowd than Davis, Hendry et al.

Don't take my word for it. Jimmy 'Whirlwind' White, his protégé and the man who inherited his mantle as People's Champion, says with feeling: 'Alex is the greatest player who has ever lived. I'm supposed to have influenced a generation of youngsters, but Alex influenced me, everyone. There's never been anyone to touch him – and there never will be.' White, one of the few people to stand by the fallen idol throughout his troubled times, adds with a smile: 'But he's a nightmare to be with unless he's on top . . . unless he's winning.' Even Steve Davis, his most bitter 'enemy', describes him as 'the only true genius the game has ever had'.

Higgins, said to have been banned from more hotels and clubs than he could possibly remember – including Blackpool's Norbreck Castle, where the main tour qualifying events used to be held – even got himself turfed out of White's local in Surrey on one memorable occasion. White left Alex supping a pint and nipped out for an hour or so on business. When he returned he found his pal standing outside the pub: he had been banned, not just from there, but from the bookmaker across the road as well. The publican said, 'I'm really sorry, Jimmy, but we just couldn't take any more of him.'

Jimmy's wife, Maureen, who had put up with countless visits from Higgins, snapped after extending the family's hospitality to the Hurricane (I've no doubt some arm-twisting had been applied by the Whirlwind) and threw him out late at night. She last saw him staggering down their long driveway towards God knows where. 'The next morning,' recalls Maureen, 'Alex was on the phone bright and breezy as though nothing had happened. He just said, "Hello babes, is James available, please?" I just laughed and shook my head. What can you say about him? He can drive you to distraction one minute and have you in stitches the next.'

The mighty Ray Reardon, six times world champion in the '70s and still playing exhibitions to the delight of his fans, says: 'Alex invented shots the rest of us could only dream about. He was an incredible player who opened people's eyes to the game. He could play every kind of side except suicide. Mind you, he'd worn out three bodies by the time he was 35 because of his excessive lifestyle. But what a player, what a character, what an opponent.'

John Spencer, another legendary figure who lost his world crown to young upstart Higgins in a stunning 1972 reversal, says: 'Alex proved you didn't always need coaches to improve your game. He did everything wrong on the table, yet was without doubt one of the greatest players ever.'

There's hardly a top player from the '70s and '80s who does not have a Higgins story – good, funny or bad. But everyone loved to play him because it was pure showbiz from the moment he strutted into the arena, playing to the gallery with outrageous shots and pots and always giving his rivals a chance to add the biggest notch of all to their guns. He was one of my three sporting idols, alongside Muhammad Ali and George Best, and to this day – 21 years on – I can recall his exact words when we shook hands for the first time at the 1980 Benson & Hedges Masters at Wembley. After I had introduced myself proudly as the *Daily Mail*'s first snooker correspondent, he told me: 'I can play shots the others can't even dream about, babes – and if we're going to be friends, you have to be honest with me and don't make things up. If I get in trouble, give me a fighting chance to put my side of the story before you write anything.'

The formula worked brilliantly for 15 years. Alex, inevitably, got into more hot spots than was good for him. These included butting WPBSA tournament director Paul Hatherell; punching harmless press officer Colin Randle in the stomach for no reason after losing a first-round world championship match at Sheffield; threatening journalists with physical violence; warning Dennis Taylor he'd have him shot; sparking punch-ups with other players and spectators; and committing a host of other 'crimes'. I always felt our friendship would stand the test of time because, over the years, I'd always been sympathetic to him in print and in person.

I enjoyed his company and spent many a long hour enthralled by his tales. He was a fine raconteur, then. But it couldn't last – nothing ever did with Alex, as several players and pressmen warned me. We had our one and only bust-up after his farewell appearance at the Crucible Theatre in the 1994 world championship. Higgins had been beaten 10–6 by young Ken Doherty (a fellow-Irishman from Dublin who had idolised him as a kid and still looked up to him) and had rowed with referee John Williams, one of several officials with whom he never saw eye-to-eye. I had the impertinence to ask why he had persisted in arguing when it was obvious the senior referee would not change his mind. His response, after reams and reams of waffle and a heated debate between the two of us, was to snort: 'The only Hennessey I talk to these days is cognac – three star.'

These after-match press conferences are broadcast around the Crucible Theatre on monitors and Jimmy told me it had provided great late-night entertainment in the players' room. But I was heartbroken because I'd always discussed things rationally with Alex, either over a pint in private or during press conferences. Yet I was confident we would make up when next we met – only to be told by a pal, 'Higgins says you've gone over to the other side.'

In fact, some years later, thanks to Jimmy, I did my damnedest through my employers, Express Newspapers, to get Alex a handsome sum of money for telling his tragic story about the cancer operation he faced. But after several days of negotiations, he left bewildered a top reporter who thought she'd seen everything, from famines to wars, after leading her a merry dance through the streets of Manchester with much subterfuge. Finally, he asked his harassed bank manager, 'How long will it take for this cheque to clear?'

'Today's Thursday, so with the weekend coming up it will take seven days,' came the reply.

'Seven days?' croaked Higgins. 'I haven't got seven minutes,' and he promptly threw away £13,000 for a one-hour interview. The reporter, armed now with an exclusive Higgins story which had cost her not a penny, went back to the *Express* office in Manchester and wrote the next day's centre-page spread.

For years I harboured a dream to write a warts-and-all book about the Hurricane because I'd heard dozens of tales from players – many hilarious – and lived through some of his adventures myself. And when he threatened to have me shot following the cheque incident, I felt this was probably as good a time as any to do it. You never know!

My grateful thanks are due to the unstinting efforts of good pal, snooker businessman and fan Freddie Madden: through his Global Visions company, he commissioned *Eye of the Hurricane*, trusted me to produce the book and worked tirelessly to get it off the ground. Clive Everton, the accepted critical voice of snooker, helped me so much in my early years. Journalists Terry Smith and John Dee have been superb allies and friends over 21 years, while Roger Lee, the world's leading snooker and billiards historian, joke-teller and impressionist extraordinaire, also pitched in with valuable material. Phil Yates, star of *Snooker Scene*, TV and a million other outlets, has always been a terrific sounding-board.

Former WPBSA tournament director Ann Yates (the headmistress) gave me some terrific tales and also kept me on the straight and narrow (well, almost) over a sometimes fiery two decades, during which we forged a lasting friendship. My thanks extend also to the many players who have befriended and trusted me over the years – John Spencer, Ray Reardon, Willie Thorne, John Virgo, Jim Meadowcroft, Tony Knowles, Steve Davis, Stephen Hendry and Jimmy White among them – and who have provided me with so much help and so many insights into the most complex sportsman there has ever been. Finally, my special thanks to Val Sainsbury, who read and reread every word and 'bullied' me into writing every day for eight months.

John Dee told me during my research for the book, 'Your trouble will be what to put in and what to leave out, because there are a million Alex Higgins tales.' I trust I have found enough to keep you entertained, so here is the Hurricane, warts and all. Fasten your seat belts and hang on tightly.

John Hennessey
September 2000

One

JAM-PACKED BEGINNINGS

'My baby, my baby!' he cried. The new World Snooker Champion had only one thought on his mind as he lifted the 1982 title in front of an ecstatic Crucible Theatre crowd. Alex Higgins had done it again, ten years after his first triumph at Sheffield, and was desperate to share the magical moment with his family. His beautiful wife, Lynn, dressed in a blue chiffon dress and carrying baby Lauren, stepped into the arena to be with her husband.

It was a memorable scene and the photograph, used in countless newspapers and magazines across the world ever since, never fails to bring a smile to my face. Hours earlier, prompted by Higgins, I had helped him fuel up on vodka and Coca-Cola to withstand the mighty challenge of the evergreen Ray Reardon. And hours afterwards, during Alex's celebration party back at the Grosvenor House Hotel, I spilled a pint of bitter all over Lynn's dress – accidentally, of course – and she was still too excited to be upset.

I was in my element. My long-time hero had regained the world title he cherished after so many abortive attempts; and there I was, chatting away with him until dawn. He must have gone through at least one bottle of vodka during the final day and God knows what else afterwards. At 5 a.m. Lynn had disappeared and Alex leaned over and asked, 'Am I drunk?' Astonishingly, he looked and sounded stone-cold sober, and I told him so. 'We've had a big row because she thinks I am pissed and she's stormed off to bed,' said the Hurricane.

World exclusive? Hold the front page? Not in those heady, fun days as snooker imposed itself on a TV-hooked nation – via such characters as Higgins, 1980 champion Cliff 'The Grinder' Thorburn, '79 champ Terry 'Griff' Griffiths, '81 title-holder Steve 'The Nugget' Davis, six-times champion Ray 'Dracula' Reardon, the emerging Jimmy 'Whirlwind' White, and so many others who became household names in next to no time.

The self-styled People's Champion had struck again and millions were celebrating all over Britain. Who cared about a silly row anyway? Little did I know that the rot was to start setting in soon after that. Lynn and Alex split up the following year for the first time; then she left him, acrimoniously, some time after the birth of their son, Jordan. Little did I know, either, that our friendship was to disintegrate 12 years on, after what was to be his final appearance at the Crucible. But that's for much later.

The rise of Higgins began in Belfast in the early 1960s and, almost in the blink of an eye, reached hurricane force within a decade. There's no doubt that he revolutionised the game and gave it to the masses. Where there had been dingy billiard halls after the Second World War, posh snooker centres began to spring up all over the British Isles. Where those on the dole used to sit around watching, playing or just drinking the odd cup of tea to keep out of the cold, now people from all walks of life flocked to the new-wave centres, which were complete with dining areas and bars where the wives could sit and natter in comfort while their partners enjoyed their snooker.

It was a far cry from the austere '40s and '50s, as Britain got back on an even footing slowly but surely after the war. Food rationing was gradually phased out and food became available more readily. Those of you who are old enough to recall sweet coupons may also remember the huge type of glass jar which housed jam and was worth threepence in old money (just over 1p) when empty, washed and returned to the local grocer. It also paid for a frame of snooker in one particular club – the Jampot – just off Belfast's Donegall Road. The mystery of what went on behind the closed doors there captivated an excitable nine-year-old who passed by on his way to school every day for years. Alexander Gordon Higgins was transfixed by the coloured balls and the 'sticks' used to push them around the green-topped tables and into the six pockets at the Jampot – and life would never again be the same for that skinny wee kid. Today, tragically, having scaled the heights, Alex finds his world is in shreds. Where he once enjoyed the luxury of up-market hotels and homes, the only roof over his head now is a bungalow in Lisburn – some five miles outside Belfast – populated mainly by pensioners. Higgins, recalling his early days and meteoric elevation in the game with Brough Scott in the *Sunday Telegraph*, said: 'I found I had an eye to watch people, to look at their actions. I was very good at memorising things, people's mistakes, the rights as well as wrongs . . . that if you hit the ball in this direction, perhaps you might create something. Improvisation, I suppose, like Lester Piggott in the St Leger on Ribero.'

The horseracing analogy is particularly apt because, by his own admission, Higgins has blown a fortune on so many nags which just haven't run as fast as he, on many occasions, has done to the nearest betting shop. Horseracing is still one of his favourite subjects. I once told him at Kildare, during the B&H Irish Masters, that my kid sister owned a horse called African Chimes which had won quite a few times. Alex immediately rattled off: 'Used to be a syndicate horse, now owned by Wheatley, ridden by Emma O'Gorman, trained by her father Bill at Newmarket with 18 wins.'

In that *Sunday Telegraph* interview Alex added, almost as an excuse for much of his outrageous behaviour over the years, 'I'm a product of the '60s, which spawned a few wild characters, and I suppose I grew up with a lack of respect for authority – and it's been with me ever since. I've been off-beam hundreds of times, but I'm not some sort of nutcase.'

Sadly, some would argue with that assumption because that is the very impression he has portrayed so often – especially in recent years when he has dominated headlines for all the wrong reasons. A look through his press cuttings makes for horrifying reading. Falling out of a first-floor window and breaking his ankle . . . being stabbed by a girlfriend . . . mugged while extracting money from a cashpoint machine in the early hours of the morning . . . stabbed by the same girlfriend after living in her back-garden caravan . . . attacked by a man wielding an iron bar (apparently) . . . The catalogue of woe appears endless since his fall from snooker grace; and each twist on the downward spiral either adds to, or subtracts from, his legendary status, depending on how you view the faded Hurricane.

Little did Harry McMillan know, when he let young Higgins step into his spit-and-sawdust establishment, that he had a world snooker champion in the making. The quick-witted youngster took the best of everyone's game in the Jampot, then moulded his own phenomenal skills around them. He was soon bunking off school at every opportunity – just as protégé Jimmy White was to do in Tooting, years later – and within three years he was earning up to £7 a week. This was a fortune in those days, especially for a 12-year-old kid. As little Sandy (his family's pet name) grew older, he realised that the beckoning shipyards of Belfast were not for him – but neither was snooker, because he knew there was a limit to how much hustling could be done locally.

At the age of 15, Alex answered a newspaper advert for a stable lad at Eddie Reavey's Berkshire stable in East Hendred, near Wantage – and his life took an amazing turn. Amazing, because he'd never even sat astride a horse, yet Higgins recalls having an affinity with our four-legged friends. At just under 7st he was an ideal weight for riding out, and he dreamed of being the next Piggott.

'Yes, I had my dreams,' he says today. 'A young boy going across the water . . . I think I'd have had the hands for it – and hands and eye and feet co-ordination, which is the link to every sport. But I didn't get the chance. Mrs Hilary was the stable cook and her breakfasts took me up to 9st 7lb in two years.'

That wasn't the only drawback. Alas, 5 a.m. starts and mountains of manure to shift daily hardly suited the Belfast kid, who sought regular comfort in the betting shop opposite the stables. Thus the dream was over before it had even reached the track, even though Ronnie Harper, sports journalist and snooker correspondent with the *Belfast Telegraph*, recalls clearly that Alex told him he had one mount, at Haydock Park.

There was another factor, explained by Eddie Reavey's wife, Jocelyn, in the 1986 Higgins autobiography *Alex Through the Looking-Glass*: Eddie, being from Northern Ireland, 'went out of his way to take on Belfast lads. But I could see the same self-destruct instinct in Alex that I'd noticed in Eddie. Ulstermen seem to have a terrible death wish about them.' She goes on in the book to describe Alex as 'a nice lad underneath. He had ability as a horseman but no staying power. As a worker he was well nigh hopeless and specialised in being a general pest. He was just a starved rat from the slums, yet he was very good to me after Eddie died, and kept in touch.'

A damning indictment, indeed. But Higgins still had the snooker bug and he headed for Leytonstone, on the fringe of London's East End, where he worked in a paper mill and otherwise honed his skills on the snooker table. A year later he was back with his family, but that London spell had improved his game no end. His first century break followed swiftly at the age of 17½ (kids are knocking them in at 12 and under these days), by which time he was playing tough, league snooker for Belfast YMCA.

By 1968 he was crowned Northern Ireland amateur champion, then all-Ireland champ after beating the Republic winner. A year later he was leading Belfast YMCA to a sensational victory in the Players No. 6 UK Team Trophy against Glamorgan's Penygraig Labour Club at Bolton – the first time he had performed competitively outside Ireland – and it was to change his life forever. John Pulman, rated one of the all-time greats, who was able to bridge the gap successfully between the Joe Davis era and modern snooker, presented Higgins with the trophy. He was then beaten by the youngster in an exhibition frame.

It gave Higgins a taste of what might be. His performance that night was noted by *Bolton Evening News* journalist Vince Laverty (a great pal of John Spencer, who had just become World Professional Champion). It was also noted by another aspiring snooker youngster, Lancastrian Jim Meadowcroft, who recalls in his book *Higgins, Taylor and Me*:

> I'd heard from a friend how good he was . . . Just how good I discovered that night. Alex was team captain and he sent in Billy Caughey first in the three-man event to do battle with Terry Parsons, the Welsh amateur title-holder who, years later, became world amateur champion.

16

And that's how Terry played that night. The scores were based on aggregates and by the time he'd finished with Billy over their two frames, the Irish lads were trailing by 154 points. Enter the man who was, in the space of three years, to put modern snooker on the map. Alex opened with a 56 break against John Shepherd, and when he finally sat down, the Belfast team were a few points ahead and I'd just witnessed the most amazing snooker I'd ever seen . . . He had the ability to crash home balls from all the angles. We spoke briefly afterwards and he said he was planning to return permanently to England, but I couldn't believe it when he arrived at my club in Blackburn a few weeks later. Of all the places he could have picked, he chose the one where I practised daily with Dennis Taylor. And it didn't take him long to get established after he moved into a little flat above a newsagent's just by our Post Office Club (also known as the Benarth).

Little did Meadowcroft know then that Higgins hadn't just arrived in the area on spec. A shiver had run down the spine of Laverty when he saw Higgins in action: he knew instinctively that this lad had the ability to make a big impact in England because he played unheard of snooker – raw and aggressive. It was to be the start of a legend, the like of which snooker had never seen. And never will see again.

*

VINCE LAVERTY
Local Bolton reporter who helped bring Higgins over to start his pro career.

I was working on the *Bolton Evening Telegraph* as a sports reporter and I was also wrapped up in snooker because I played to a fair level myself. John Spencer and I had been in the side who had won the Lancashire team championship for about nine years and through that and my job we became great pals.

I went along to cover the Players No. 6 final for my paper at the Bolton Institute of Technology. Like everyone else in the area, I'd heard about Alex's exploits with the Belfast team, written about them in my preview for the big clash, and couldn't wait to see him in action. What I saw was a real eye-opener. I'd written a feature about Joe Davis, the God of snooker, only recently and I can remember Joe telling me players should go for shots only if they had an 80:20 chance of potting them. But here was this 20-year-old going for just about everything that night and most of the time it came off for him. The crowd loved it because none of them had ever seen snooker being played like that.

I never spoke with Alex that night, but his performance got me thinking and I called John to tell him all about this great people-puller. Don't forget, even the top players didn't earn fortunes in those days and when John, who had won the world professional championship the previous month, raised his exhibition fees to 12 guineas [£12.60] a night , there was an uproar. All the players were happy to earn a few quid here and there in money matches, and perhaps the odd £200 for winning a tournament, which would be spread over a few days, even a week.

But I discussed with John and local promoter Jimmy Worsley the idea of inviting Alex back to Bolton for a big five-day challenge match, over 41 frames. I could see us all getting a decent pay-day out of it, as well as giving Alex a chance to come back over. I got his address from someone and wrote to his mum with an all-expenses-paid invite. She replied, saying Alex was all for it and within days, it seemed, I was meeting this frail-looking kid at Bolton's Trinity Station.

We hired the same Institute of Technology hall at £25 for the week and set it all up properly with tiered seating and accommodation for about 600 fans. Word spread rapidly and before we knew it, we had a sell-out on our hands with tickets at 10 bob [50p] a shout. And, of course, it was a raging success. Not even John, a renowned long potter, could cope with Alex's swashbuckling style.

He played like the Errol Flynn of snooker and beat John 23–18 over the week, having received a two-black start per frame, as was the norm when top amateurs took on the pros. Alex had already heard that Lancashire was a real hotbed for snooker, with the likes of the up-and-coming John Virgo on the scene in Manchester. John Spencer and I also had a good tickle, earning about £140 each. But we had reckoned on more and it was only when we went through all the receipts that we realised that dear old Jimmy – long dead now, sadly – had his entire family working there all week as well. But we weren't worried because the promotion had been a great success.

Alex stayed for a while with a mate of mine who had an Irish wife, then with Jimmy for a few weeks before moving off to Blackburn. There he linked up with Dennis Taylor and Jim Meadowcroft at the Post Office Club. I lost track of Higgins for a few months, although the stories of his achievements were spreading like wildfire.

If he made three centuries, say in Preston one night, you can be sure the bush telegraph would relay the information to Bolton, Accrington, Blackburn – anywhere in those areas – within a day or so. He built up an enormous following rapidly and clubs were packed out wherever he played. A pal of mine was asking what had happened to Alex one evening and I couldn't tell him for sure. We were off to Blackburn's Cavendish Club for a regular night out with the lads and you had to take a lift up to the club. As the doors opened at the top, there was Alex, drunk as a skunk, being thrown out by two bouncers. 'Hello Alex,' I said with a grin. 'And how are you doing these days?'

A lot of people thought of him as a thick Mick, simply because he came from Ireland; but he was actually very astute, and he had a photographic memory for horses. Soon after he arrived, I asked him about his likes and dislikes and, to my surprise, he reeled off music, horses and snooker as his favourites in that order. You could list all the runners, say, at Lingfield, and he'd tell you the jockeys, weights, trainers, owners – every possible thing about each horse. He also became adept at doing crosswords, the sort of tough ones you get in *The Times* and the *Daily Telegraph*.

Alex once gave me the best piece of advice ever and to this day I regret never taking him up on it. I had an idea to launch a magazine called *Cue World* to project the players more and we had a pow-wow round at John Spencer's house one night to discuss ways of getting it known. There was Alex, Dennis Taylor, John and a few others all putting up suggestions. Then Alex said, 'Why don't you print 5,000 and give them all away?' I was horrified, naturally, because it would have cost a bomb. In fact, it was a great idea because it actually took months and months for *Cue World* to take off when we might have attracted a decent circulation right from the off.

It's terrible to see just how much he has declined over the years and I suppose we are all guilty of aiding him to an extent. Alex was quite a shy person off the table, but on it he had a certain arrogance. He always seemed to be surrounded by people who said they would help him but were actually only out to help themselves. Many of them wanted him to stir things up because it generated publicity. I suppose he was like a David Beckham, always attracting attention whatever he did, good or bad. I once managed Alex for six months and it was a nightmare. I was forever getting calls from promoters saying he hadn't turned up – and I've kept the documented evidence to prove it.

In a way, I was like a father to him, but like everyone else I didn't put my foot down firmly enough. I tended to gloss over his imperfections because he brought so much excitement to the sport. He had so much charisma and magnetism and satisfied thousands of fans, especially in the early days when there was no snooker on telly except for *Pot Black*. For all his faults, though, he had certain values, and they were good values, and he would take notice at times.

Yet he always seemed to need that adrenaline rush to produce his best snooker. Some years later he was playing fellow-pro Paul Medati in a best-of-five match and went two down. Lynn, later to be his wife, was watching and said something. With that he clocked her one and I couldn't believe it. But in the next frame he banged in a big century. All through his career he seemed to create diversions to get that adrenaline fix; but it didn't work in later years, of course, as his game went backwards.

RONNIE HARPER
Belfast sports journalist who befriended Higgins in the early, raw days.
I've worked at the *Belfast Telegraph* for many years and have always been interested in new sporting talent because Belfast has a habit of producing glorious failures. But I was apprehensive to say the least when a snooker player at the YMCA told me about a new boy joining the club who was good enough to win the Northern Ireland Championship. Now snooker had always been really strong in the city and I laughed it off.

What a shock I got the following year when the cheeky wee lad walked off with the magnificent NI trophy after beating former champion Maurice Gill, a player of no mean repute. Higgins had made a huge name for himself – especially locally – and he had the crowd literally hanging from the rafters on that memorable March night in 1968 with a 4–1 success, winning much as he pleased.

Yet I was amazed at Alex's preparation for his first individual final of any note. The previous night I travelled with him on a 90-mile car journey for an exhibition in Derry and we didn't leave the venue until the early hours of the morning. But that was typical Higgins. He loved snooker, lived snooker and never tired of talking about it.

He went on to win the All-Ireland title that year, with an easy win over Dublin's Gerry Hanway, and was back in the NI final 12 months later, confident he was on his way to more glory. But what a shock he got as Dessie Anderson, a former champion, rattled off a 4–0 win in 90 minutes. But the shock did him the world of good, in my opinion, because the following night he compiled a century break in a charity match against Anderson and never looked back.

His fantastic potting was the talk of the country and it was inevitable that he would follow in Jackie Rea's footsteps to England and the bright lights of the professional snooker circuit. The impression I formed was that Alex didn't play a frame of snooker but attacked it, and so it was to prove. But there were many, many heartaches for him on his way down, having scaled the heights; and, tragically, he eventually joined the list of Belfast's glorious failures.

I couldn't honestly say I got to know Alex really well in the years that I knew him. Did anyone? He always struck me as a loner and often sat on his own. I used to wonder what he was thinking about at those times. When I first heard of Alex's illness I was horrified. I called his sister, Jean, and asked if she would contact him for me. I wanted to know if there was anything at all I could do for him. But he never called me back.

Two

THE LEARNING GAME

Now came the big challenge: could Higgins live up to all the expectations he and his burgeoning fan club held for his future? The answer was swift in coming because his ability to rattle off centuries, almost at will, made him the focus of attention at the Post Office Club. Two members who were to have an influential bearing on his career couldn't help but notice all the fuss he was creating. Jack Leeming and John McLaughlin, who ran bingo halls, soon made themselves known and agreed to manage him.

Cards offering his services were printed and distributed and an advert placed in the snooker magazine alongside those of Jackie Rea, John Spencer, Ron Gross, Gary Owen and others:

ALEX HIGGINS

Snooker's most exciting young player

Irish champion 1968

Runner-up 1969

Available for exhibitions, demonstrations etc.

And that was it. After practising for 10–12 hours daily, Higgins would then take himself off to whichever club required his services. Bear in mind that he was a still an amateur, so the handful of tournaments available to Spencer, Ray Reardon and co. were beyond his reach at this stage. It would be hard for anyone who wasn't around in those days to comprehend the snooker scene because there was little organised snooker for amateurs or pros.

People complain that there is too much snooker on TV these days, but 30 years ago it was practically non-existent and the only way to watch a professional was at a club. The club scene was booming and players like Jackie Rea thrived. He was a world-class player and was always in demand because he weaved a comedy routine into his act. John Virgo freely admits he was inspired to do his impressions of the other players after watching Rea in action; Dennis Taylor was also influenced by this little Ulsterman, who was to figure large in the life of Higgins over the next couple of years.

By coincidence *Pot Black*, the BBC2 one-frame competition which helped launch colour TV, was introduced just a few months after Higgins had made his first impact in Bolton. But that was a long way up the road for him. Next, in January 1970, still aged only 20, he was accepted into the professional ranks. Higgins celebrated by beating Rea 22–19 over three days; another new pro, Graham Miles 11–3; then Spencer 6–5 in a thrilling £100 challenge match. The Rea victory was significant because it alerted Irish officials that at last they had a player capable of challenging their long-standing pro champion for his crown. But that would not be for nearly two years – and then it was a week-long match spread over various venues in the Republic of Ireland.

A lot of snooker was to be played by Higgins before then, however, including several losing clashes and the odd win against Spencer – from whom there is no doubt he would have learned to enhance his safety play no end. Wins over other newcomers John Dunning and David Taylor (remember the Silver Fox?) added to his reputation.

There was also the small matter of his first world championship. Higgins came through his qualifying round 16–5 against Ronnie Gross, a top amateur who had won the English Championship three times in his heyday. I must explain that the world championship bore no relation to what we see today. There was no Crucible Theatre and no 17 days set by each year to stage them. Instead, players arranged their own matches until the latter stages and the event took up to a year to play. For instance, Alex began his challenge in March 1971 and finished in February the following year.

Meanwhile Higgins – now managed by Dennis Broderick, a salesman with a Lancashire firm of bar fitters – kept running up against an in-form Spencer, who had regained his world title the previous year having lost it to Reardon in 1970. There was no room, either, for Higgins in the Park Drive 2000, a tournament for top pros which had been launched the previous year. In fairness, he was still an untested, fledgling pro although Reardon, having beaten him 5–4 from 3–0 up in a challenge match, fancied him to do well in the world championship. 'His safety has improved and he could cause a lot of players some headaches,' predicted the Welshman. If only he knew.

Higgins continued to build his fan club in the north and in October he completed another rung on the world ladder by beating Maurice Parkin 11–3 in his second and final qualifying stage in Sheffield. Parkin was impressed with his young rival, but couldn't see him getting past Reardon or Spencer. Surprise, surprise, Jackie Rea was his first-round opponent in the November, just two months before their projected Irish showdown. Alex got himself bang in the mood with a typical flourish, cracking three consecutive tons during an exhibition at Liverpool's Lockheed Club – the first centuries ever recorded there.

And so for Rea: this time Alex prospered 19–11 at the same Sheffield club over four days, after his opponent had pulled out all the stops with his best snooker for 15 years. Rea, who had ruled the Irish roost for 24 years through lack of competition, knew his national title was in serious danger. And so it proved. The five-day match began in Collider and ended in Dublin after much drama. Before then, though, came Alex's world championship quarter-final match with ten-time title-holder John Pulman – a giant from the old school who was steeped in the rock-solid ways of Joe and Fred Davis and was rated in the same breath as the brothers. Higgins had the greatest respect for this Devon man, who would become a top TV commentator in later years, and they developed a fine understanding.

This was all-out war, however, because Pulman was determined to prove he could live with the whipper-snappers of the day. Pully did his level best to keep his rival in check. But there was no holding high-speed Alex who, by this time, was being advertised as 'Hurricane Higgins'. He ran out a 31–23 winner and now the snooker world simply had to sit up and take notice – even if the national press were, for the most part, oblivious. In fact, although Alex was gaining a reputation as a boozer, his life off the table was largely sheltered from the press and it wasn't until after he lifted the title that the stories started appearing regularly.

Higgins was thrilled to beat Pulman: he regarded him as his first TV idol, having seen glimpses of him on the box years earlier. 'His cue action was immaculate and his safety play was probably second to none,' recorded Higgins. 'Now, here was a living legend standing beside me at the table, but I wasn't overawed because I had supreme belief in myself and had worked out a battle plan.' Higgins knew full well that Pulman was another of the superb percentage players and decided to go for the throat from the off. As he said, 'Attack with brute force and frighten them to death. The plan worked and I felt quietly elated to have beaten a great champion.'

Pulman, who befriended me early in my snooker-writing career, used to rave about Higgins and Steve Davis, even before the latter had made his mark. 'Alex is a genius with the quickest snooker brain of anyone,' he said one night over his usual glass or two of Bell's whisky. 'He was at his best when he beat me in 1972 and it's a shame you couldn't have seen him then. But his temperament was always fragile and he was so highly-strung that you never knew which Higgins had come to play. His was a God-given talent, but he couldn't always capitalise on it because of the way he was made.'

After that momentous win over Pulman came Alex's Irish title challenge and by this time Rea knew exactly what to expect. Higgins thought the world of him because Jackie, or Jack as he was also known, had taken him under his wing. 'He was a lovely man and full of fun,' says Alex. 'He was a bit of a father figure to me because right from my early days, Jack was the only Irishman I knew on the pro circuit and he used to tell me tales about how Joe Davis ran snooker single-handed and that what he said went. He was also an attacking player, but old Jack was past his best when we met.'

In fact, Rea was able to hold Higgins to 4–3 on the first night in Collider and by the same score in Dublin the following night, when Higgins enjoyed all the running. What ensued in Limerick on the Wednesday paved the way for a new champion, Rea being brushed aside ruthlessly as Higgins took the session 9–0. He won 6–3 in Shannon the following night and he clinched the title by gaining the three frames he needed for a 21–12 success in a beautiful little Kilkenny town called Graignamanagh (by coincidence the birthplace of my lovely Mum, Cathleen, who became a Higgins disciple much later and would say Hail Marys on hands and knees whenever her beloved 'Old Higgy' or 'My Poor Alex' performed on TV). The final evening, in a posh Dublin hotel, was reduced to an exhibition, watched by famed singer Josef Locke and many other Irish celebrities. Again, Higgins triumphed.

The records chart Alex's progress throughout the week, but Rea is adamant that Higgins won the crown on that momentous night in Limerick and that he himself went on to have the last laugh during the exhibition on the final night. Whatever, a new Irish king was crowned and Higgins could not have wished for a better warm-up for the two biggest challenges of his young life which were to follow.

*

JACKIE REA
Northern Ireland's greatest player until the appearance of Alex Higgins, with whom he struck up a friendship that has lasted ever since.
At the peak of his form, I'd put Alex up there above every one of the modern stars, including Stephen Hendry and Steve Davis. He was a mercurial player, able to improvise with incredible results. I'd been playing for about 30 years before he arrived on the scene and I'd faced the best – including John Pulman, Fred Davis and his brother Joe (the greatest of all, in my opinion, who taught me so much about the game when he was in his heyday).

Yet Alex played shots I'd never seen. Ray Reardon always said Alex invented shots and he was absolutely right. I used to stare in amazement at some of the shots he played using the cushions to get back into the pack after playing past the blue into baulk. It was completely unorthodox and revolutionised modern snooker.

I first encountered him around 1970, when he was Irish amateur champion. We played a few exhibition frames but, quite honestly, my eyes didn't exactly pop out because we were just smashing the pack open early on and treating the crowd to lots of decent breaks. I'm 79 now, but in those days I was a huge star in my native Belfast and pretty big in England, too. I'd ruled the Irish roost since 1947, when I won the All-Ireland championship, and I held it for something like 24 years because there were no challengers until Belfast-born Higgy came along.

He'd just turned pro and we played for a week all over the Republic of Ireland in early 1972. We were pretty even until the fourth night, which was staged in Limerick. I then discovered how he had obtained the 'Hurricane' nickname because he had absolutely blitzed me off the table with the most amazing snooker I had ever seen. He won all nine frames and I honestly never had a chance to get in. Every time I got to the table I always seemed to be trailing by 60 or 70 points and that's the night I lost my title. It wouldn't have mattered who had been there the way he played. When he was at his best and playing close round the back spot, his cue action was very good. But with the long ones he threw everything into it. His head moved, his elbow jutted out and he did everything wrong. Yet if you studied him closely, he was perfectly still at the crucial moment of impact.

We always had a decent drink after each session and we became good friends as a result of that tour. We got to know each other well and I knew he was destined for great things. In fact, I told RTE (Radio Telefis Eiran) after the Limerick whitewash that I'd almost certainly played a future world champion. And Alex proved me right just a few weeks later when he stunned everyone by beating John Spencer, who was in a special class alongside Reardon in those days.

Curiously, I always used to beat Alex when we played exhibitions. He never knew when I was going to make him laugh and was always wary while he was at the table. We'd play three frames of relatively serious snooker, opening the balls up early on. Then Alex, who was never into trick shots or comedy, would retire to the bar and I'd do the funny stuff for half an hour or so. He'd then come back for a final frame with a few beers inside him and I nearly always stole his limelight by pinching that one as well. But it was all good fun and we had some smashing nights.

Although I say it myself, I was a decent player and could hold my own against most players, thanks to Joe Davis. I must have had something because he okayed my pro ticket (his word was absolute law in those days) and took me on tour with him all around the world. Everyone thought he was a stern so-and-so because that's how he came across. He was actually a very funny man off the table, but when we played, I was the clown to his straight man and it worked well.

But even in those early days I was worried about the amount of booze Alex packed away. He'd turn up for the odd exhibition smashed and I used to lecture him about it. But it was like talking to a brick wall. By coincidence, he moved to Cheadle with his wife Lynn and their two kids in the early '80s and we saw quite a bit of each other because I was just down the road in Cheadle Hulme, where I've lived in the same house for 40 years.

Alex was a diamond with my three kids. He'd pop round the day after playing an exhibition, say, empty all the loose change from his pockets and give it to them. They worshipped him and always looked forward to seeing him.

But it wasn't always sweetness and light. He once insulted my wife Betty and upset the both of us. I'm only a little fellow, probably smaller than he was in those days, but I was so angry with him that I laid him out – he didn't know that I'd been in the Commandos and could more than look after myself. I knew it was only because he had been boozing, and, sure enough, when he sobered up he was full of apologies to Betty and me. And he's never ever put a foot wrong in front of her since.

Another booze-related time, I received a phone call from the local police station in the early hours of the morning. Would I please bail out a Mr Higgins, who was in a cell? 'What's the little beggar done this time?' I asked. 'He's kicked-in the Marks and Spencer window and says he will refuse to pay up,' said the police officer.

I belted down to the station and was eventually confronted by Mr Higgins, who was more than the worse for wear. 'You took your bloody time,' he complained. I asked him what on earth he was playing at and he swore blind he had simply been standing in front of the shop when the window just shattered. Never mind that there were dozens of people who saw him do it after he'd been ranting and raving about the company employing slave labour abroad for the manufacture of their clothes.

I agreed to take him home after a copper told me Alex would probably be fined about £25 for being drunk and disorderly and made to pay for the damage when he appeared in court later that morning. With that, I drove him straight back to my home; as soon as we arrived, Alex said, 'Get the scotch out, Jackie.' But I told him in no uncertain terms that he would not be putting any more booze down himself. I ushered him up to the spare bedroom and locked the door.

Betty knew nothing about it, so, when she got up in the morning and heard all this moaning and groaning, she wondered what on earth was happening. I put her in the picture quickly, then set about getting Alex ready for his court appearance. 'I'm not going to any frigging court,' he hollered. 'And I'm not paying any fine.'

'Oh yes you are,' I shouted back through the door. 'So get yourself washed and dressed and smartened up.' And I warned him: 'If you don't go, Alex, they will issue a warrant for your arrest and you'll probably end up in prison.' That did the trick and Higgy kept his nose clean for a little while. But there has always been the maverick in him, which is why he has always been in trouble.

Alex and I once played a four-handed, Ireland v. England match in Galway. We were to play John Pulman and Ray Reardon for a big jackpot (the winners to get twice the amount as the losers did) plus individual appearance money. When we got together I said to Ray, 'But you're a proud Welshman.'

He replied, 'For that kind of money I'll be a proud anything they want me to be!' Typical Ray. Always an eye for the main chance.

Anyway, we agreed to split the money evenly but Alex wouldn't have it. He was playing so well that he was absolutely certain we'd finish in front. In the end we talked him round, but would you believe it? – he then went in to see the organiser and told him some cock-and-bull story about how he needed the money up front. Your man fell for it and Alex was off to the bookies before you could bat an eyelid. The outcome was inevitable and Alex was forced to play the entire week for his appearance money only. Mind you, he was such a hero that people were always plying him with drink. One lunchtime, he literally fell in through the door of the hotel where we were all staying. 'I'm not playing today,' he informed me, 'I'm not up to it.' I was furious.

'Oh yes you bloody are,' I roared at him, then frogmarched him to his room, filled him full of black coffee, locked him in and let him sleep it off. That night he was sweetness and light, fully sober, and played some great stuff.

It saddens me greatly that he has fallen so far from such a great height. With his extraordinary ability, he should be sitting in his mansion, watching the world go by and making the occasional public appearance for bundles of money.

But he just wouldn't, couldn't conform, and wouldn't leave off the booze. He even pretended at one tournament in the '80s that he was on the wagon and was drinking milk whenever he played. Sure enough, there was a jug filled with the white stuff on his table whenever he played and Alex sat there content, sipping away at the milk. Unfortunately, it transpired that this white stuff was well spiked with vodka. He had a good run in the tournament, though.

Because he opened up the modern game and helped attract all the accompanying wealth, Alex felt it was his divine right to make fortunes. But no one had that right and he got himself into deeper and deeper water as the booze seemed to flow more and more when he was playing. It sounds as though I'm a real puritan because of all my complaints about Alex's drinking. Anyone who knows me, however, will tell you I can sup with the best – but only after work has finished.

He was usually very reliable, as far as I was concerned, although once he asked and got a week's money up front and did a bunk. I was left to play against people in the audience, but I did my regular comedy stuff and it worked out OK in the end.

He once surprised me by refusing a decent week's exhibition work in Dublin. The deal was £1,000 a night for him and half for me, with all expenses – and I mean all expenses – paid. He'd been going through a lean patch, workwise, and I was convinced this would cheer him up. 'My fee's £5,000 a night,' said Higgy, and no matter how hard I argued that it would at least get him up and running again, he refused point-blank. I phoned the promoter and told him the bad news. 'But I'm pretty certain I can get Jimmy White over instead,' I told him.

'That would be great,' replied the promoter. 'Jimmy's also a great hero over here.' With that, I called Jimmy and the little rascal couldn't believe the deal. Needless to say, he was on the next plane over. We had a fabulous week, doing exactly the same routine as I used with Alex. Jimmy loved it. Both he and Alex were too serious about their snooker to mess around and Jimmy didn't play trick shots, either. So after the opening three frames, he would repair to the bar while I got the laughter.

I'd pull off a really difficult trick, then look under the table and shout, 'Did you see that one, Alex? It was a belter' – pretending he was lying there drunk. The crowd loved it, even though they'd probably seen my act before because I used to do that sort of thing all the time. One night, Jimmy was in the middle of a big break and the club's phone rang. I shouted, 'That'll be Alex. Tell him about Jimmy's break and what a good time we're all having.' It went down a storm as well. I'd also used that one several times to great effect because Alex was so big over there that the mere mention of his name would raise a great cheer.

I wish he had realised at his peak just how much he meant to these people who roared him on. But I believe he took too much for granted and in the end it all rebounded on him.

I retired from competitive snooker when I was 70. I'd travelled the world and lived out of a suitcase for nigh on 50 years, and I just ran out of gas in the end. I wanted some home life. But Betty is a nurse, so I hardly saw her during the day anyway. She'd be off to work and I'd be off to the bookies and the pub. But after six months of kicking my heels, I yearned for the action again. A local club asked if I could coach some youngsters and, over the last few years, my classes have built up nicely. It keeps me occupied.

I've often wondered whether I might have made a difference to Alex if I could have chaperoned him through his turbulent times. But in my heart I know it would have been an impossibility. He's had more managers than most football clubs over the years, and no one has ever really controlled him. But I still consider him a true friend, and I wish with all my heart I could turn back the clock for poor old Higgy.

Three

THE FINAL FLOURISH

Higgins was back on familiar ground when he tackled Rex Williams in the world championship semi-finals at Bolton in January 1972, this time at the Co-operative Hall. And, as former world-class referee Jim Thorpe wrote at the time in *World Snooker* (the magazine to which he contributed regularly): 'Beyond all shadow of doubt, it will be remembered as the greatest professional match ever staged there. After 61 frames of vintage snooker, 22-year-old Higgins emerged the winner, but my pen cannot capture the tension and electric atmosphere in which the final frame took place.'

Just as Willie Thorne, many years later, was to rue a missed blue against Steve Davis which effectively wrecked his career, so Williams had to live with his failure to sink a blue ball which would almost certainly have led to him ensuring his place in the final against John Spencer. At 29–30 after a wonderful see-saw battle, Williams compiled a magical 61 break to tie it all up and force a last-frame shoot-out; and with Higgins looking even paler than usual, the odds were on his normally unflappable opponent.

But as Thorpe recounted, 'Even Williams, who had remained so calm throughout the match, appeared to be affected. I detected a slight tremor in his cue action which had previously been so correct. The spectators were so quiet that I thought they had all gone home. But this only emphasised how the vital situation had been transmitted to the crowd via the players.'

Nevertheless Williams, world billiards champion at the time, appeared to have forged a winning opening when he led 28–14 with only five reds remaining (a measure of how tight it was) – only to miss a blue off its spot into the centre pocket, inexplicably. Higgins responded with a break of 32 then missed a difficult yellow. Superb tactical play featuring fine snookers from both players followed. Then the Irishman threw off the shackles after potting yellow, then green, and cleared to pink to clinch his final place at the first attempt. Not until Terry Griffiths some seven years later did a first-year pro get that far.

There were some amazing twists throughout the match. Higgins led 4–3 after the first session, yet Williams, steeped in billiards as well as snooker, had shown his quality early on with a 70 break. Higgins took the opening two frames of the evening and fans sat back, expecting Williams to be blown off the table. Instead, the man from Stourbridge took complete control and won the last six frames to be 9–6 ahead overnight. Yet Alex's recklessness accounted for the last three frames and it seemed as though his lack of experience would contribute to his downfall.

That seemed to be confirmed when Williams also won the first three frames the next day, for nine in a row, and two of the next four to lead 14–8. It looked ominous for his young rival, but Higgins showed his own mettle with that gritty spirit which was to rescue him on many an occasion throughout his career. No one would have pointed a finger had he folded against the vastly more seasoned Williams. Instead, breaks of 58 and then 80 enabled him to pull three back immediately after the interval.

Williams snapped the sequence with a 59 and although Alex hit back again, Rex took the final frame of the night to restore his four-game advantage at 17–13. The tension mounted when play continued the next day, Rex taking a leaf out of his rival's book by sinking breaks of 64, 82 and 65; but Alex still managed to win four of the seven frames in the afternoon session, to trail 20–17. They shared the first four frames in the evening, but Higgins, mixing caution with flair, took three of the last four to get within breathing distance again at 23–22 down.

As if that were not enough, the two gladiators served up a dish fit for royalty on the final day. Higgins kicked off by winning the opening two frames to lead for the first time since the opening day, which must have seemed like months ago to the little jack-in-the-box. But Williams won the next and pinched another on the black to regain his lead at 25–24. Higgins responded with three in a row, starting with a black-ball finish before Williams won the last of the afternoon.

The excitement was almost unbearable as Higgins launched the final session by going 28–26 in front, only for Williams to make it all square. Alex tip-toed back into the lead, but dogged Rex hit back with a fine break of 64 to draw level again at 29–29, with just three frames remaining of their epic semi-final. Williams had the next frame at his grasp, only to miss a relatively simple yellow, thus enabling Higgins to gain a vital advantage.

Then came the splendid pressure break of 61 from Williams, who, to his dismay, undid all his good work by missing that blue to blow it. But what a sensational match, and what a choker for Williams. 'It was the best I'd ever seen Rex play and he always looked the likely winner,' recalled Thorpe. Higgins felt justice had prevailed because he believed

Rex had employed dodgy tactics – even before a ball had been struck, as the match was postponed three times at his opponent's bidding. 'By the time he'd changed his mind for the third time I was getting pretty fed up,' he says. 'Whether it was gamesmanship or not, I don't know, but it cost me money because I had to turn down some bookings.

'I wasn't happy with Rex Williams's antics, but I wasn't worried about Rex Williams the player because I knew I would triumph in the end. It took me three days and five sessions to get level because I went hell for leather and tried to blast him into oblivion. And I'll give Rex some credit because he hung in there well. But even at 30–30 there was no doubt in my mind who'd be the one to crack. He missed a vital blue that could have put him in the final and left me a half-chance.'

Williams, generous in defeat, said: 'I knew Alex was good and I realised just how good in the end. As for rearranging the date, I was sponsored by Watney Mann and my diary was packed with engagements.' (Many moons later I sat up all night with Rex, Alex and John Pulman and marvelled at their collective knowledge of snooker, and roared at all the funny tales they came out with from touring the world. No sour grapes, that's for sure.)

From Bolton Higgins was in action again, before he'd hardly had time to draw breath – this time in the plush surroundings of Sheffield's City Hall, in what was undoubtedly a forerunner to today's luxurious Crucible Theatre, just a stone's throw away. Higgins had been booked to play 1970 world champion Ray Reardon, in front of spectators seated in the comfort of tiered armchairs. The crowds couldn't wait for the two-day encounter.

Reardon battled his way through thick fog and arrived punctually. He was followed (in the nick of time) by Higgins who was sporting a huge black eye – not the last of his career by any means – and several stitches in his face. Higgy looked terrible. He said he had been involved in a car crash three days earlier and had discharged himself from hospital that morning against medical advice to fulfil his obligation. In fact, he'd been involved in an almighty punch-up at a club the previous night after claiming a member of the audience had simply leapt out and thumped him in the eye – never mind that Higgy had been throwing insults at him all night . . .

'I should have seen it coming but if I'm guilty of anything, it's not sensing how angry some people get when I offend them,' said Higgins – and he actually meant it. 'It developed into a full-scale contest: arms, feet, everything. I was in bad shape, but you should have seen the other fellow. Fighting with one eye shut isn't easy and I took more punishment than was good for me. It put me in hospital overnight when I should have been practising for the Reardon match.'

Higgins even tried a practice frame at the Elite Club in Accrington the next day, wearing a patch over his eye, but to no avail. In desperation, he cut an eye hole in the patch and promptly fired a 97 break. Ready, then, for the mighty Reardon. Alex began with a 73 to the crowd's delight, but wily Reardon, with top breaks of 58 and 48, finished level at 4–4. Higgins, minus the patch, cut loose the following night to win three of the opening four frames, with breaks of 54, 84 and 68, so quickly that the crowd hardly had time to blink between shots. Not to be outdone, Stoke-based Reardon took the next to be 7–6 down; but Higgins had the final word, taking the next game and wrapping it up with a 66 to clinch a 9–6 victory against the steeliest of opponents.

Reardon recalls: 'No doubt every player can relate a tale or two about his experiences with Alex and I have one or two fond memories, including the one at City Hall. In those days, comfortable seating and air conditioning were almost unheard of, yet the City Hall had both and a great deal of luxury besides. Amid all this Alex arrived with one massive black eye, the other one the worse for wear as well, and still knocked me off the table. Amazing! And earlier in his career I played him the day after winning the 1970 world title. It was at the Stanley Institute in Burscough in front of a packed audience and Alex fired in a big break. A voice from the audience promptly cried out, "Seventy-eight in one minute 34 seconds." It was the first time I'd ever heard anyone being timed for a break. When I potted a loose red he'd left over the pocket, I turned round and said, "One red, one second." There was a deathly hush, then the whole place erupted, with Alex joining in.'

Thus, battle-hardened after two gigantic clashes in every sense of the word, Higgins was in the perfect frame of mind to launch his final assault on Spencer's world crown. And he did not disappoint. There was yet another obstacle for him to overcome before then, though – in the shape of John Spencer. While Higgins was busy carving his name with pride throughout the north, the Park Drive 2000 tournament had been introduced by the tobacco company for the world's leading players and was now in its third series. Higgins was invited to take part, along with Spencer, Pulman and Reardon, the players facing each other three times in a league table.

By an unfortunate coincidence the final featured Higgins and Spencer at the Civic Centre in Radcliffe (Spenny's home town) in a dress rehearsal for the real thing. Spencer won 4–3 but Higgins, who writes of a titanic battle over several days in *Alex Through the Looking-Glass*, was convinced he had the measure of the defending champion. And so he marched on Birmingham's Selly Park British Legion with confidence running high.

Curiously, while Higgins was awaiting the biggest match of his young life – a match that would ultimately shape his future – fellow-Ulsterman Dennis Taylor was making his own inroads into the game. Still an amateur, Taylor won the East Lancashire All Star Invitation tournament against Northern champion Doug French, a result that must have helped persuade him he was reaching the stage where the pro game beckoned.

And so to the world final. This, incidentally, was covered nationally by only Clive Everton (for *World Snooker* and *The Guardian*), the *Daily Mirror*'s Ted Corbett (who was to be a great inspiration to me when I started out) and Higgy's great ally Ronnie Harper, from the *Belfast Telegraph*. A far cry from the turn-out these days at the Crucible Theatre, where up to a hundred journalists descend each year from all the snooker-playing countries.

Spencer, already twice world champion, was a hot favourite because of his enormous experience at the highest level; but Higgins, as the underdog and challenger, had the crowd on his side from the off. And what a crowd, perching on the makeshift tiered seating of scaffold boards stretched between metal beer barrels, and wandering about the hall with pints of beer by the trayful – it really was a sight to behold.

Oh yes, it took place during the infamous miners' strike. The British Legion, allowing for the power cuts which afflicted every household throughout the land, made contingency plans with their own generators. They had been promised a classic from the stylish left-hander from Radcliffe and the young gunslinger by way of Blackburn via Belfast. And that's exactly what they got, with Higgins completing his meteoric rise by ousting the defending champion over six thrilling days. An enthralled Everton wrote in his first edition of S*nooker Scene*:

> On the week's play, Higgins thoroughly deserved to win. Over the 69 frames, he missed only one sitter and very few pots that lacked a considerable degree of difficulty. Without playing quite at his fastest, except for some inspired spells, his speed was still remarkable and his use of check-side and screw was at times amazing. To this he added consistency, an extremely competent safety game and the temperament to seize his chances. In contrast, Spencer never looked completely assured and it was largely through determination and experience that he was able to keep the winning margin so narrow.

The match began only minutes after a power cut had finished, so at least they got off to a bright start, Spencer taking the opening two frames. Higgins won the next, then made a dashing 60, only to miss a pink with a possible century on. They finished the session at three apiece and no real damage done by either player; then started the next with the emergency lighting on, because of a power cut.

It was to the players' great credit that they managed to keep going, for the temporary lighting threw unnatural shadows at both ends of the tables, and Spencer and Higgins responded brilliantly. Higgins opened with a 47 to be 4–3 up and Spencer responded with a fabulous 101 clearance. When Alex rattled in a 46 and 30 to win the ninth, the three evening frames thus far had taken just 26 minutes. He also took the tenth, but John prevailed in the last two of the night to repair to his bed at 6–6. It was a satisfactory opening day and Spencer flourished when play continued, a fine 109 taking him into a 9–7 lead. Higgins came back to 9–8, then delighted the crowd by hammering in a long red to spark a break of 41 from which he eventually drew level again – a rare cocked-hat double on the last red enabling him to compile a precious 22.

So, 9–9 and a long way to go, but Spencer lessened his burden with the first two frames of the evening session. They shared the next four to leave the champion 13–11 ahead going into the third day with no real hint of any serious damage from Higgins, who began the next day with a quick-fire 48 to narrow the deficit to one frame. Back came Spencer with two in a row for a 15–12 lead and he finished 16–14 ahead. They split the first two evening frames; then a 75 clearance by the Ulsterman left him just one behind at 17–16. By the end of another night of tense, unremitting snooker from both sides, it was 18–18. There was still all to play for at the halfway stage, with the winning post still miles away.

Day four loomed large and a missed final pink by Spencer proved costly as Higgins took the lead for the first time. But by the end of the session they were even-Steven again at 21–21, with no hint of the explosion to come that night. Higgins won the first three frames and was beginning to look comfortable for the first time, while Spencer appeared decidedly edgy. The Hurricane then flashed in a trademark 65 to be 25–21 in front as the roars from the crowd grew louder and louder. And he completed the 6–0 whitewash of the champion with enthralled fans clamouring for more. As Clive Everton recorded, 'The pots flew in from every conceivable angle.'

As if Spencer weren't in enough trouble, he and his wife Margot were stuck in their hotel lift for 25 minutes on their way to the afternoon session on the fifth day following a power cut, while buoyant Higgins warmed up with a four-minute century in the British Legion's billiards room. He then made a swift 50 break, when play got under way, to stretch his lead to 28–21. But gritty Spencer clawed his way back into it with two consecutive frames.

Higgins restored his six-frame advantage, but Spencer responded to get back to 29–25. The Irishman, though, with the bit between his teeth, extended his lead to 32–28 and could scent victory as the evening session finished. Higgins, up bright and early for the final day, sharpened his cue with two tons in his warm-up. He secured the opening game with a 40, but Spencer demonstrated his greatness with his third century of the match – a 123 break which could have so easily been a 136 clearance, had he not fluffed an easy pink.

He followed that with a 52 to get within three frames of a nervous-looking Higgins at 33–30; and when Spencer won the next as well to be just two frames in arrears, the tension was electric. However, just when you thought the 21-year-old was on the wane, back he came with a fluent 82 break to go into the final session of a thrilling encounter 34–31 ahead. Higgins won the opening game that evening, to be just one tantalising frame from a historic victory. And when Spencer failed to take the opening chance in the next game, Higgins struck victoriously with a 94 (his highest of the match) and 49, to be crowned the youngest snooker king of all. His prize money, believe it or not, was a paltry £480. But at that time, the Joe Davis trophy was far more important to Higgins.

'I wanted to do a Cassius Clay and shout from the rooftops, "I'm the Greatest",' says Higgins. 'But for once in my life I bit my lip. I was the youngest champion, I'd come up the hard way and I'd done it at the first time of asking. In one fell swoop I'd taken away snooker's "misspent youth" image and I'd broken into the élite band of pros who had tried to keep the game a closed shop. Despite the poor prize, I realised there was a lot of money to be made from the game.'

Ronnie Harper, still with the *Belfast Telegraph* and still seeking fresh talent some 28 years later, says: 'It was one of the most enthralling experiences of my entire career. I watched every ball potted and felt so proud at the end when Alex finally made it. I also saw him win the 1982 title, but with his unique talent, he should have won so much more.'

Ted Corbett, now specialising in cricket for the *Sunday People*, actually wrote a Higgins diary that never materialised into the book he had envisaged. He recorded:

Imagine the scene. A British Legion hall not far from Edgbaston cricket ground but a million miles from Wembley or Wimbledon. On a good day and with a bit of a squeeze, it may hold 500 snooker fans if they are all as thin as Alex and standing shoulder to shoulder. Whichever way you look at this 'championship venue', it is much too crowded.

And the noise! Chairs bang, doors slam, people talk, pint pots crash, stewards shout, the referee calls the points and the marker answers. You cannot hear yourself think. The lights, powered by a nervy generator to beat the strike, flicker and fail. Spectators actually walk near the table as the players line up their shots. To play! It must take strong nerves to play championship snooker anyway. Here, those nerves must be of steel or, better still, as though Higgins were absent altogether. Oh yes, I know what my verdict was a year or so ago. Nerves like alarm bells. Not this week. Just a frightening, frantic energy, a boiling desire to win, a flyweight rush towards destiny.

Because he has nothing to lose and because he is only a week of concentrated effort away from the title – his title.

Like Muhammad Ali, he spends so long convincing other people he can win that he now believes it, too. Higgins sips his beer between shots, bites his nails and revels in the strain. I hear and see that he drinks too much, sleeps little and is too often in the wrong company and worries too much about a girl back home in Oswaldtwistle. But how will he handle his new fame? Not calmly, I fear. There are already unpleasant tales about his behaviour, yet he has always been polite, even deferential, towards me.

Corbett was right in there at the start of a legend and recalls Higgins telling him before the final: 'A London evening paper has asked me to be the new George Best, so I've just done my birds and booze act for them.' Higgins then begged Corbett to persuade Best to attend the final, but the wayward Irish genius didn't want to know, saying, 'I don't fancy that.'

Years later, Higgins told me how he and Best had been drinking together in a Manchester nightspot when Best slagged him off for playing poorly in a recent match. 'I didn't think much about it at the time,' said Higgins. 'But we were there until the early hours of Saturday morning and George went on to play a real stinker that afternoon. Who on earth was he to tell me I'd been playing badly?' Generally, though, they got on well and had a memorable meeting in Dubai in the early '90s. Higgins was competing in the Dubai Classic, while Best had a regular coaching contract there. They made an odd couple beneath the palm trees, though – Higgins dressed casually but immaculately, as usual, and Best in a foul-looking turquoise shellsuit.

*

JIM MEADOWCROFT
Former pro and Higgins sparring partner and now a respected TV summariser.

I could only make one day of the championship and, as luck would have it, I chose the Thursday to watch my great pal Alex in action against my own particular hero. I wish I could have been there for the entire week – but I was still an amateur, working in a factory, and I had twin daughters.

Alex met me and suggested I practise with him before the afternoon session. I'd hardly expected that, so I hadn't brought my cue. But Alex just said, 'Never mind, we can both use mine.' He'd play a few shots then hand it over when he missed and by the time we'd finished, he was in good heart and well tuned up. He'd more than held his own against Spencer up to that point, which was quite an achievement against such an accomplished player, and he was happy to share the six afternoon frames. The score was 21–21 going into the evening session and what followed was absolutely incredible. It wasn't the type of snooker we are used to seeing today, but the standard of potting was supreme. It was attack, attack all the way with every shot in the book and more besides coming from both players. Alex and John were so talented and the total clash of styles made the match irresistible as a spectacle: John, smooth and creamy; Alex, erratic, edgy, hungry and really desperate to win the title. I couldn't have picked a better session of the final to watch, apart from the one in which Alex clinched the title.

What I saw on that March night in 1972 more than made up for anything I'd ever seen before or have done since. Alex won all six frames and you can't even begin to measure how good he was. There will never be another Alex Higgins. He was a genius. I can remember only one pot missed by either player – a quarter-ball cut aimed by Alex into the corner pocket, which he overdid.

The balls returned almost to the same position and John played an identical shot and also missed. But Alex was playing so well that if he'd been allowed to carry on, I firmly believe he would have won the title there and then. From his point of view, the worst thing that could have happened was for the session to finish. Alex had stolen the show in the first five frames and what happened next is still as fresh in my mind today as it was all those years ago.

Alex took control coming up to the colours in the final frame of the night and potted a tremendous green. Instead of doing it the simple way, the way which would have taken all the pressure off the shot, he wanted to demonstrate just how masterly he was. So instead of just dropping the green in and stunning the white over for the brown, he smashed it in, coming off three cushions with reverse side. It was awesome as the applause began on that shot and he was so quick to get on the brown that it was still building as he thrashed that ball in with a similar shot – this time coming off two cushions. Instead of the cheers dying, they just grew louder and louder as the blue and pink followed in rapid succession.

By this time the noise was almost deafening and then the strangest thing happened. When a cue ball hits the object ball, which then hits the pocket, it makes a loud noise, similar to the one you hear on TV. But by the time Alex got down to complete the most marvellous session of his young career, you simply couldn't hear a thing. I never heard either the white making contact with the black, or the black crashing down. It was magic, pure magic and as the ball slammed into the back of the pocket, Alex scooped up the white ball and walked off in his own inimitable style to deafening applause. It remains one of the most memorable experiences of my life.

REX WILLIAMS
Former World Billiards Champion, twice WPBSA chairman and an old-school snooker player right out of the Joe Davis mould.

Alex had the sharpest brain of all and no one could size up a situation, or learn new shots, with the same speed as he could. And he was so unorthodox. As Ray Reardon pointed out, we always played to a pattern – the one laid down by Joe Davis – until Higgy came along.

After all these years, people still ask me whether I have always been haunted by the blue I missed against him in the 1972 world semi-final, which would have given me the match. I always say the same thing: 'I got over it fairly quickly, because I had a living to make and it was always on to the next challenge.'

In some ways I was unlucky that Alex played John Pulman in the previous round because he learned so much about safety during that match. Before then he relied on his outstanding potting and break-building; but Pully was a tremendous safety player and Alex realised he would have to match him to get the better of him, and that's what he did. I was astonished just how quickly he picked up on things in our match. I'd play a particular safety shot and about three shots later he'd play the same one.

As chairman of the WPBSA Board, and chairman also of the Disciplinary Board, I had to confront Alex several times. At one hearing, everyone was so antagonistic towards Alex that I couldn't help feeling a little bit of sympathy for him. He couldn't help what he was – his brain was so mixed up. Alex is the most mixed-up person I have ever met. I remember saying once: 'All this is very well but would you like to spend even one day inside that body? He has to spend every day inside it.'

But he was a remarkable player with, as I've said already, the most astute snooker brain of all. And he could be such good company when he was in the right frame of mind.

Four

NEW DAWN

If Alexander Gordon Higgins thought he had cracked it, he was in for a shock. The youngest world champion ever, to be sure, but that did not mean his rivals were prepared to roll over at the very mention of his name. In fact, quite the opposite. His phenomenal success merely served as a spur to his opponents, as he discovered shortly. And the Fleet Street knives were being sharpened as his reputation as a hard-living, hard-drinking, gambling, womanising, hell-raising sportsman came into focus.

Thames Television tracked the new world champion's every move in preparation for a half-hour documentary, which included footage of Higgy beating deposed title-holder Spencer 4–3 and his subsequent defeat by him. That was his first big eye-opener, a 25-frame challenge match against the Bolton star at Wallasey Civic Hall less than two months after his great triumph. Spencer gained partial revenge with a 13–10 win and rubbed it in a little when, after collecting the £150 prize, he helped himself to all but twenty quid of Alex's winnings following a personal sidestake. But Higgins, being Higgins, was back in pocket two days later when he beat his old adversary 6–3 at Neath for a winner-takes-all £100 jackpot. A paltry sum by today's standards – Mark Williams pocketed £240,000 for clinching his first world crown at Sheffield in 2000 – but still way above the national wage.

Life was hectic for the young world champion and his days and nights consisted of travelling the length and breadth of the country earning his corn. And remember, Higgins didn't drive – he gave up after one abortive attempt to learn – so unless he could scrounge a lift from the likes of Jimmy Meadowcroft or even Dennis Taylor, it was buses, cabs and trains. That added so much time to his journeys. No wonder he leapt at the chance to be chauffeur-driven in a gleaming Rolls-Royce, many years later, in a venture that was to signal the start of his dreadful decline. But Higgy soldiered on as best he could from one engagement to another, packing them in wherever he played.

His next big threat came from Pulman, by coincidence, at Selly Park

British Legion, which had become home for Higgins for that glorious week in March. This time he tasted defeat, going down 19–14 to the ten-times world champion over the three-day event. Pulman knew his age was against him, especially with the new-wave players such as Ray Reardon, Higgins and Spencer redefining the way that snooker was being played. And in a bid to stave off Old Father Time, he trimmed his considerable bulk by two stone. 'They all pot well, but there's nothing new in potting,' observed Pulman, a rigid disciple of the Joe Davis, Leicester Square Hall era (when players were all steeped in billiards knowledge and employed rigid safety and precise positional play). 'If Joe missed a long one it was an event, and Walter Donaldson was the finest long potter I ever saw.'

Higgins was his usual self, with a mixture of brilliance and carelessness, and absent from his world success performance was the consistency he had shown a few months earlier. He maintains his beloved cue, which had stood him well since his amateur days in Belfast, had been broken accidentally on his way to the venue. Yet the grit, his stubborn refusal to accept defeat, was evident as he pushed the rejuvenated Pulman all the way until the final evening, when the Devon man ran off the three frames required to complete his £500 success.

Higgins's star was in the ascendancy. Having moved on from John McLaughlin and Jack Leeming to their pal Dennis Broderick, he then switched to London-based Snooker Promotions under the guise of West Nally (broadcaster Peter West and Patrick Nally) and the personal touch of Simon Weaver, who must have aged overnight. Under this umbrella, with mounting 'crimes' against his name in England, the next Higgins adventure took him Down Under – courtesy of Pulman – for the summer. There they played against Australian stalwart Eddie Charlton ('Steady Eddie', as he became known in Britain, years later on the circuit), who ran the game there for many years. Curiously, during a two-day stopover in Singapore on the way out, Higgins and Pulman treated a huge shopping-mall crowd of 3,000 to an exhibition of hexapool – a peculiar form of pool which never took off.

It was mayhem at first sight for Higgins, who fell in love with Australia, its women and gambling – and he even married an Aussie girl two years later. On this occasion, however, he settled for snooker before revealing his true colours. He won and lost against Paddy Morgan, a fellow Belfast man who had emigrated recently, before getting stuck into his tournament with Pulman and Charlton, who beat him 19–17 in the final. Higgins admitted: 'He was better than I gave him credit for. He was solid and never missed a thing.'

Wide-eyed Alex, who lived it up to the full on his first visit to anywhere outside Britain, couldn't believe what was going on around him. 'It was like Chicago in the days of Prohibition,' he recalls. 'Sydney in the '70s was almost like London in the '60s . . . a swinging city full of women, money and massive gamblers, and that suited me down to the ground.'

But he was lucky to make it back to England after an extraordinary incident one night when he was thrown out of a casino for accusing 63-year-old Norman Squires – a much-respected local pro with hundreds of centuries to his credit – of being an old no-hoper, on the snooker table installed on the top floor. 'I was giving him a 65-point start and had won three frames,' says Higgins. 'True, I did call him a no-hoper and I got into a fight with some of the regulars who objected. Pandemonium broke out. I was screaming and shouting when a big hand landed on my shoulder and a broad Aussie accent drawled, "Stop shouting at my boys, sport."'

Higgins, as diplomatic as he was to prove in later years, responded with the words 'shut up, you old bugger', and was promptly lifted off his feet by two huge bouncers and dumped in the street. But the Irishman, on learning the identity of who was at the other end of the big hand, wrote an apology on a scrap of paper while sitting in the gutter and asked for another chance. Joe Taylor, renowned as the Godfather of Sydney, according to the miscreant, accepted the apology with grace and the two forged a lasting friendship until his death in 1980. To the amazement of the club's regulars, Higgins rattled in a 112 when he resumed his match with Squires. 'That's why they call me the Hurricane,' Higgins assured them – then promptly kicked off his shoes, stripped to the waist and played on, barefoot.

Sadly, old Norm passed away three years later while playing at the same City Tattersalls Club he had graced for 30 years. Far from being a 'no-hoper', he had actually led John Spencer 6–3 in the 1970 world championship before fading badly, and he was a superb money player. Even at 66 he was playing for up to $3,500 a frame. He was a legendary figure and would even give poor players a 150 start, which meant he needed snookers from the off. Yet he wasn't a hustler in the accepted term, because he was always open about his ability. Spencer said, 'Norman was a smashing bloke and I had some of the best laughs ever with him.'

There was another stopover on his way back home for Higgins, this time in India, where he disgraced himself even more. He was scheduled to give three exhibitions in Bombay and various others spread over a three-week period in other states. Behind the scenes he had tried unsuccessfully to get extra cash so that his girlfriend, Liz Kendall, could join him on tour (she told the *Sun* newspaper they were engaged and were getting married later in the year). Yet there was no hint of the havoc to come when he launched his tour with an opening 109 break, to the delight of a capacity Bombay Gymkhana crowd. His subsequent booze-fuelled behaviour, during which he said he had no intention of doing any more exhibitions in India and that he would be on the first plane home in the morning, stunned onlookers, and members of the Billiards Association and Control Council of India. Vice-chairman R.K. Vissanji was quoted in the *Times of India* as saying, 'During the 25 years of my association with the game, I have never seen such disgraceful behaviour.'

Higgins appeared to have a mini-breakdown and his entire control and reasoning deserted him while at the table. He announced that he would not play on without being paid (there was no money involved as such – his contract stipulated a generous, all-expenses-paid holiday) and then decided to do some trick shots, which were totally alien to his nature. As the heat got to him, Higgins stripped off his long-sleeved shirt and carried on playing, much to everyone's disgust. He was soon fully clothed again when he realised people were offended and he apologised for his behaviour. But it put a dampener on the evening and spectators, aware only of his snooker reputation and hoping to witness the magic of the Hurricane, left disgruntled.

Higgins made it clear to another Indian official, Wilson Jones, the former world amateur billiards champion who attempted to mediate, that he did not like his country, the food or anything else there. So that was his India trip. Ten frames, over and out.

By this time Higgins's misdemeanour record was growing almost daily at home and abroad. He explains his behaviour in India thus, in *Alex Through the Looking-Glass*: 'After my experience there I don't care if I never set foot on Indian soil again. If they had a £5 million tournament in Bombay and invited me, I'd insist they send Bombay to England. It's the most disgusting hole it's ever been my privilege to fall into.'

He then complains of a nightmare journey, having been collected from the airport at 5 a.m. and then taken to Nataraj Hotel – a 'splendid establishment', as he recalls:

> Cripples and beggars sleeping in the foyer and cockroaches crawling up the wall of my bedroom. I even invited Wilson Jones to my room to witness the biggest cockroach I'd ever seen – as big as a fist. What a night. I woke up every few minutes just to check there wasn't some other insidious creature creeping up on me.
>
> I'd agreed to do the organisers a favour by appearing on an expenses-only deal. I was told it was a poor country and not to expect a fat purse. The attraction was that the Indians were partial to offering presents instead of cash. I played Indian champion Girish Parikh on a dreadful table and made a 109 break with my first hit which, under the circumstances, wasn't bad going.
>
> One bright spark then offered several thousand rupees for a 100 break. I said, 'But I've just made one. What's the point of me coming

all the way here for nothing only for you to offer prizes after the event?' That did it for me. The temperature in there was way over 100 degrees so I stripped off my shirt, knowing it would upset them – and they were beside themselves with indignation. I'd played five frames before I saw the colour of anyone's money. I was knackered, with sweat dripping from every pore when a millionaire called R.K. Fasanjay [*sic*] walked across and offered me the night's star prize. It was a little tin cup. I told him where he could stick his sanctimonious offering.

I admit I'd had a few drinks, but the official version that I 'offended members by drinking, insulting the organisers and taking off my shirt' has to be put into perspective. According to reports, the Indian authorities 'put me on the next plane'. The truth is that I made my own way to the airport and was more than happy to get out. I got to the airport in time to meet Liz. She was a well-known equestrian at one time and worked at a famous London nightclub called Churchill's. I said, 'Babe, it's good to see you – we're leaving on the next flight.' It cost me £350 for the privilege of getting back on to the plane with her.

Higgins had already left a trail of bad conduct behind him in England. He caused a rumpus at Hartlepool, where he demanded his exhibition match with Spencer be stopped because of the poor lighting. 'I complained to the promoter several times, but he did nothing,' says Higgins:

> There wasn't even a light over the table and it would have been ideal if I'd wanted a game of blind man's buff.
>
> I conceded in the eighth frame after being fouled. Spencer told me not to be a prima donna and we had a blazing row in front of everyone. We'd have come to blows if they hadn't held us apart. I turned to the promoter and said, 'You're an arsehole to put on a thing like this.' I apologised the next day, but the damage had been done. The spectators were hissing and booing because I refused to carry on, but then I remembered the world championship at Selly Park in the power cuts. It had been Spencer doing all the moaning there, yet I beat him. Eventually, I came round to his view that the show must go on and I went on to beat him again – virtually with a white stick.

Fiery Higgins, on edge because he was trying to give up smoking, also landed in the soup at Ilfracombe, where he hurled his new cue, spear-like, at a spectator who had wound him up. Alex was promptly frogmarched out of the room to cool off. Fortunately for him, the cue remained in one piece.

On his return to Britain, Higgins was confronted with the TV documentary in which his first manager, John McLaughlin, said, 'Alex had only three vices – drinking, gambling and women.' The director, Christopher Goddard, said, 'He inhabits a world which is essentially shoddy and tinselly.' Commentator John Morgan reflected, 'Snooker was a game on the dole,' and suggested Higgins had resurrected it. He added, 'It is sometimes rather patronisingly referred to as the working man's chess, as if working men can't play chess.'

Higgins himself recalled, 'They deliberately set out to show the seedy side of snooker. They filmed me at this club where there was green mould running down the walls outside. When they saw it, they said, "Great – just what we want."'

Astonishingly, despite his world title fame, Higgins was little known outside the north. Peter Black, the *Daily Mail*'s esteemed TV critic of the day, wrote: 'I'd never heard of Higgins and it seems the other professionals do not care much for him. But of his standing as a player there can be no doubt. The combination of speed, accuracy and touch was phenomenal.'

The *Daily Express* critic was similarly baffled as to who he was and the *South Wales Echo* reported, 'He's the World Champion, but who had ever heard of him?' Nancy Banks-Smith wrote in *The Guardian*, 'For some time I thought Hurricane Higgins was a bullfighter. I still feel he was a bullfighter and changed when I wasn't looking.' To balance that, the *Daily Mirror* recorded: 'ITV came up with a real winner. Higgins has upset the pros who've been at it for 50 years. He's young, cocky and, as he says, unbeatable.'

Clive Everton, severely critical of the programme, wrote in *Snooker Scene*: 'Goddard feared that the snooker public would be disappointed with the actual play, but the sequence in which he cleared the table with a break of 104, captured perfectly the image of Higgins at his best.' Everton also disputed that Higgins was solely responsible for the game's upturn in fortunes, saying: 'His world title earned a blaze of publicity but the game was booming well before then and *Pot Black* must, in any case, be regarded as the most important single influence in selling snooker to a general public.'

Goddard added: 'What I think we show is that there is no real glamour in the life Alex leads. I think at the end of the film, a lot of people will say, "Poor sod."'

Everton summed it up, saying: 'Higgins comes across as an extremely lonely and vulnerable figure with the Cassius Clay-type remarks ("There's no doubt about it, I'm the Greatest at the moment . . .") masking a chronic insecurity of which his undisciplined, almost frenzied lifestyle, is another symptom.' The following month, having learned that the programme had reached 20th in the ITV ratings and 25th in the joint BBC–ITV list, Everton concluded: 'It may well have had to some degree a public relations effect.'

It was soon business as usual for Higgins. He beat John Spencer 4–2 in the plush surroundings of London's Café Royal to earn rare praise from Joe Davis: 'His entry into the game will do a great deal of good, and if more players could reach his standard it would be better in every way. Great players don't come along every night, but Higgins has come to the front in such a short time that I can hardly believe it.' Praise indeed from the maestro.

There was little love lost between Higgins and Spencer by this time and they seemed to be in each other's pockets nearly every week. It meant the spectators were given far better value for money than they might have expected, because there was no such thing as an exhibition match where these two were concerned. Every clash was a blood-and-thunder affair. (Imagine a Steve Davis–Higgins scenario in the '80s or Ronnie O'Sullivan and Stephen Hendry today, but without the animosity.) Higgins was beaten for the second time by Spencer in the Park Drive 2000 final, this time losing 5–3 in a low-scoring match at Belle Vue.

It was the sixth successive strike by Spencer against him and he polished off the year in grand style, beating the 23-year-old Ulsterman 38–37 in an absolute corker of a £500 challenge match at Radcliffe Civic Hall – scene of other great triumphs by the hometown hero. In a nip-and-tuck encounter, Higgins won 8–7 on each of the first three days. Spencer then rattled off six of the first seven frames when they resumed, only for Higgins to reply with the next six. But the northerner won the session 8–7 to be just 31–29 behind going into the final day.

Again there was some startling snooker served up by both players who, since their initial meeting just three years earlier, must have known each other's game inside out. Spencer kicked off by sprinting 7–1 ahead, and Higgins retrieved the balance of power with another six in a row but lost the final two nerve-racking frames to a pumped-up opponent. Higgins felt the daily travel from his Accrington base may have affected his play, but was generous in defeat, conceding: 'It couldn't have been any closer and what a shame someone had to lose.'

But the storm clouds were gathering over the Hurricane, whose boozing, birding and betting reputation – on top of his penchant for attracting trouble – was fast gaining momentum.

*

RAY EDMONDS
Twice World Amateur Champion and now a top BBC TV commentator.

I remember playing an exhibition one night in my home town of Grimsby and someone introduced me to this skinny little kid and asked if I'd give him a frame. He was only about 17 and I had no idea whether he could play or not. I broke off and smacked the pack open from the back to give him a chance to do a bit. Next thing, he's potted the lot and brought the house down.

Years later, when Alex had won the world title and was famous, he was back in Grimsby for an exhibition. I had been invited along and saw a chap there who had never liked me. He collared me after Alex had performed and said, 'Edmonds, you're an arrogant bastard and you always will be.' It didn't bother me, because I'd been called a lot worse in my time; but Alex happened to be standing next to me and leapt to my defence, saying, 'Everyone knows Ray's a great player, but he gave me every opportunity to show what I could do when I was a kid. He was the star of the show, yet he spread the balls everywhere and invited me to show what I was made of. If he were arrogant, there's no way in the world he'd have done that, so show some respect and apologise.'

Alex has been in and out of trouble all his career, but I've never forgotten those two incidents. He has a decent side to him and I'm sure a lot of people would agree with me.

Five

BACK TO REALITY

He was still world champion, if not with the world at his feet, and Higgins must have been exhausted with the wall-to-wall snooker, slotted in between all the hell-raising. He was involved in *Pot Black* for the first time – and almost the last, after yet more turmoil – and he had a world title to defend. And the announcement of Park Drive's first involvement in the championship was the best news snooker had ever received.

The cigarette company, delighted with the packed-house response from their 2000 series, injected £8,000 – with £1,500 for the winner, a fortune in 1973, especially against the £480 Higgins received for winning the crown a year earlier. In addition, the company introduced an eight-table system at Manchester's City Exhibition Halls, with a Wimbledon-style Centre and No. 1 Court, and spread the event over 13 days in April (a taste of Crucible things to come). It was a revolution for the world championship with record prize money; and even first-round losers collected £100.

In addition, Bruce Donkin, steeped in snooker via Riley's equipment manufacturers, was to oversee proceedings. Only a few years later Donkin, a great friend to all the players and officials, would be MC at the Crucible, watched by millions each day as he ushered players into the arena. There was also a record entry of 24 (more than 500 battle for 16 unseeded spots, nowadays).

All this, and Higgins was installed as top seed, although No. 2 seed Spencer was the favourite and Reardon was placed at No. 3: the world's three best players in their rightful places, even though there was no official rankings chart. The usual suspects were below them: Fred Davis, Charlton, Williams, plus a newcomer from Canada, Cliff Thorburn. The Canadian was to become another great Higgins adversary over the years and he once administered instant justice with a swift kick in the Irishman's nether regions. Needless to say, Higgins showed him a fair degree of respect – off the table at least.

There was yet another clash of titans when Higgins was beaten 23–16 by Spencer in a three-day match at Aberdare, sponsored by the Welsh ruling body – one of a series of fund-raising activities for their run-up to the world amateur championship. Spencer was in tip-top form. Higgins, meanwhile, seemed unduly off-colour. But he raised a smile when presenting the world trophy to Ray Edmonds, a familiar voice to BBC TV these days as a snooker commentator. Higgins then drew a 1,000 crowd for the Men of the Midlands final at Wolverhampton: he took the £500 top prize with a 5–3 win over Reardon in the final of a round-robin series that also featured Pulman and Spencer. The highlight of the tournament was when Higgins beat Spencer 5–1 at Walsall, then fired a 114 in one of the 'dead' frames in under three minutes, Spencer responding with a 120.

An interesting diversion to Higgins's build-up to his world title defence came when he took on Dubliner Noel Miller-Cheevers (a property developer and a wily amateur) at London's Eccentric Club – a wonderful place which lived up to its name in every respect and was to be the venue for my all-time favourite Higgins story some years later. Miller-Cheevers won the £500 sidestake by beating Alex 3–0 after receiving a 40-point start (he must have been grinning all the way home). Miller-Cheevers was responsible some years later for snooker's International Club, which prevails today and has teams and venues scattered the world over. He also played a prominent part in Jimmy White's early years, and returned to help him out at Sheffield a few years ago. 'He's the best "second" I've ever had,' said White, alluding to a boxing term.

Higgins completed his warm-up with a marathon 29–21 defeat by Gary Owen, the Brummie who emigrated to Australia. It should have been a worthwhile challenge for Higgins because Owen was an out-and-out safety player, employing the tactics that the champion was sure to face in the coming weeks. But Higgins displayed little patience, tossing away frames with reckless shots and displaying only hints of magic (notably a 123 clearance).

And so to the 1973 Park Drive World Championship, run by Snooker Promotions at Manchester's City Exhibition Hall, where the game's future was defined – one venue and all over in a couple of weeks – though not without hiccups. The event attracted no fewer than 25,000 fans, which matches easily today's Crucible Theatre attendances, on a pro-rata basis, and demonstrates the enormous pulling power of snooker in the early '70s. Unlike today's two-table set-up, there were eight in action from the start, which caused unrest at various tables as the cheers went up.

Higgins was chomping at the bit and resplendent in white Oxford bags, as opposed to the normal collar-and-tie suited affair standard for daytime play in those days. He drew veteran Londoner Pat Houlihan and sailed through 16–3, but with the maximum amount of fuss. He won the opening session 7–1, then returned to the venue 22 minutes late for the evening start. He was greeted with a storm of booing, which increased as he attempted to explain away the delay. He was, he said, attempting to sponge-clean his trousers, which had become stained from his leaning over the table all afternoon. He claimed he also had to re-tip his cue, which had split during the afternoon play.

A likely story, felt the crowd. So did tournament director Donkin. All laid into Higgins. These days, of course, a player is docked one frame for every ten minutes of his absence – as John Virgo discovered to his cost when he arrived 20 minutes late for the second day of his 1979 UK final against world champion Terry Griffiths and saw his 9–5 lead shrink by two frames in an instant. But it took Higgins just a few minutes to win the crowd over again, with a rip-roaring 78. That was enough to demoralise Houlihan further and with Higgins chatting away to girls in the table-side seats throughout the evening, he had no chance. Higgins wrapped it up 7–0 for a 14–1 lead, then shared the next four frames on the resumption to settle it with not a century in sight. Spencer and Reardon also came through, as did the evergreen Fred Davis, who whipped Blackpool newcomer David Greaves 16–1 and was to prove a terrible thorn in the side of Higgins in what turned out to be a classic encounter, including a delay for rain. Honestly!

The contrast in styles – Alex, all action, all a-twitch against dependable Fred, schooled and steeped in billiards and old-style snooker – was a dream. Davis led 4–1 and was 67–29 up on the final yellow of the sixth frame but somehow contrived to lose on the final black as Higgins fought brilliantly to stay in touch. Davis took the session 5–2 but Higgins, who has always loved evening play, enjoyed a 6–2 advantage with some vintage play to lead 8–7 overnight.

Fred took the first game of the evening and was preparing to mop up the blue, pink and black when water began to drip slowly on the table. Yes, rain actually stopped play. As Clive Everton observed in *Snooker Scene*: 'Even allowing for the fact that this was Manchester, it was ridiculous. But there was no alternative but to chalk-mark the position of the balls, put the covers on and wait for the roof to be plugged by a party which included Simon Weaver.'

Eventually, Davis took the frame and went on to carve out a 12–10 lead. But Higgins closed the gap to 14–14 that evening. Even then, as a wearying Davis began to feel the pace, the 60-year-old had a great chance to get to within a frame of victory. Yet he missed an easy pink and that was his last shout. The 30th frame, tinged with mistakes, finally fell to Higgins on the last few colours and he was within two matches of retaining the trophy. But the enormous effort required to get past Davis told on him and to his dismay, and that of all his faithful followers,

Higgins blew up in his semi-final clash with Eddie Charlton.

The dour Aussie (who started losing his hair in the '70s, then 'grew' it again miraculously in the '80s and today has a magnificent, gingery-brown thatch sitting proudly on his bonce) began well and continued in the same vein during the evening. A strangely subdued Higgins didn't even twitch as the axe was lowered on him progressively. At one stage he was so low after missing an easy cut on a frame-winning black that he surrendered by picking up the white as it travelled towards baulk.

Manna from heaven for Steady Eddie, who forged ahead 12–3 overnight. There seemed no way back for an increasingly dejected Higgins – and so it proved, Charlton running out a comprehensive 23–9 victor. Higgins blamed his new cue (remember, his old one was smashed beyond repair two months earlier), while Charlton said: 'Pressure had a lot to do with his performance and I feel he has an awful lot to learn about the game. Whether he is capable of learning remains to be seen.' Higgins himself agreed he was in no shape to defend his title. 'I'd burnt the candle at both ends and in the middle,' he admitted. 'I'd discovered the demon drink and I'd had my nerve-ends shattered by a 100 m.p.h. lifestyle. I'd even lost my battle against the weed and was smoking again even before the championship.' A decision he must rue bitterly now.

Meanwhile Reardon, who trailed Spencer 15–9 after two days on the adjacent table, fell further behind when the title favourite increased his lead to 19–12, needing just four more to reach his third world final. But Reardon, seemingly inspired by the Higgins demise, fought back to secure a remarkable 23–22 victory; then he polished off Charlton 38–32 to clinch his second world title after losing the first seven frames (Jimmy White was to do the same against John Parrott in 1991, but on that occasion the deficit was far too great for him to make up).

In the wake of Alex's title failure was a £100 rap over the knuckles for his past and present indiscretions. Among these was turning up late for a world championship session and wearing unsuitable clothing – a green velvet suit on one occasion and those white Oxford bags (West Nally's idea, apparently, to jazz him and the game up a little). Yet for all the harm he had caused on his travels, he was always a dapper dresser whatever the mood or occasion and surely offended no one with his bright clothing. He was later fined £200 following complaints from the Indian Association and others.

Again Everton, the only full-time snooker chronicler of the time, records: 'On the whole, Higgins has harmed snooker much less than he has harmed himself. The contrast between the way he dresses and the traditional tuxedo outfits of the other pros is all to the good. But it is obvious to anyone who has spent time with him that Higgins is living on his nerves, as his compulsive drinking, womanising and gambling bears out.'

Everton's account continues with the observation that Higgins 'has, it seems, almost a death wish or a desire for self-destruction which, unless he starts to control his impulses, could lead to a decline as abrupt as his rise'. A spot-on assessment of the star's fragile character. And it would be nine long, frustrating years before Higgins was to lay hands on the coveted crown again.

Yet there was plenty of mileage to be recorded until then, plenty of scrapes – and plenty of heartache for him, because the Irishman never won a title of any significance until the Benson & Hedges Masters in 1978, a fact barely believable considering his towering talent. Even worse was the decision of Pontin's not to include him among the eight invited professionals for their inaugural Festival of Snooker (top prize £1,000), which went on to become one of the great weeks in the calendar, where the public had the chance to rub shoulders with the stars (and it is still going strong today).

Around this time Alex's management company, Snooker Promotions, began to have serious doubts about their ability to control the wayward star and Patrick Nally set up a new associated company to handle his affairs. Nally said: 'If he could keep his temper and control himself, he could be a tremendous asset to the game. However, if he is going to act as he has done on his recent tour of Australia and India, his future is extremely doubtful. But the new company have made it clear to Alex that there are standards of behaviour to which he must conform.'

Fine in principle, but not so easy in practice. Shortly afterwards, Higgins was criticised by officials at Llay British Legion in North Wales for failing to appear for an exhibition. He said he was dining with his mother in Preston on the night and had misread his diary. However, he pledged to cover the costs of the evening and promised a return visit a few weeks later.

But there was a cocktail of good and bad for Higgins before the year's end. Spencer toppled him 8–2 in the Norwich Union semi-finals at London's Piccadilly Hotel after Alex had beaten Dennis Taylor and the emerging Thorburn to get there. He then lost a third-place play-off against Charlton and must have been well pleased to see the back of 1973 – except that he announced his departure for Australia at the end of December for three months, and his forthcoming marriage to Cara Hauler.

Another slice of heartening news for him among all the slings and arrows was the gratitude of the B&K Club in Watford. They had engaged him for an exhibition and were delighted with what they got. Snooker secretary D. York wrote in *Snooker Scene*:

> We booked him to appear at 8 p.m. and he arrived at 6.30, then left
> his cue at the club while I took him around Watford to find a hotel.

We got back at 7.30 and Alex started his exhibition at once. He played 13 frames and not the nine as advertised and played at such speed that the referee had a job keeping up with him. That night finished at 1 a.m. and the next day, I phoned him to ask if he would like to return to the club for a drink. He came down at lunch-time and played another seven frames. That's not the end of the story because that same evening he was back at the club playing nine more frames, again in perfect style. On behalf of our members, I'd like to say Alex was just great.

And so to Australia, where Higgins duly married Cara – with Reardon, on tour out there, in attendance. She was four years older than him and the daughter of a racehorse owner. That suited Alex fine because he was able to indulge in his favourite pastime. But, like so much in his life, there was no stability and the marriage petered out three years later when he met Lynn. She was to become his second wife in 1980 and the mother of his children, Lauren and Jordan.

Higgins, who got into a few scrapes Down Under in early 1974, returned for another tilt at the world title at Manchester's Belle Vue announcing that his Hurricane days were over and that he had reformed. Sadly, it all finished in bitterness and anger and another fine. He produced some of his finest snooker to breeze past Southampton pro Bernard Bennett in his opening round and came up against Fred Davis for the second year running in the quarter-finals. No rain this time, but there was certainly a major storm. Higgins had built a 13–9 lead against the veteran (fully recovered from a heart attack suffered some months earlier but seemingly uncomfortable in the early stages) and looked set for his third successive semi-final.

But old Fred, belying his 61 years, fought back with three in a row, thanks to an unfortunate incident in frame 25. Higgins looked set to take the frame as he built a 32 break, but referee Jim Thorpe called him for a push-shot on the blue. Even Davis stood back from the table, suggesting it was an error. Higgins protested long and loud to no avail, then landed himself in hot water by telling the official: 'You should read the fucking rule-book.'

Davis went on to take that frame but when Higgins responded with a 54 to win the next, it left his opponent needing the last three frames for an upset win. Surely he couldn't? Oh yes he could. With Higgins on edge, Davis hit breaks of 91 and 45 to set up a final-frame shoot-out and took that as well for a 15–14 win. To his credit, Higgins accepted defeat gracefully, but the push-shot verdict still rankles with him today and, needless to say, Thorpe has never been on his Christmas card list since. As Higgins said, 'Every player I spoke with agreed it was a fair stroke and that I'd been robbed of a possible semi-final place. It disrupted my concentration and Davis sensed my mind had gone. Once more I'd blown it through no fault of my own. The sad thing, from my point of view, was that I'd fallen over backwards to mend my ways and lose my wild-man image. I might as well have not bothered.'

Having lost with dignity, Higgins then queered his pitch by launching into a rant against sponsors Park Drive and referee Thorpe in the pressroom, eventually being shown the door after threatening to fight one journalist. Reardon went on to claim his third world title and Higgins was consigned to the sidelines. Thorpe said, 'I'm convinced I was right. If there had been any doubt, I would have kept quiet. I was just doing my job. I knew the push-shot was on when Alex went for the shot from the way the balls were placed and the way he was about to play. As he played the shot I called foul and then, of course, Alex got annoyed and there we were, arguing right in front of the TV cameras and I was embarrassed.

'It's forgotten now,' he went on, 'but Alex murdered Fred in the next frame before going off the boil. I was crucified by the press and TV and that upset me for a long time.'

Curiously, Thorpe himself was dumped from the 1981 world championship by promoter Mike Patterson, who decided he had called Dennis Taylor for a push-shot incorrectly in his second-round clash with Canadian Kirk Stevens (a great Higgins pal). Thorpe was actually jocked off the match after that session and senior referee John Williams took over. It can't have pleased Patterson or Thorpe when Dennis, grinning widely, told me after the championship: 'It was more a shove than a push!'

Not surprisingly, Higgins parted company with Snooker Promotions soon after his world title failure. He teamed up with Maurice Hayes, vice-chairman of the amateur game's ruling body. Hayes had put together a stable of players under the umbrella Q Promotions Ltd, including Graham Miles and Canadian Bill Werbeniuk, plus John Virgo and Willie Thorne (both still amateurs at this time). The Irishman was billed as THE NEW ALEX HURRICANE HIGGINS. It led to an immediate tour of Canada for exhibitions but, ultimately, it would end in tears for Higgy and co.

The main event, the Players' International, was held in Thorburn's home town, Toronto. It was won by the ever-improving Canadian, who beat Dennis Taylor in the final. Taylor had beaten Higgins 8–6 in a magnificent semi-final in their first big-time encounter as professionals.

Taylor, who would enjoy a love-hate relationship with Higgins over the following two decades, said of his fellow-Ulsterman in a Burnley newspaper on his return home:

We know Higgins is a bit of a case but he is a great snooker player –

perhaps as good as any the world has seen. But normal human beings would drop down dead if they tried to live like him, if they stretched themselves to that degree. Yet if he tried to change at all, if he stopped to think, he'd no longer be Higgins. The beauty of Higgins is that he is magnificently ignorant. He doesn't know what the hell he's doing, yet when he goes to the snooker table he makes magic happen.

Higgins had enjoyed a short tour of Auckland, New Zealand, on his way out to Canada and impressed the Kiwis in a dozen exhibitions with his great break-building and general demeanour – so much so that he was invited back the following year, where he treated fans to 15 exhibitions, including 27 centuries. And although he was frowned on for some of his observations and criticisms, in the main he was well received. 'I found him good company and a gentleman at all times,' said Fred Hawken, president of the Auckland Billiards Association. 'In my opinion, with some encouragement from the right quarter, he could become an asset to this great game.'

That was but a brief respite, however, and the Higgins downward spiral continued when he resumed in England, losing 9–8 in the Norwich Union semi-finals to jet-lagged world champion Reardon (who was just back himself from a one-month trip to New Zealand and Australia). Higgins was still up among the top men but unable, seemingly, to get his hands on a trophy of any sort; while winner Spencer continued to prosper, as did Reardon. Then his luck changed in the £3,000 Watney Open at Jim Williamson's purpose-built Northern Snooker Centre in Leeds, complete with proper matchroom.

But, for the umpteenth time in his torrid career, there was more controversy, though not of his making. He came through a superb semi-final against Reardon 13–11, but only after the Welshman and some onlookers felt there had been a vital scoring error in the sixth frame. The scoreboard showed Higgins trailing 58–37 on the colours, yet some felt the score should have been a conclusive 78–37 in Reardon's favour. Higgins cleared the table to be 4–2 ahead while confusion reigned and Reardon demanded and got the removal of referee and marker; but his rival went on to win. He then toppled Fred Davis 17–11, demonstrating his new-found ability to cope with long, drawn-out safety play and capturing the £1,000 first prize.

Then followed the inaugural Benson & Hedges Masters, now the longest-running sponsored show of all and acknowledged as the *crème de la crème* of invitational events in England and in Ireland. It provided Higgins with one of his greatest triumphs, as well as one of his most abject failures. But in 1975 he was a disappointing 5–3 loser to Rex Williams in the quarter-finals, missing a series of easy shots after whitewashing Werbeniuk 5–0 in the opening round at London's West Centre Hotel. Predictably, Spencer and Reardon contested the final, the latter losing another nail-biter 9–8 to his closest rival.

There was yet more heartache to follow when Higgins, after beating David Taylor 15–2 and Williams 19–12 in the 1975 world championship (held in Melbourne, Australia), went down 19–14 in the semi-final against Reardon after sharing the first 20 frames. The Welshman completed a hat-trick of titles and his fourth in all with a do-or-die 31–30 success against home favourite Eddie Charlton. Reardon had led 16–8, then trailed 29–23 before pulling off the most sensational win of his career. The peculiar seeding system saw No. 1 seed Reardon pitched against No. 2 Spencer in a quarter-final which developed into a classic, the Lancastrian falling 19–17.

Reardon offered some complimentary words about Higgins after their match, saying, 'People don't appreciate what a great safety player he is. He negotiates the baulk colours beautifully. He doesn't pot as well as he did in the year he won and he doesn't have the same inspiration, but he's always dangerous.' Reardon added, significantly, 'Alex played quite well when he was more or less on his own. He seemed to play worse when he had his followers around him.'

Spencer accentuated his misery with a 9–8 win in a match sponsored by Benson & Hedges in Dublin's National Boxing Stadium, just outside the city (yes, they did take the ring down for the night). Then he took Alex 8–6 in a match to celebrate the opening of Potters, the Geoff Lomas-owned, John Virgo-managed club in Manchester to which Higgins was to gravitate. In fact, he and Lomas were already pals and went on to forge a partnership of sorts in the '80s.

While Higgins floundered, Maurice Hayes strengthened his Q Promotions stable with the addition of Thorburn, Spencer and Dennis Taylor. Not bad going: two world champions, two in the offing and a host of other talented prospects. But there was a little ray of sunshine for Alex in Canada, where he won the Plus Cigarettes tournament. It attracted a huge 81 entry, with players from the US, the UK and Canada. Higgins thrilled his many fans there with a 147 in practice – his fourth in all – and went on to beat Pulman 17–7 in the final to claim the $5,000 top prize.

There was another bright ray for snooker in general that year when W. D. and H. O. Wills agreed to sponsor the 1976 world championship, under the Embassy umbrella. The deal was secured by Maurice Hayes. For snooker it would, subsequently, open the door to riches untold over the next 25 years and open the eyes of a TV-watching nation accustomed only to the one-frame *Pot Black* series (from which Higgins had been banned, incidentally, after his initial, unhappy foray in 1973). But Higgins still had the proverbial mountain to climb in his search for gold.

JOHN DEE
Journalist and long-time friend of Higgins, involved in the current snooker scene as *Daily Telegraph* correspondent.
I promoted exhibitions around the West Midlands in the '70s and Alex often used to play for me, as long as I drove him to the clubs. We were travelling home one night at about 1 a.m. and Alex was desperate for a drink. 'You must be mad, Alex,' I said. 'Look at the time – there's nothing open now.' He kept insisting I must know somewhere, and I did. A pal of mine ran the King's Hill Tavern in Wednesbury and I knew he enjoyed a late-night lock-in sometimes, so I drove there. The place was in full swing because they'd had a darts match that evening.

Alex lapped it up, challenging the players to £1 a throw nearest the bull. He won a few quid and lost a few and, funnily enough, I bumped into an old pal recently and he recalled taking a tenner off Higgins, who had actually paid up. All the food laid out for the darts match had gone and Alex said he was starving. The only thing left was a bowl of beetroot and Alex kept wandering over and pulling out a slice. By the time we got back in the car at about 3.30 a.m. his hands were blood red and it looked as though he'd murdered someone. And don't forget, beetroot juice stains like nothing else and is hard to remove, so he must have had a bit of explaining to do over the next few days.

I enjoyed his company over the years and we had some good laughs. He had a soft spot for my wife and often used to drop in when he had time off. But I saw the nasty side of him for the first time in the mid-'70s when he played John Spencer in a Men of the Midlands challenge at Pelsall Labour Club, just outside Walsall. He'd beaten Spenny 5–1, the crowd had enjoyed the show and, as was the case in those days, they played the dead frames. Alex made a magnificent clearance up to blue and they loved it. But then Spencer did the same, clearing up to the pink and Higgy went mad. From being the most charming man in the world, he turned and was so sour to everyone. One old boy asked him politely if he could have his autograph and he just said, 'Fuck off.'

But he could be such a funny man at other times. A mate of mine pulled me in the street one day and asked whether Alex could write. I said, 'Of course he can. What on earth are you asking me that for?' He told me Higgins had played at Dudley Town Hall the previous night and had a rubber stamp with 'A. Higgins' on it – not even Alex or Hurricane. He sat there for ages banging this stamp down on whatever was put in front of him. Apparently, he'd had it made in Hong Kong and thought it was a brilliant idea. I suppose there must have been so many complaints that he soon dropped it. But I bet that stamp is worth a fortune now.

It's the same with his cue. As far as I'm concerned, I've got the one he won the 1972 championship with – I'm pretty certain of that, yet I've read of two other people who swear they've got it.

Sadly, he's hardly had a civil word to say to me for years. I'm not the only one, that's for sure. But I saw him about three years ago and he was very pleasant. He didn't look too bad and I told him so. But that was before his throat operation. Since then he has lost so much weight and he must be a walking miracle. But like many who have come into contact with him over the years, I still have a soft spot for Alex. Mind you, a psychologist once said he was as near as you can get to a sane man bordering on insanity.

Six

THE LONG ROAD BACK

He was ranked No. 3 in the world, but Higgins was still trawling the country, working his socks off and spreading the Hurricane gospel to all and sundry. Alex was better known in the North, naturally, because he was based in Lancashire and tended to work out of there. But he set the South alight on two glorious evenings at Fishers Centre in Acton, where he played local favourite Patsy Fagan – from the other side of the Irish border in Dun Laoghaire, just outside Dublin – for a £2,000 jackpot. This was a far greater prize than any world championship one to date. It would be the equivalent of, say, Ronnie O'Sullivan playing Stephen Hendry for £275,000 (if you consider that Mark Williams, 2000 World Champion, reaped £240,000).

Fagan had become a great favourite in London and had come through some thrilling money matches against the big-timers. But nothing ever matched this one for raw excitement. Such was the occasion that £1.50 tickets were swapping hands for up to £20 and spectators, crammed into the centre, were given full value. Fagan had just been turned down again for pro status by the WPBSA and was decidedly unhappy about the decision because he had forged a considerable amateur reputation for himself.

He received a one-black start and was 5–5 overnight. The following evening saw Fagan lead 9–7 and, with the tension mounting by the shot, Higgins win three in a row before the home player took the last two for a famous 11–10 victory which, incredibly, is still talked about with reverence today. Sadly, poor Patsy never fulfilled his outstanding promise, though he made an early, dramatic impact when accepted as a pro, only to freeze while attempting a rest shot on TV for a Rest of the World side in the World Team Cup. It signalled the beginning of the end of his career before it had hardly taken off and was considered one of the great snooker heartaches of all time.

Higgins then returned to the real world when he was beaten 7–2 by Spencer in a Champion of Champions event in Middlesbrough where, curiously, the butt of his cue snapped in the third frame. Having seen first-hand just what he did to his cue over the years, it came as no surprise to me. Alex was always fiddling with the length and weight of his cue, sawing lumps off, sticking them back on, adding lumps of Plastic Padding, rubbing them down, then hacking them off, drilling holes in the butt and pouring in lead. You name it, he did it. Yet with his staggering ability, you'd think he would have been able to play with any old cue.

But all the players are the same as far as using their own special cues is concerned. Hendry once offered a £10,000 reward when his cue was stolen during a Grand Prix event at Reading. Steve Davis had a replica made by master cuemaker John Parris when his old cue, filched from Plumstead Working Men's Club when he was a nipper, finally gave up the ghost. Even little John Higgins spent a tortuous year messing about with his cue before Parris sorted it out for him and was rewarded months later when the Scot lifted the world title in 1998.

John Parris also dealt with Alex's cue from time to time and chuckles at the memories. 'He'd phone up, come dashing round with his Burwatt Champion and expect me to drop everything and alter it on the spot,' said John. 'When I told him it would take a while, he'd just say, "Well, I'll wait, babes", and he would. I didn't have the heart to turn him down and would drop everything else to accommodate him. But he was always charming.'

The second Benson & Hedges Masters was switched to the luxurious New London Theatre, where 1,500 fans packed in for the semi-finals and final. Sadly for Higgins, he lost his opening round 4–1 against Graham Miles, who was toppled by Reardon in the final. Higgins returned to Dublin's boxing stadium for another B&H event, this time involving Spencer, Miles and Dennis Taylor, to do battle in what was to be a forerunner to the sponsor's Irish Masters in the magnificent setting of Goffs Horse Showring in Co. Kildare.

This time Higgins had to swallow a 5–0 thrashing in the final by Spencer – and on Irish telly. But Alex was far from a spent force and he made history one night with a 16-red clearance while playing Willie Thorne in a challenge match at Leicester YMCA. Higgins was left snookered after a Thorne foul with all 15 reds still on the table. He took brown as his free ball and green as the colour, then proceeded to knock in 15 reds, 10 blacks, 5 pinks and all the colours for a remarkable 146 break. Yet Higgins, who went on to whitewash Thorne 10–0, did not realise the significance of his achievement while play was in progress. 'I didn't give it a thought and I've been kicking myself ever since,' he said. 'I took pinks with three of my last four reds, but I could have got on the black just as easily.' The extra three points would have given him an unheard of 149 clearance – two more than the standard maximum.

And so to Manchester's Wythenshawe Forum for the start of the Hurricane's 1976 Embassy World Championship challenge. He got just the opener he needed with a humdinger of a first-round match against Cliff Thorburn, whose blossoming presence in the snooker world worked wonders for the game in Canada for a while and helped add an international flavour to the proceedings. Higgins won 16–14, but only after Thorburn had endeared himself to the breathless crowd with his sure-fire potting to lead 13–10.

Higgins staged a fine recovery to win the next two. But when the Toronto player went 14–12 up with one needed for a shock victory, the Irishman pulled out all the stops. Despite their appreciation of Thorburn, Higgins was a firm crowd favourite and they lifted him through the last stunning three frames to nail down a win which seemed to bode well for his chances of going all the way. And he almost did, reaching a final tinged with controversy not of his making but leaving him deflated again.

The sponsors, in their wisdom, decided to split the event in two: one half of the draw took place at Middlesbrough Town Hall and the other in Manchester. While Higgins and co. drew fans galore to the Manchester venue, Reardon and his rivals played to sparse audiences. Nevertheless, it all boiled down to a winner at each venue coming together at Wythenshawe for a final showdown. No prizes for guessing who came through his half of the draw at Middlesbrough, but the smile had long departed from Reardon's face because of what he considered poor playing conditions. The Welshman, in thunderous form, saw off John Dunning 15–7, Dennis Taylor 15–2 and Perrie Mans 20–10 to claim his final place. Higgins had a much tougher route, going from Thorburn to old rival Spencer and beating him 15–14 as well to reach the semi-finals. Then came a revenge win over Charlton, who cost him his crown in 1973 at the same stage. This time Alex crept home 20–18, but with high hopes of reclaiming the title he always felt was his by right.

Reardon, though, having had to change to Manchester and feeling unhappy with the Wythenshawe Forum set-up, was soon complaining about the glare and dazzle coming off the BBC TV lights. For once, Higgins remained relatively calm but it was obvious from the poor standard of play from both sides that something was amiss. Reardon, with a run of five consecutive frames, opened an 8–5 lead on the first day. But his mood grew grimmer as the next day wore on. Higgins won the first three frames to be all-square, then completed the afternoon session 10–9 ahead, with the champion complaining bitterly about the way the table was playing. Efforts were made during the interval to improve it, but Lady Luck frowned on poor Higgy again when play resumed. Whatever his faults, he didn't always deserve his on-table treatment, and when referee Bill Timms decided Higgins had failed to escape from a snooker, there was uproar.

Eventually, play continued after Higgins told the official: 'I'll have to accept it, but you're wrong,' while sporting Reardon spoke volumes when, having been awarded a free ball, merely asked his rival to play again. Reardon took the frame and later ran off another five frames in a row to be 15–11 ahead with half the match gone.

Again, the 1972 champion won the first two frames on the third day then, curiously, elected to play left-handed the red which would have left Reardon needing snookers. He missed; Reardon didn't and went on to extend his lead to 19–13, but not before another altercation involving Timms and a free ball for Higgins. A fuming Reardon complained at the interval about the standard of refereeing and it was no great surprise when Timms announced he was unable to carry on because of kidney trouble, appointing John Williams in his place.

As the match drifted further and further away from Higgins, so his play became more and more patchy and Reardon slept comfortably on a 24–15 overnight advantage. That was swiftly transformed the next day into a 27–16 success, his fourth world title in succession and fifth in all as Higgins subsided meekly. You can't help but wonder, though, how many times referees – unintentionally perhaps – were able to disturb the Hurricane's fragile balance. Higgins says poignantly, 'I never had any doubts about my ability. The problem was getting into so many scrapes because of my erratic temperament. By my very nature, I would never achieve a great level of consistency. That's my appeal and my downfall rolled into one.'

There was partial revenge for Higgins against the now five-times world champion the following month. He played brilliantly – shades of his carefree 1972 days – to beat Reardon 6–4 in the Canadian Club Masters final at the Northern Snooker Centre, Leeds, to pick up £1,000. He was also ranked world No. 2 behind Reardon. However he craved the world title, never mind all the accompanying glory and revenue, more than anything.

But things would get worse for Alex before they would get better. His manager-agent, Maurice Hayes of Q Promotions, was exposed as nothing more than an enthusiastic amateur, despite enticing sponsors into snooker. Hayes, it seems, took bookings and deposits from various clubs around the country but forgot to tell the players. As a result, Higgins was attributed unfairly with letting many of his fans down. The failure of Hayes to provide Embassy with a full breakdown of their first world championship left their future involvement in jeopardy and he dropped out of the scene rapidly leaving many questions unanswered.

At this time, Dennis Taylor was beginning to make a name for himself on his travels with his quality of snooker, plus the trick shots and comedy he began injecting into his exhibitions. The phone rang during one and, quick as a flash, the Irishman said, 'If that's the Hurricane, tell him I'm still ahead.' More than a shade of Jackie Rea – and Taylor also admits to being influenced by that perky little Ulsterman who started the whole comedy ball rolling. 'There's nothing new in trick shots,' says Rea today. 'I learned all mine from Joe Davis, who got his from Willie Smith, who got his from someone else. They were all passed down the line.'

With the essentially American game of pool beginning to make inroads into Britain, Higgins departed from the big table to beat Warren Simpson in the Australian Open final. He would later join forces with old enemy Eddie Charlton, promoting a new type of pool game in Britain. Its popularity has soared since those days and Steve Davis and Jimmy White, though still full-time on the snooker circuit, appear regularly on Eurosport in international competitions promoted by Barry Hearn.

Higgins travelled to Romford, the new Essex headquarters of Steve Davis and Barry Hearn (who had recently taken over the Lucania chain of snooker halls) to compete in the first Lucania pro-am. It was a typical old-style billiards hall, with a tea bar and nothing else except a derelict room to one side filled with junk, until Hearn's arrival. I was working on the *Romford Observer* right next door to the club in Arcade Place at the time and we used to pop in for a frame or two at lunchtimes, never dreaming that the likes of Higgins would be displaying his skills there within two years.

In fact, Vic Harris, a more-than-useful Essex amateur who delivered soft drinks for Schweppes for a living, began frequenting the club and we struck up a friendship. My first attempts at writing about the game revolved around Vic and his adventures in the English Championship, which he went on to win in 1981. I travelled a few miles up the road to Basildon one evening with Vic to see him play an exhibition match against John Spencer, who had been deposed of his 1972 world title by Alex shortly before. I was amazed at the professional's prowess, especially his long potting, and likened him to a Rolls-Royce purring round the table. But Vic was already my hero, so Spencer had to be No. 2 on my list then – before my meeting with Higgins, of course.

I was working and missed the whole show, but to my utter delight Harris beat Dennis Taylor and Higgins to win the Lucania title – while kid Davis gave a glimpse of what was to be by beating Harris in the Lucania National championship to reach the final. Higgins was extremely disparaging about the club and the fans who gave snooker the Romford Roar, led by former pro footballer Mark Lazarus (he scored QPR's winner against West Brom in the 1978 League Cup final at Wembley), but they didn't half get their own back on Higgy in the years to come.

Mark's brother Joe, a decent amateur boxer who also arranged unlicensed shows and took part in them, is still fighting fit at 61 today. He remembers shouting 'Come on, Vic' after Higgins had missed a shot and being challenged by the Irishman: 'Hey big mouth, put your money where your mouth is.' Joe took the bait, then realised he had only a few bob on him. 'I'll be back,' he told Higgins, then strode out to his car and drove round to rustle up some cash from friends. He arrived back in time for the interval, having scraped together £100. Lazarus confronted Higgy, saying, 'Right, Alex, I've got a ton that says Vic beats you.' Higgins sneered and responded, 'I don't bet in peanuts.' Joe, the most mild-mannered of men until roused, lunged at him and actually got his hands around his throat. 'I was so angry,' he told me. 'If the boys hadn't pulled me off him, I don't know what sort of damage I might have caused. He then went on to threaten my brother Mark that he'd get the IRA to shoot him, but Mark just laughed at him.'

From then on, though, whenever their paths crossed, Joe remembers, Alex would mutter 'Hello' and walk on. 'I've got no time for him, never have,' says Joe. He now coaches promising young Basildon pro Stuart Bingham, who scored the greatest upset in modern snooker history when he toppled seven-times world champion Stephen Hendry in the first round of the 2000 Embassy World Championship. 'I accept he did more than anyone to put modern snooker on the map, but from what I saw and what I've read, he treated everyone like rubbish. Well, he picked on the wrong bloke with me.'

Meanwhile Higgins, who was to pick on many more 'wrong blokes' in his time, travelled back across the Atlantic for the Canadian Open in Toronto. There he beat bright 18-year-old homegrown prospect Kirk Stevens, Bill Werbeniuk and Bernie Mikkelsen, but lost 17–9 to his nemesis, Spencer, in the final. However he compensated partially against a rejuvenated Spencer with a 140 break in their seven-frame challenge match afterwards.

Soon afterwards came the news that was to revolutionise professional snooker – thanks to Mike Watterson, a quality amateur whose wife Carol (now deceased), returned to their Chesterfield home from watching a play at Sheffield's Crucible Theatre and told him it would make a fantastic venue for snooker. Watterson popped in and liked what he saw. Within months Sheffield had become the home of snooker and Watterson, who was worth a good few bob even then, was on his way to untold riches. Deservedly so, because he was ultimately responsible for the professional circuit which exists today (although his aptitude for gleaning sponsorships far surpassed today's efforts).

It was then back to Australia, this time for the World Matchplay Championship – devised by Eddie Charlton and sanctioned by the WPBSA, but not *the* world championship. It was an incredible scenario and when Charlton beat Reardon in the final he was acknowledged by some, even in Britain, as the new world title-holder.

Higgins went as far as the quarter-finals before bowing out to Paddy Morgan. Alex, on the map in every sense but not the honours board, had a year of mixed fortunes in 1977. He opened his Benson & Hedges Masters challenge at London's New Drury Lane Theatre with a 4–2 win over South African Perrie Mans. Then he fell in the semi-finals in a patchy match against rookie pro Doug Mountjoy, the Welshman who stunned the snooker world by going on to beat world champion Ray Reardon 7–6 in the final. Another big one had eluded Higgins and he must have despaired of ever seeing his name on a trophy again. Worse was to follow in the Embassy World Championship, staged at its new Sheffield home in the tailor-made Crucible Theatre venue and offering a staggering £17,000 in prize money.

But before then he secured a precious win over Reardon in another B&H event in the Republic of Ireland, this time at Leopardstown Race Club. Also competing in the round-robin event were Graham Miles and Dennis Taylor, whose opener against Higgins produced an absolute corker. Higgins opened with a 61; Taylor responded with a 71, then sat back and spectated as his rival ran off breaks of 66, 78 and 126 for a 4–1 win.

Breathless stuff. But when Reardon beat Higgins by the same score on the first day, it was anyone's match. Finally, on the third day, it boiled down to a one-frame play-off between Taylor and Higgins for the right to play Reardon in the final. When Taylor opened up a 57 lead it looked all over for Higgins, but an error by Dennis was all Alex needed and he leapt in with a lightning 70 clearance. He then toppled Reardon 5–3 in front of an ecstatic crowd to enhance his reputation still further with the Irish.

Alas, his dreams fell apart for another year at the Crucible, the venue that saw in the game's greatest era and was to become the theatre of heartache and triumph. Higgins faced hot newcomer Doug Mountjoy in his opening round and was pipped 13–12 in a thriller, a do-or-die black down the rail sending Mountjoy clear. It was a nightmare for Higgins and the sponsors. Or so they thought, until BBC viewers began switching on in their millions. It was the widest exposure yet for the sport and the popularity was to gather in pace in the next decade. Spencer notched the third and last of his world titles, beating Thorburn 25–21 to make history by becoming the first Crucible champion.

But Higgins rounded off the season in spectacular style when he took Pontin's by storm. Only TV's *Pot Black* entrants were invited as professionals to compete in the Professional and Open events at the popular holiday camp jamboree at Prestatyn in North Wales, so Higgins, having been shunned by *Pot Black*, flew solo. He took advantage of a new ruling, allowing pros to compete in the Open section by conceding 21 points per frame, and joined the rank and file in the toughest of all pro-ams to win.

The toughest, because the qualifying rounds – known as the Sheets – are played on what can only be described as holidaymaker tables and over a two-frame aggregate score. In effect, the pros were conceding 42 points per match, sometimes to quality amateurs. But it was a marvellous format because it meant ordinary, bread-and-butter club players had a chance of tackling a famous name.

Higgins came through the Sheets in a style reminiscent of his great world title victory five years earlier, and endeared himself further to an ever-growing army of fans with every shot. He had only one qualifying stumbling block in the shape of Billy Kelly, a left-hander from Manchester who was certainly a cut above many of the entrants.

Kelly, with his huge start, led by 104 points with only four reds remaining in the opening frame and sensed a famous success. But Higgins, accompanied by a tidal wave of support, rose to the occasion and nicked it by 12 points. He went on to secure victory on the colours in the next frame. No one had ever recovered from such a deficit and from there Higgy grew in strength as the competition was whittled down to the last 32. He beat Doug French and Murdo McLeod (both to turn pro in the '80s) 4–3 downstairs on the show table, then blew Reardon away 4–0 with one of his greatest displays ever against the maestro. That took him into the semi-finals, where he beat Fred Davis by the same score.

The final was watched by an incredible 2,000 spectators (remember, the Crucible holds fewer than 900). Alex conceded 25 points per frame to new English amateur champion Terry Griffiths and won 7–4, teaching the Welshman a lesson to remember. Mind you, Terry was to pay him back in spades over the next few years when he gained his pro ticket. The Irishman proved conclusively that although he was regarded as a nonconformist, he truly was the People's Champion. And didn't he deserve the whopping £1,500 top prize? Such was the impact Alex's success had that his achievement is still spoken of in glowing terms today by snooker people.

Sadly, it was to prove a mere pebble on the beach for nearly a year. Higgy's next big test came in the Canadian Open in Toronto and by this time he had joined Reardon and Spencer at the International Snooker Agency (ISA). This was formed by Del Simmons, a Surrey-based entrepreneur who couldn't believe how poorly paid the top players were, and how they were usually obliged to handle their own affairs, when he booked Spencer for an exhibition at his home town of Weybridge. So Simmons, Reardon and Spencer put their heads together and formed the agency (all three were directors), which attracted several classy players.

Del was to prove a giant for Higgins, and the game generally, before his untimely death from cancer some years ago.

Good news for TV fans came when Alex was welcomed back to the *Pot Black* fold for 1978 after an absence of five years – not that it concerned him overly, because he had little time for the one-frame event that offered great projection for pros. He made his negative views clear on several occasions, much to the chagrin of commentator Ted Lowe who devised the event and had a major say in which eight played each year. But the marriage lasted just one season before Higgins was bombed out again. 'We're always looking to show new faces,' said Ted Lowe – who promptly welcomed back 65-year-old Fred Davis for the 1979 series.

Meanwhile, the most hilarious event ever staged loomed in Canada. The Canadian Open was always a must for players, but this year the regular Toronto venue was unavailable and so – to the astonishment of players and officials alike – it was held in a big top with a live circus going on next door (complete with dancing elephant) plus a steel band and a non-stop dance group in adjoining tents. It was either that or cancel the tournament. And what a to-do. The fierce heat led to swarms of flies and impossible conditions, yet even today the event is remembered fondly by the players.

Higgins, revelling in the abnormal conditions, beat Thorburn 9–6, then Reardon 9–7 in the semis after leading 8–3. And there was Spencer waiting for him in the final for the second year running. Not for the first time, they clashed in a verbal confrontation which sowed the seeds of unrest between Higgins and ISA. But he was still bubbling with pride from his Pontin's win and saw off the old enemy 17–14 with an array of shots and positional play which had the watching Joe Davis shaking his head in amazement. And even the next-door elephant trumpeted his approval.

Higgins went from one circus arena to another when he headed to Blackpool Tower Circus ('40s and '50s home of the legendary Fred Davis–John Pulman–Walter Donaldson world title shoot-outs) for the inaugural UK Championship, which was sponsored by billiard ball manufacturers Super Crystalate and promoted by Watterson. But Higgins failed to juggle his act successfully as Irish newcomer Patsy Fagan stole his thunder with a début title win 12–9 over Doug Mountjoy. Higgins reached the semi-finals, only to be ousted 9–2 by Mountjoy after a spanking first-frame 129. He was distracted midway through the match by a spectator complaining of not being able to see. But Alex was 6–2 down at that stage and it probably did not affect the outcome – but he was so finely balanced, who knows what went on inside his head at the time?

There was yet another barrowload of controversy during the

tournament but, mercifully, Higgins was not to blame. Willie Thorne, a more-than-promising newcomer, was accused of a deliberate miss by Rex Williams in their second-round match. The row rumbled on after Thorne's win and he was disqualified, then reinstated. London-based Fagan made another big impression when he beat Higgins 4–2 at Wembley Conference Centre in the Dry Blackthorn Cup, put on by boxing promoter Mike Barrett in January 1978. That doubled Fagan's earnings to £4,000 in just a month, with Higgins pocketing £1,000. The Hurricane was beginning to roar again, though, and he defended his Irish title successfully with a 21–7 defeat of Dennis Taylor at Belfast's Ulster Hall on a table with tight pockets, tailor-made for his precision potting.

'It was like a bad dream,' said a bewildered Taylor, who had always given as good as he got throughout their formative years as amateurs and professionals. The pulling power of Higgins and, to a lesser extent, Taylor, attracted more than 4,000 spectators over three days, alerting sponsors B&H that there was definitely a huge market for snooker in Ireland, either side of the border.

Even better was to come for Alex. Two days after that success, the two Irish rivals were back over in England, contesting the B&H quarter-finals at the New London Theatre. Again, Higgins emerged victorious 4–3 after a much tighter match. A quickfire 5–1 win over Reardon took him into a final confrontation against Thorburn, who had beaten Mountjoy and Spencer, and what a cracker it turned out to be. Higgins roared into a 3–0 lead and was clearly looking for an early night. But the dogged Canadian had other ideas and won the next three to reverse the pressure. It went tit for tat from then on until, at 5–5, Higgins won the next two for a 7–5 win.

The £3,000 jackpot was more than welcome, but for Alex it signalled a genuine return to the big time after all those years in the wilderness watching Spencer and Reardon, then newcomers Mountjoy and Fagan, steal his thunder at every turn.

*

VIC HARRIS
Former English amateur champion, who turned pro under Barry Hearn and has been a great inspiration to Essex players for years.
I'll never forget the year Alex went through the Sheets at Pontin's because we were all dead chuffed for him. It was a fabulous achievement and he had the whole place rocking at Prestatyn. I'd been around a few years on the amateur circuit without quite breaking through and I bumped into him on the stairs coming down

from the main snooker room at Pontin's one evening. 'Harris, you're useless,' he said. 'You can't play snooker to save your life.' I just laughed and replied, 'Alex, I can take that from you – you're absolutely right.'

With that, he said, 'I'll play you for £100 over seven frames,' and I agreed. Back we went up the stairs and got cracking. Before I knew it, I was level at 3–3 with everything resting on the final frame. Alex opened up a 49-point lead with only three reds left and he wanted the black off its spot to win. As he walked past me he said, 'Good game this, Vic.' Unfortunately for him, he missed and I dished up to win. Needless to say, his face was thunder, but he paid up and I just kept smiling. He was an incredible player and I'm pretty certain just about everyone learned something from him because he was so sharp – and such a character.

We were playing in Canada once and I happened to have the room next to him in the hotel. We checked in during the evening and I was knackered and decided on an early night. At about 2 a.m. my phone rang and it was Alex. 'D'you fancy a drink, babes?' he asked. I couldn't believe it. It was so late and, anyway, everyone knows I'm teetotal. About an hour later there was a knock on the door and Alex said, 'Well, d'you fancy a Chinese, then?' When I stopped laughing, I told him it was far too late and we left it at that.

Blow me, the next night I'm in bed again and there's a terrific ruction going on in the corridor. I rolled over to get back to sleep and all of a sudden there's a knock on my door and two security officers are standing there. 'Excuse me, sir, but we've been informed there's been some trouble and your room number has come up,' said one of them. I told them to try next door and, sure enough, Alex had been having a row with someone.

He was really wound up and lots of verbals went on. But in the end they quietened him down and went off. Alex said, 'Come in, babes, I want to show you something. I invited a girl up for a drink, but there was something dodgy about her and I thought she might be after my money when my back was turned.' With that, he opened the window and hauled in some string with a sock tied to the end. He was giggling as he opened the sock and shook all his money out. 'I'm far too clever for them,' he said.

I just cracked up. It was a whole new world to me.

Seven

BLACK AND BLUE ALL OVER

The tide had turned and surely now Higgins could march on the Crucible Theatre, confident of regaining his pot of gold at last. But he just couldn't resist another couple of outbursts before the Sheffield jamboree. He let fly in the J. W. Lees Trophy pro-am event in what was a home fixture for him at Potters Club in Salford. Higgins, playing John Hargreaves in the semi-finals, arrived late, then went 3–1 down at the interval against the mild-mannered amateur, who was receiving 14 points per frame. Then he started, complaining bitterly that he wanted the balls to be changed because they were 'sweating'. Hargreaves reasoned that they were OK for him, and was told for his troubles: 'I'm the professional – you're the amateur.'

Higgins then clashed with old referee foe Jim Thorpe, who told him the balls were staying where they were, and for that received a verbal long pot from the Belfast man. Alex then suggested they place the balls in a hot oven, to which Thorpe again responded negatively. Finally, to pacify an overheated Higgins, Thorpe and Hargreaves agreed he could put them on top of a radiator in a container. It was a farcical turn of events and just showed what Higgins got away with in those days. Nevertheless, Hargreaves went on to beat him 5–3, then toppled Virgo 5–2 in the final – and, backed by Thorpe, filed an official complaint about the behaviour of his opponent.

There was more trouble at the Ipswich Corn Exchange when Higgins was beaten 7–3 by Patsy Fagan in an invitation event. Higgins, trailing 6–3, accused the referee of disturbing his concentration by moving after he had missed a simple shot. He then refused to play out the dead frames, as was the custom in those days to give spectators full value for money, unless he could bet on the outcome. Fagan, the last person in the world to get involved in trouble, agreed to play best of three for £100 – for the sake of peace – and Higgins got his just deserts when Fagan beat him again and donated the money to charity. Fagan was such a decent man and a great player to boot and what happened to his career was heartbreaking; but more of that later. Higgins stormed out, refusing even to collect his runner-up cheque. The promoter vowed that he would never be welcomed back. That was to become a recurring pledge from other organisers over the years, and not just in England.

But all was sweetness and light when Higgins returned to Ireland – south of the border this time – for another four-man B&H event, at Goffs, in Naas, Co. Kildare, which was to become the home of the Irish Masters. Spencer beat Mountjoy to win the tournament in front of an enthusiastic 1,000 crowd, with Higgins behaving himself throughout. And so, primed once more for world championship action in his own inimitable, impossible way, Higgins set sail for Sheffield.

Awaiting him in the first round was Fagan, itching no doubt to put his troublesome opponent in his place again. But what a dish they served up for fans at the Crucible, battling through 25 frames before Fagan snatched a memorable 13–12 victory by winning the last three frames. At 12–10 up, it seemed Higgins had only to stay cool to make progress. Fagan went 41–0 ahead in the next frame, only for Alex to hit back with a 66. Yet his miss on the green left the door ajar for Patsy who cleaned up to win on the black, then pipped Alex with a superb black in the 24th frame to level at 12–12. With two black-ball finishes both going Fagan's way, the crowd were going wild with excitement. But when Higgins took a narrow lead in the final frame after missing an easy red, and then laid a snooker, Fagan appeared to be at the end of the line. But he played his way out of it, fluked a snooker himself in the process, then cleared the colours up to the pink to record a breathtaking win. So Higgins was out of it again almost before he had begun.

He left the arena in tatters, little knowing an even worse fate was in store for him 12 months down the line. Fagan fell to Fred Davis in the next round and Reardon rewrote the history book again by beating Perrie Mans in the final to take his fifth title in six years and his sixth in all – a modern record which was to stand until Steve Davis equalled it in 1989 and Stephen Hendry overtook it in 1999.

The 13-day championship marked a turning point for snooker because the BBC, realising they were looking at and sitting on a goldmine for viewers, increased their coverage to nearly one hour a day – a mixture of live play and highlights – and audience figures shot to an unprecedented six million for the final. There was much rejoicing all round. The tournament was tinged with sadness, however, when 77-year-old Joe Davis, watching his brother's every shot in the semi-finals against Mans, complained of pains in his back and was taken back to his hotel, ashen-faced. He spent the next day in bed and was then driven to his London home, where he collapsed on the pavement. Joe, without whom snooker would never have seen the light of day publicly, underwent an operation lasting more than six hours; and although that got him over the crisis, he was to die two months later.

There was a typical Higgins postscript to the championship when he was involved in a skirmish with Graham Miles at Caerphilly during a round-robin one-nighter. It must have been hilarious to witness this, because winner Miles, a peace-loving man, generally, who looked so innocuous, got a mouthful of abuse from Higgins as he went to collect his £500 winner's cheque. Alex, who felt Graham had enjoyed the run of the balls, called him a 'jammy bald bugger', at which Miles took a swing at him. He missed and Higgins, in shying away, overbalanced and tumbled into the crowd. Once they got backstage, the rumpus continued and I seem to remember Higgins ending up with a black eye – although his version of events differs. Promoter Ray Davies was said to have fined them both £200. They clashed again in Pwllheli one night and apparently knocked six bells out of each other. Miles begs to differ, saying today that it was 'just a tiff blown up by the press. There was nothing to it, really.'

Higgins went from bad to worse during a subsequent event at Middlesbrough's TUC Club when he faced the up-and-coming Steve Davis – who was beginning to create big waves on the amateur scene – in an 11-frame, £300 challenge match. Davis, given a two-black start per frame, was 4–1 up after the opening night (I could never understand why they spread so few frames over two nights), so Higgins challenged local amateurs and support bill Dave Martin and George Wood, who were to turn pro later, to play money matches. He lost both and in doing so forfeited his guaranteed purse for the two nights. No problem for the promoter, but big problems for the petulant Hurricane, who threatened not to return for the second night. In the event he did, only to finish a 6–2 loser – Davis showing shades of the class which would propel him to greatness in a few short years with an 82 clearance.

A scathing report in *Snooker Scene* recorded:

> Although no one likes losing, mature players learn to cope with these setbacks, but Higgins is all too prone to sulk, lash out or simply dull the pain with drink. His capacity for self-destruction is terrifying. Indeed, his behaviour is such as to virtually invite someone to attack him . . . He was lucky, many felt, to escape from the TUC Club unscathed after the incident at the Davis match. All the danger signals are raised as far as his personal future is concerned and he is badly in need of the right kind of advice before it is too late.

The magazine article summed up the Higgins situation to the letter and, sadly, it could have applied to any stage of his turbulent career. He neither listened to, nor heard, any words of wisdom from well-wishers, and he paid little heed to any of his managers as his career lurched from one self-made crisis to another. And it was still only 1978. His next jaunt was the defence of his Canadian Open in Toronto, where he notched the fourth 147 of his career while practising. Higgins beat diminutive Canadian Mario Morra (dubbed 'Short Sticks' when he arrived in England as a pro in the '80s), then Steve Davis 9–8 in a quarter-final thriller.

But he was shocked rigid by 19-year-old British junior champion Tony Meo, who won their semi-final 9–7 for the finest result of his fledgling career. Meo was beaten 19–17 by Thorburn in the final, but his performance left no one in doubt that, along with Davis, he was one to watch for in the future.

On his return home, Higgins also lost to Vic Harris in the Lucania pro-am semi-finals at Romford. Harris, in turn, was beaten in the final by his Romford stablemate Davis, who was taking his final bow as an amateur. Higgins picked up what was for him a measly £60, which makes you wonder why he travelled all the way down from Manchester to a venue he hated with a vengeance.

He observed in *Alex Through the Looking-Glass*:

> I hated the sinister bunch of hangers-on who followed Steve Davis around. I first met them down at Romford in the late '70s when Barry Hearn booked me for a series of money matches at a seedy little dive called the Matchroom. Little did I realise I was being used as fodder for Davis. Hearn was nurturing his talent and a troupe of East End desperados were growing fat gambling on his ability to take on all-comers. Don't get the idea Davis started off in some romantic little corner of London. The place was full of tin ashtrays ingrained with dirt and if you asked for another cup of tea it came stale and cold in the same chipped cup you used last time. You had to stand up because there was nowhere comfortable or clean enough to sit down. I detested being asked to play in those conditions and there was no love lost between me and the Hearn camp from that moment on.

Alex has the most vivid memory – and the most colourful imagination. I lived in Romford then and I know what I saw and heard. Yes, the Matchroom was shabby, because there were no vast wads of money in Hearn's bank account at the time. He'd recently bought the Lucania chain of billiard halls and was only a kid himself, dipping his toes in shark-infested snooker waters. As for the bunch of East End hooligans who, Alex recalls, jumped on the Davis bandwagon: they were the same crowd who had frequented the Lucania long before the arrival of Hearn and they were dead proud to have one of their own – two, in fact, with Harris – who could take on the big boys. Sure, they were loud, sometimes even raucous. But even Higgins went over the top when he said, 'They came from all over docklands and screamed and shouted like banshees.'

Most of them were, in fact, locals. They meant no harm and I'm sure Alex would have loved regular support like that instead of being surrounded by the hangers-on and parasites who varied from tournament to tournament. And don't forget, these Romford guys followed Steve through thick and thin, spending fortunes travelling with him and staying in guest houses and hotels. True, some weren't the kind of people who frequented the genteel surroundings of Plumstead Working Men's Club, where Steve began his long journey of discovery alongside his smashing dad, Bill; and yes, they won bundles betting on their boy. But he loved it when that Romford Roar went up. And incidentally, when Hearn *did* hit the heights with Davis, he sold off the Lucania chain for over £3 million but retained his Romford centre: there he created a luxurious, exclusive club from the fag-ends of the old one, with huge office quarters downstairs from where he ran his Matchroom base for many years until converting the whole place into a professional boxing gymnasium and moving his headquarters into a sumptuous new property a few hundred yards away.

The whole set-up can't have frightened Higgins that much, because he offered his services to Hearn some years later and was shattered to be rejected out of hand. 'I knew I'd have to sell my soul, but I also knew this company would take charge of everything, even down to paying the electricity bills,' he said. 'Hearn turned me down point-blank and said I was impossible to manage, but I don't think I was. I put bums on seats and sport depends on people coming through the turnstiles.'

Barry actually chatted with me about it at the time (around 1982) when I was sniffing round for a story, having heard whispers about the link-up, and what Alex said in his book years later simply confirmed it. 'He would have been a nightmare,' said Hearn, who had recently embraced Griffiths and Meo into the Matchroom team. 'Can you imagine me losing sleep over Steve when he is out of sight? Higgins is a great player but I know I'd be letting myself in for a 24-hour headache every day. I just don't need the aggro because things are going so well with Steve, Tony and Terry.'

Higgins had one more big trip down south before the 1978 UK Championship at Preston's Guild Hall. Armed with the knowledge that he had been at his best in winning the B&H, he must have felt confident about his chances of lifting the £2,000 in the *Daily Mirror*'s Champion of Champions – promoted again by boxing man Mike Barrett at Wembley Conference Centre.

Higgins beat Mountjoy in the four-man event to qualify for a final clash with Reardon, who won 6–1 against a suffering Fagan. He had been haunted by the 'yips' with the cue rest for the past year and had also hurt an arm in a car crash some months earlier. And, though crowds weren't huge in the big arena, those who attended were treated to a wonderful exhibition of snooker from both players. Reardon took a comfortable 9–5 lead in the 21-frame showdown and looked home and dry; but Higgins, as so often in front of an appreciative audience, raised his game and won the next four to be level. He even took a substantial lead in frame 19, only for the Welshman to conjure a 77 clearance to regain his advantage. This clearly took the wind out of his opponent's sails and Reardon raced through the next frame to wrap up an 11–9 victory.

The world champion then praised Higgins, at the same time paying himself a back-handed compliment: 'Higgins usually plays well against me because he builds up for it and treats me with the proper respect. He sometimes loses to other players because he believes he can beat them without really trying. He lives for performing in front of a crowd and, if they get behind him, it usually lifts him. Once he gets a charge going he is very difficult to stop, but when I won the 19th frame he looked like someone who had been travelling at 100 m.p.h. and had suddenly hit a brick wall.'

Higgins took defeat well, saying, 'It was a good match and I feel there's only Reardon and me now.' Little did he know . . .

For all his bravado, Higgins was well below par when he opened his account against close pal Jim Meadowcroft at Preston's Guild Hall in the Coral UK Championship. Superb new sponsors and a superb new venture which, sadly, was where the start of Higgy's ultimate downfall would take place some years on. Meadowcroft, who on occasions had acted as chauffeur to Alex and offered a well-worn shoulder to cry on whenever necessary, had every opportunity to pull off a shock victory; but he just could not get his break-building going and Higgins went through to a quarter-final meeting with Fred Davis, who tested his on-table patience to the limit. Higgy went 5–0 and 8–2 up against the veteran. Fred scratched his way through the next two and looked set to make it 8–5 until the Irishman fluked the black and went on to secure a 9–4 win.

So far so good, but Higgins, now odds-on favourite to capture the second-most prestigious title behind the world crown, ran into Mancunian David Taylor in the best form of his life. Taylor, much to his own delight, raced into a 7–1 lead and effectively killed off the Higgins challenge in that first session because he needed just two more for a place in the final. He achieved the lead by stealth and accuracy, punishing Higgins for his many unforced errors without ever scoring heavily. Higgins came out after the interval stoked up; but though he took the opening three frames, it was never going to be enough and Taylor was left celebrating a famous 9–5 success. That pitched him against 1977 runner-up Mountjoy in the final – but the Taylor bubble, which had floated along happily throughout, was pricked by the Welshman, who added the UK title to his B&H success with a 15–9 win.

The odds against Higgins winning another important title seemed to lengthen with every tournament, though he was still making his mark in lesser events. The Castle Open at Southampton was a case in point. He'd won it the previous year and Alex, coming in at the last-eight stage, beat Perrie Mans and Mountjoy to reach the final, then saw off Fred Davis 5–1 with an exceptional spell of attacking snooker. Wembley's Conference Centre was his next stop on the competitive agenda and Higgins had a fresh opportunity to thrust himself right back to the fore in the B&H Masters as defending champion. It all went to plan as he beat arch-enemy Charlton in the quarter-finals and Mountjoy 5–1 in the semis.

Alas, the best-laid plans of mice and men . . . facing him was South African Perrie Mans, a demon potter who cared little for the finesse of break-building or positional play. Perrie's idea was to smash down every red ball possible, hope for a colour and run for cover if none was on. Snooker players in the main are tidy creatures of habit. They like to know all the colours are on their spots, so they don't have to keep looking around the table. Obviously these do get dislodged, when reds are missed or when the white cannons into them inadvertently, but just watch any half-decent pro – or even club player these days – and they do their utmost to make sure all the spots are covered correctly. Not so our Perrie, who attacked everything with a zest which opponents found off-putting. True, his safety was solid and his spectacular long-potting made him a great favourite with spectators. Higgins won the first two frames, then could only watch as Mans swarmed all over him, taking six in a row. And when the defending champion forced a respotted black, then went in-off unluckily from a ridiculous angle, he must have known his number was up. Mans ran out an 8–4 winner.

Higgins was down but not out, and the cancellation of Eddie Charlton's World Matchplay Championship Down Under a month or so before the official world championship would have brought a smile to his face. There was never any love lost between the two players and Charlton was adamant Higgins would not play in his event. Higgins was fully entitled to compete as a high-ranking pro, and even considered legal action against the Aussie at one stage, even though the WPBSA sanctioned the event and okayed the ban. But the collapse of sponsorship left Charlton red-faced – and a good few pros wondering how they would fill their empty engagement books. I'm sure Higgy will have reminded Charlton of this embarrassing flop from time to time. Just to pass the time of day, you understand.

'I was the only one of the top 13 pros not invited, just because I told some club official over there to bugger off when he forced me to wear a bow-tie,' said Higgins. 'I had a lot of good friends in Australia and they thought it was diabolical. I don't deny my behaviour over there has been a little rowdy at times, but how many Aussies do you know who are shrinking violets? It was cancelled in the end, which was a catastrophe for the organiser – it couldn't have happened to a nicer fellow.'

Higgins enjoyed a nail-biting 5–4 win over Reardon to win the Tolly Cobbold Invitation round-robin event at Ipswich. This also featured Steve Davis, who whacked Alex 4–0 early on, only to lose by the same score against Reardon. Those who saw the final will never forget it because the standard of play was exceptional, even by the standards set by these two great warriors. The nine-frame showdown took less than two hours' table time. The breaks weren't earth-shattering – a 68 and 80 by Reardon and a couple of 60s from Higgins – but the quality dazzled everyone. When Reardon hit a 49 in the final frame to lead 57–8, it looked all over. But the Hurricane, sensing blood, fired in a rapid 63 to clinch the match at one of his favourite venues. He told me he loved playing for the Cobbold family, whose roots were deep seated in brewing and Ipswich Town Football Club. They always treated him like a king and he responded on the table, blotting his copybook there just once.

Alex had a special date at Ulster's Belfast Hall, where he defended his Irish title against Patsy Fagan, but before then he found himself at Romford, playing new pro Steve Davis over five nights and 63 frames. Needless to say, Davis won 32–23 in another exciting encounter which realised three centuries by the resident pro and one from Higgins, plus many other high breaks from either side. Barry Hearn knew these head-to-head clashes could only be of benefit to the Davis education and the only reason such players as Reardon, Higgins, Griffiths and Thorburn went along with them at Fortress Matchroom was because they were paid exceptionally well. Higgins described them all as 'cannon-fodder', but they all had a choice.

During the Davis heyday of the '80s, the 16-year-old Stephen Hendry played him over six consecutive nights throughout Scotland and was thrashed each time. His canny manager, Ian Doyle, having read of the Davis exploits at Romford, turned it against the Hearn camp despite the miserable scoreline. On paper it cost Doyle a small fortune, but as he said, 'How else could you get six solid nights of matchplay with the greatest player of all for that sort of price? Davis hammered my boy because he knew how dangerous he could become and wanted to put him in his place.

'But it had the adverse effect', he continued. 'Instead of being scared off, Stephen took strength from it and went on to become even greater than Davis. And I made a few bob out of the whole deal with gate receipts.' No wonder Doyle and Hearn were to fall in and out of the commercial bed regularly over the next 15 years. They came from the same pod, always with an eye for the main chance, and linked up in many lucrative ventures.

Higgins marched on the Ulster Hall determined to prove to his adoring public there that he was still Ireland's best player, having seen off Dennis Taylor's challenge the previous year. Despite putting on a quieter face than normal, he was in superb form against Fagan, hammering him 21–12 and treating unbelieving eyes to a 100 m.p.h. century into the bargain. Higgins fired home a 122 break in just 2 min. 45sec. (Maltese pro Tony Drago made a century in 2 min. 12 sec. as a young amateur) and even today, 'Rocket' Ronnie O'Sullivan – by far the fastest break-builder in world snooker – would have to go some to match that. 'I'm a rhythm player and when I find that rhythm there's not another man in the world to beat me,' said a jubilant Higgins.

It was terrific stuff, though considered small fry in the broad context of the game. It also gave Higgins a perfect warm-up for the Embassy World Championship, fast approaching its third year at Sheffield. None of the pundits gave Welshman Terry Griffiths a second glance as they pored over the betting odds and automatically worked out who Higgy would meet in the quarter-finals. The quiet, unobtrusive former English amateur champion had all but quit the pro circuit after his shocking baptism, losing 9–8 to Rex Williams in a UK qualifier at Romford after leading 8–2. But sometimes fate takes a hand and someone up there must have decreed that the 1979 world championship would throw up a fairytale of mammoth proportions.

Higgins swiftly avenged his UK defeat by David Taylor with a comfortable 13–5 opening-round win, while Griffiths took just three more frames to beat Perrie Mans. The Ulsterman, who destroyed his Welsh opponent in that memorable Pontin's final while conceding 21 points a frame just two years earlier, must have been looking ahead at the draw as well. But it just didn't work out that way as Griffiths matched fire with fire in what is generally considered among the greatest of matches played at the Crucible Theatre. The opening four frames went by in a blur, Higgy firing two centuries and the Griff enjoying two black-ball successes. Higgins rushed out after the break to impose himself on the upstart and won four frames in a row to finish the session in good shape at 6–2 up.

Remarkably, Griffiths won three consecutive black-ball games to narrow the gap to just one, before Higgins hit back with two of his own to be 8–5 ahead and still well in control. Or so it seemed. The Llanelli man, who had never experienced such an atmosphere, was supposed to fold at this stage and leave it to the wise old pro to show him the ropes. But Griffiths, despite this soft-looking exterior, was solid steel inside and he came back at the 1972 champion with a devastating ton and two other frames to be all-square at 8–8. The Crucible crowd were in uproar.

Griffiths was first to strike when the breathtaking match resumed, only for Higgins to grit his teeth and come back with a 63 frame-clincher. So it was 9–9 and still in the balance. They swapped the next four frames and then came the crunch: Higgins missed a dolly back when leading 55–0 with a century beckoning. It could well have broken Griffiths, but instead he took up the challenge, clearing with a 67 to go 12–11 up and be within a frame of safety. Back came Higgins to force a final-frame shoot-out, but you could almost see in his eyes that he knew he'd blown it.

Sure enough, Alex was forced to sit and spectate as Terry put together a winning 107 break on top of his six black-ball finishes. So for the third year running, Higgins had been edged out by a frame. He wouldn't have been human had he not left the Crucible in despair. 'I watched distraught as Terry made that century to beat me, and he has proved to be a constant thorn in my side ever since,' said Higgins.

As everyone knows, Griffiths went on to beat Charlton in the semi-final, thanks to an amazing fluke at a crucial time. He then told TV presenter David Vine, in his lilting accent, 'I'm in the final now, you know.' It couldn't have happened to a nicer chap and when he went on to beat Dennis Taylor in the final, a new star was born and the public had another champion they could call their own. Higgins, always acknowledged as the man who thrust snooker into the limelight, would have to concede that Terry's incredible success, watched by millions, brought home the message that the sport was live theatre – live drama encapsulating every emotion. The BBC had a hit 'soap' series on their hands, starring real 'actors'. The snooker boom was on its way.

The knife was twisted deeper by another Welshman, Reardon, shortly afterwards when he met Higgins at Ulster Hall over two days in a 37-frame Guinness-sponsored challenge match. Higgins lost his proud, unbeaten record there, going down 19–9, and he lost the nine-frame exhibition that followed as well.

Around this time, from within the confines of the amateur game, emerged a London kid called Jimmy White. He had just become the youngest English champion at 16. Already friends with Alex, he was to play an important part in the Ulsterman's life during the next two decades.

Higgins spent the summer of 1979 licking his wounds, then returned to Toronto for the Canadian Open. He'd been there earlier in the year with Dennis Taylor, winning a Northern Ireland–Canada match against Thorburn and Stevens. But it just wasn't to be. After cruising through his opening two rounds, he came up against Thorburn in the semi-finals and went down 9–6 after leading 4–2. Griffiths, with his new-found celebrity status, went all the way to the final. Squeezing past Stevens 9–8 in the semis, he fell to Thorburn 17–16 from 10–3 down in a marathon-style match which was to be their trademark whenever they met. Again the conditions were sweltering, which made life difficult for the players.

Next came the inaugural State Express World Team Championship at Birmingham's Haden Hill. Higgins and Taylor linked with old pal Jackie Rea there to form the Northern Ireland team, which finished third. Wales (Reardon, Mountjoy and Griffiths) whacked England (Spencer, Fred Davis and Graham Miles), in the final. But the event will be remembered only for poor Patsy Fagan's inability to use the rest while playing for the Rest of the World team. You could see close-up on TV the anguish on his face as he tried and tried without success to push his cue through to the white ball; I'm sure millions must have sympathised with the little guy with a big heart.

Fagan tried so hard to overcome the psychological problem, but it kept returning to haunt him. He finally gave up a game which promised so much when he had ruled the London roost, become UK pro champion at his first attempt in 1977 and stunned Higgins a few times. Patsy was already struggling to contain the problem when Alex beat him in the Irish Championship earlier in the year, but there is no doubt he would have become a formidable rival to Higgins and Taylor had the demons not gripped him.

In fact, Fagan reached the Coral UK Championship quarter-finals a month later, and so did Higgins, only to fall on his face against that man Griffiths. A huge crowd had assembled and again they were not disappointed. It seemed impossible that the pair could supply an action-replay of their Sheffield extravaganza, but they did. This time, though, the world champion opened a 5–2 lead, only for Higgins to roar back with five in a row – including a 104 – to go in front 7–5. But Griffiths, armed with his new status, reversed the pressure slowly but surely. He got back to 7–7, then fired a 118 to demoralise Alex and finished him off in the 16th frame to win 9–7.

To my utter dismay, I missed the match. It was my first tournament as *Daily Mail* snooker correspondent, but I was allowed out to cover the last stages only and arrived a day too late to meet Higgins. I'd already met Griffiths at Romford when he joined the list of 'cannon-fodder' a month earlier. Instead, I met Dennis Taylor for the first time. He had just been beaten 9–5 in the semi-final by John Virgo, who was to provide me with my first 'exclusive'.

Dennis couldn't have been friendlier and within minutes we were swapping jokes like old pals. And that's how it's been ever since . . . except that he never acknowledges a new joke by me. He nods, laughs then says, 'Oh yes, I heard it told a different way, but the ending's the same.' But you can bet your boots he'll be telling Virgo and whoever else he can find the same joke within minutes. He's a great guy and a great ambassador for snooker, and I always felt it was such a shame he and

Alex never got on. He had good reasons for keeping a safe distance, even in those days, but Higgins would go on to give him the clearest reason of all.

Virgo went on to claim his one and only major title when he defeated Griffiths 14–13 in an astounding final (during which the BBC cameramen went on strike, I believe, and failed to record John's final-frame triumph). In fact, I was partly responsible for Virgo getting his hands on the UK trophy because at 11.30 on the Saturday morning, with John leading 11–7 overnight, there was a huge panic on at the Guild Hall. Virgo was due to resume at midday but he believed play started at 1.45, as it had done all week. No one appeared to know where he was staying. Most players were at the Crest Hotel, just a five-minute walk from the venue, but John had told me he was booked into the Charnock Richard motel, some ten miles down the M6.

I had no idea there was a panic on until promoter Mike Watterson happened to ask if I knew where he was staying. 'We've tried everywhere locally,' said Mike, 'I'm blowed if I know where he is.' I couldn't believe my luck and raced to a telephone. 'John,' I asked when he answered his phone, 'what the hell are you doing?'

'I've just had a nice bath,' he replied, 'and I'm lying on my bed in my dressing gown watching the racing on TV.'

'John,' I screamed, 'you should be here – you're late.'

He said, 'Don't wind me up. We don't start until 1.45 and I'm having a nice lazy morning.'

In the end, after much pleading from me, John believed me. Within minutes he was being driven up the M6 and then had to charge through the crowds in Preston carrying his case, unable to get near the venue in the car because of all the shoppers. He arrived in the arena 30 minutes late for the kick-off and was docked two frames. Though decidedly unhappy about this decision, Griffiths was forced to accept it. A huge cloud seemed to gather above the table as the reluctant Welshman won the next two frames. But Virgo held himself together to win 14–13, and with no other Fleet Street reporters around – they had left to cover football matches – I had my exclusive. But I still hadn't achieved my goal: to meet the Hurricane.

That was soon put right by Henry West, who managed Virgo. Henry, a wonderful rogue of a character who really could have sold snow to the Eskimos, had been around the scene for years. He flogged snooker tables and equipment and co-owned one of the first luxury snooker-leisure clubs in the country. It was situated at the back of Bentalls, the huge department store in Kingston-upon-Thames, Surrey, where I grew up. It was built on the site of an old spit-and-sawdust billiard hall where, as a 12-year-old, I poked my head around the green double doors for a dare (one lunchtime after bunking off with best pal John Folan and the gang during the dinner hour from St Joseph's School, half a mile away). Unlike Alex and his Jampot experience, I found the dingy, low-lit surrounds intimidating and never had any desire to hang around, although – like so many in the early '70s – I became hooked on the televised *Pot Black* exploits of Reardon, Spencer and co., never dreaming that in time I would get to know them all so well.

By 1979 Kingston Snooker Centre was in full flow, with John Virgo not only installed as resident pro and coach but living with the West family in Shepperton, Middlesex. That was where I first encountered him – on a miserable, drizzly Friday morning just three weeks into my new role as snooker writer with the *Daily Mail*. I was tackling my first big interview – a feature on Virgo and his hilarious impressions of the other players, which were to go down a storm with TV audiences in the '80s. There was no one else in the club except the girl serving coffee and after a cuppa and a quick chat, John got down to business, showing me a few trick shots in an attempt to get warmed up.

I made appreciative noises but nothing was developing. As John said, there was no atmosphere and it was difficult for him to get into his stride without a proper audience. I then had an inspiration after one trick shot. 'How would Alex play that?' I asked. With that, my interviewee clicked into gear and I spent the next 30 minutes rocking with laughter. Neither of us could have known that John was just weeks away from his only major title and I was heading for my first *Daily Mail* exclusive. Yet it was to be a good while before I knew just how closely Virgo and 'Alec Kiggins' (as he pronounces his name) were entwined via their days at Potters.

West, a former boxer and useful snooker player, whose brother Wally mixed with the best amateur players around and ran the women's game, was the Yul Brynner of Surrey. And like Brynner in the classic Western film, Henry hand-picked his own Magnificent Seven. They were led by Virgo and Fagan. John had been lured south from Salford to further his career after reaching the world championship semi-finals himself that year. The other members of the stable were Jimmy White, his best pal Tony Meo (17), Tony Knowles, Joe Johnson and young Terry Whitthread – an outstanding prospect at 14, tipped to follow in Jimmy's footsteps, though sadly things never worked out that way and it is years since he has even picked up a cue following the tragic death of his pretty young wife, Kim.

Higgins used to love being around the likes of Jimmy, Tony, Terry and their pals David Gilbert and Paul Mascall. They were all game for a laugh and up for a drink when, perhaps, they should have been concentrating more on their careers. They had fabulous talent, but none of these kids – not even Jimmy – ever thought about the future because it had all come too easily for them, and they mixed freely with superstar

Alex, who knew them all by name and who even let them scrounge a few drinks from him.

Meanwhile, away from the bar and back on the table, Higgins was rebuilding his act again, this time in the Padmore–Super Crystalate International at West Bromwich. This was despite being decidedly under the weather in more ways than one. He'd had raging flu, and appalling conditions outside meant a simple M6 journey down from Manchester took him six hours. His spirits were hardly lifted when he learned that Fred Davis, his first opponent, had been snowed-in at his Stourport farm. On top of a postponed match, Alex developed an ear infection which needed hospital treatment before he was allowed to go ahead. In the event he beat Fred, then Willie Thorne 3–2, and completed a sweet hat-trick by toppling his 1979 Benson's conqueror Perrie Mans 4–2 in the televised final (still a comparative rarity) to collect the £2,000 prize.

Higgins added another £1,500 to his kitty, but not without rancour, when he finished runner-up to John Spencer in the Wilson's Classic in Manchester – an event to be run over seven weeks on Granada TV in the north-west. He beat Dennis Taylor and Griffiths to reach the final, with Spencer coming through the other half of the draw. You'd think they would have been sick of each other, but for all the disputes which littered their confrontations frequently, there was a genuine bond between them – perhaps because they were each determined to prove a point each time. They had been going hammer and tongs for nearly a decade and the public could not get enough of them. This time, Spencer prevailed 4–3, but only after a heated discussion between referee Jim Thorpe and Higgins, who was called for a push-shot when 2–0 down after potting a close-up yellow and screwing the white back three feet.

Spencer was happy to abide by the official's ruling, saying, 'From where I was sitting I wouldn't like to say whether it was a foul or not, but there was something odd about the way the ball started to travel sideways before coming back.' Higgins was seething, reviving memories of Thorpe's infamous push-shot decision in the 1974 world championship which Alex believed cost him a second title. Having studied a video of the shot and without pretending to be an expert, it certainly didn't look like a push-shot to me or, for that matter, to observers who can still recall the incident.

What hurt Higgins on such occasions was that he always called himself for foul shots, even if the ref was unsighted. But Thorpe, in a perfect position to weigh up the shot, was adamant. It clearly unsettled Higgins, even though he went on to win the frame and then berated Thorpe with what can only be described as 'industrial language'. Early in the next frame he demanded that Thorpe check the black was on its spot correctly. But the referee was having none of it. Needless to say, Higgins was brought before the WPBSA beaks and fined £200 for conduct unbecoming. Yet he could hardly rail at Spencer, whose offer of a re-rack in the final frame when 24 points ahead was accepted gratefully – though to no avail.

Checking back on the decade's litany of events, I regretted bitterly missing out on what was undoubtedly a hugely colourful chapter in snooker history.

*

TERRY GRIFFITHS
Rookie pro whose 1979 world title win stirred hearts and propelled him and snooker into the big-time via TV.

I loved playing Alex because you were always sure the place would be full, making for a great atmosphere. If he hit the ball well he could be so brilliant and so unorthodox that he made me smile and it helped me relax. He was the best opponent I ever faced. I don't say that lightly. He could almost be intimidating with the crowd behind him and it either lifted you or helped sink you.

When he started wearing that fedora hat at Sheffield, he had a remarkable effect on me. As he came through the curtains to be introduced, I'd be sitting there watching from my chair and he'd lift the hat to salute the audience. As he did, so his hair seemed to rise up with the hat, then down flop again. It looked absolutely marvellous and though I was just reduced to a spectator role, I could feel the hairs on the back of my neck rising.

In my book *Griff*, I recalled my first encounter with Alex, in front of 2,500 people in the pro-am final at Pontin's in Prestatyn. I had recently won the English Amateur Championship but it looked to be a daunting task, made even more so because Joe Davis and Ray Reardon were in an audience containing about a thousand of the best amateurs and professionals in the country. A lot of players might have frozen under such circumstances, but it gave me a real kick. I remember Joe making a comment to me about Alex's play. He was all the rage at the time and was coming to the table and playing the most extraordinary shots that had never been seen before. Joe said, 'I don't know what the hell Higgins is trying to do. I don't know how he plays the game.'

I was well beaten, but it was a great experience and helped make up my mind to turn pro. I was accepted immediately and chucked in my job with Pearl Insurance a few months later. By the following April I was appearing in the Embassy World Championship at Sheffield and facing Alex in the quarter-finals. It was a terrific match because we were both playing well, but after six black-ball wins, I got home in the last frame with a 107. In all the euphoria, I did feel sorry for Alex because he had played brilliantly. What made it worse for him was that he had given up the booze for ten weeks prior to the championship and had stuck to drinking tea. But I heard him say in his dressing-room afterwards: 'Fuck the tea, I'm going back to something stronger now.'

My father, Martin, who was a regular in the pressroom, came out into the corridor to greet me when I beat Alex for the first time at Sheffield. Len Ganley was standing there with a small crowd around him. Alex walked by and Len told me later he said to Dad, 'Tell your fucking son to get off the table when it's my turn to play.' Dad apparently said, 'Alex, I'm really proud of my son and if you were my son I'd be really proud of you as well.' With that, Len said, Alex put his arms around my Dad and wept. I found that extremely moving.

He really upset me in an exhibition match at Queensferry, North Wales, a while later when, after beating me 9–1 in one exhibition, he toppled me again. Naturally, I wasn't pleased to lose a second time in front of my countrymen, so I tried to make amends with my trick-shot routine. But even that kept going wrong, and when the one with the basket didn't work, Alex, who always refused this kind of entertainment after an exhibition, leaped up and said, 'Let me do it.' I appreciate he was only trying to help, but I was the world champion in my own country and everyone booed him. We then had words afterwards.

So now a rift had formed and we were fated to meet in the Coral UK Championship quarter-finals at Preston a few weeks later. It was a cracking match and, from trailing 7–5, I won the next four frames to go through 9–7. I knew there would be trouble, so I locked myself in the dressing-room to avoid a confrontation. I always respected him as a player – the way he fought for everything – but I didn't want a fight off the table as well. Alex was swearing away in his dressing-room, moaning to Dennis Taylor about some cues he owed him, but it finally cooled down and I went outside. Who should be standing there but Henry West, an ex-boxer, talking with Alex?

I had no option but to say something, so I shook Alex by the hand and said, 'That was a great match, Alex, and anyone could have won.'

'Why do you always have the fucking luck?' he replied.

I restrained myself and said, quietly, 'If I had your talent I would never lose,' and that shut him up. Henry said to me afterwards, 'I don't know how you didn't smack him one.'

From then on, we talked when we had to, but we never really got on. I beat Alex in the Benson & Hedges Masters final at Wembley the following February after a tight first session which ended 4–4. Alex asked whether I wanted to split the prize money and because I was only interested in the title, I agreed. In those days there were so few tournaments and the prize money wasn't that great. I went on to win 9–5 and was ecstatic because it was only my second season as a pro. As luck would have it, we met again a year later in the final at Wembley and Alex led 5–3 at the interval. I was expecting him to make the same offer as last year but he said nothing and went on to win 9–6 in another fine, tactical battle. Years later, I asked Alex why he didn't want to share the prize money again and he just said, 'I fancied beating you that time.'

He once invited me to his house to stay overnight. We'd been playing somewhere up north and were due to play in London the next day and he wanted a lift. He was still with Lynn at the time and she made me very welcome. But Alex pulled up a huge winged chair, turned it around and sat with his back to me. Eventually I got fed up and went to bed. The next day, we set off and he promptly plonked his feet on the dashboard, opened a newspaper and read it all the way down to London without uttering a word. It wasn't funny at the time but, looking back, I have to laugh at some of his antics. He was great for snooker because he was such a huge personality and the fans could not get enough of him. And I really must stress again that Alex was the best of all my opponents. Bear in mind, I played all the greats, including Davis, Thorburn, White – the lot.

Eight

RETURN OF THE GOOD YEARS

I missed him at Preston, but I was determined to shake Alex by the hand when I saw him at the Benson & Hedges Masters at Wembley and, thanks to Henry West, an introduction was effected. I have never forgotten the experience and have never become blasé about snooker fans meeting their idols because the electricity generated when they do was exactly what I experienced at that moment.

'Henry,' I whispered, on seeing Higgins across the room in a backstage bar at Wembley Conference Centre, 'do you know Alex?'

'Course I bleedin' do – everyone knows Higgy,' he growled. 'Come on, I'll introduce you.' Higgins shook my hand, looked me up and down and said, 'I don't like the press because all they ever write about me is lies.' I spluttered a protest and he added, 'We will get on OK if you always get my side of the story whenever there is trouble.'

'Alex,' I said, 'I'm only interested in snooker and not what you do off the table. Your private life is none of my concern. I can't play the game and I will never criticise the way you play because I'm obviously not qualified and I'll always be truthful.'

He leaned closer and said in hushed tones, almost conspiratorially, 'I can play shots the others can only dream about, babes, and I've even invented some of my own.'

I was more than impressed, even though I didn't understand how he could invent shots for a game which had been around for so many years. Yet Reardon reiterated almost word for word what Alex had said when we collaborated for a book in 1984, and so did other players from time to time. One or two said unpleasant things about him, and Cliff Thorburn twice shut him up – once with a well-aimed flurry of fists and another time with an even better-placed boot. There was little love coming from Dennis Taylor's corner, either, but both men had plenty of reasons to keep their distance over the years.

To my utter delight, Higgins reached the Benson & Hedges final later that week, beating Fred Davis and Mans, then Reardon in the semi-finals, only to lose to the man who almost certainly cost him the 1979 world title. As Terry Griffiths polished Alex off in a Wembley thriller with a 131 clearance to complete a 9–5 win and a World and Masters double, proud Reardon – standing beside me on the steps leading up to the arena – told me, 'We just shout down a mine and up comes another great Welsh player.'

Higgins, who picked up £2,500, would have his day the following year. For now he had to concentrate on other events before he began focusing on the big one at Sheffield. Benson & Hedges, who had enjoyed tremendous support for their events already in Ireland, especially at Goffs the previous year, now launched their Masters series at the same Kildare venue (a magnificent sales showring for horses, normally) which remains a top attraction on today's circuit. The tobacco company's decision, prompted no doubt by capacity crowds, added to the growing feeling that snooker at last had the makings of a proper pro tour on the same lines as the tennis and golf boys – thanks mainly to the foresight of promoter Mike Watterson – although it would be another couple of years before it all came together.

It would also be several years before Higgins became the first Irishman to win the Irish Masters – in the most incredible fashion ever – and his first attempt ended in semi-final failure against Doug Mountjoy, who was beaten by high-riding fellow Welshman Griffiths 10–9 in the final. Nothing was ever made simple in the life of Higgins and he stirred up more trouble at the Tolly Cobbold event at Ipswich Corn Exchange against final opponent Dennis Taylor before netting the £1,500 jackpot. Trouble with a capital T reared its ugly head in the fifth frame when referee Nobby Clarke penalised Higgins for attempting to hit a red lying against the black. Whether or not Clarke was correct – he probably wasn't, according to observers – was rendered academic by Alex's protestations. He even implored the watching Terry Griffiths to adjudicate on the issue, without success, and finally called Taylor a cheat. This accusation he later withdrew.

In addition, he moaned that Taylor was standing in his line of fire (in later years he was to accuse John Williams, right behind him, of standing in his 'line of thought'). Taylor, leading 3–1, was clearly unsettled and missed out on what could have been an important victory for him. It goes without saying that Higgins was reported to the WPBSA by the referee and Taylor.

He was also reported by referee Ron Hope, who suffered a volley of abuse from the Irishman during his Demmy Pro-Am semi-final match against Jimmy White at Potters Club. Higgins, ludicrously, wore a fedora hat throughout the match. He lost 5–3 then exploded. He complained to the referee that White had played a deliberate miss when snookered in the last frame, having said nothing at the time. He also had another bite at Hope as he left the club. What Jimmy must have made of it all does not bear thinking about. He was just 17 and, like Alex, would always call his fouls. To my knowledge, throughout his illustrious career, he has never argued about decisions and to see his role model behaving like that must have been a real shock – especially as Alex had been such an inspiration to him in his formative years.

For those 'crimes', Higgins was fined £200 by the WPBSA; perhaps God does dish out his own brand of punishment at times because Higgins lost the Irish crown he had held so proudly since toppling Jackie Rea in 1972. Facing him across the room at Belfast's Ulster Hall was Taylor with more than a few scores to settle. And didn't he just! Despite appearances in two world semi-finals and a final, he had not been acknowledged as a genuine contender, but his 21–15 demolition of Higgins put him firmly in the frame. He had been accused on some occasions of 'tightening' when it came to the crunch – some would say 'bottling' – and it always hurt him to read such charges.

He proved his mettle when Higgins came right back at him. Taylor led 16–9 overnight, despite a 131 from Higgins, and when Alex won all but one of the opening seven frames the next day, Taylor's so-called suspect temperament was tested thoroughly. But Dennis came through handsomely, reeling off the four frames he needed for a famous triumph – his first big one as a professional. It must have been sweet revenge for all the brickbats he had endured over the years, but he kept his composure right to the last and resisted the temptation to rub it in against his arch-rival.

Higgins dashed to Ipswich from Derby, where he was playing in the new British Gold Cup, which featured four groups of four playing a round-robin format to produce the semi-finalists. He had already won his group, tossing in back-to-back breaks of 135 and 134 against Griffiths and celebrating in true Higgy style at Ipswich. He was then driven back to the Friary Hotel at Derby by Henry West, who decanted him at breakfast, then told all and sundry, 'Get your money on Meo.'

Terry Smith, then of the *Daily Mirror*, was having breakfast when Henry walked in and told us what a state Alex was in – 'It was like the Great Gold Rush as everyone lumped it on Tony at the bookies.' Higgins retired to his bed for a couple of hours, then proceeded to knock semi-final opponent Tony Meo off the table 4–0 despite the 11 a.m. start. Meo, a talented break-builder and rated extremely highly, could not believe it. 'He's not human,' he told me. 'No one is entitled to play like that after what he's been through.' And with a resigned grin, he added: 'I'd have probably stood a better chance if he'd been fresh.'

And so to the Crucible Theatre, where Higgins, wearing his blue fedora complete with lucky charms, returned for his ninth attempt to win back the world crown. He launched his Crucible challenge with a shaky

10–9 opener against Meo, then saw off Perrie Mans 13–6 as Higgins began to get into his stride. And now for a quarter-final showdown with Steve Davis, who had scored a sensational 13–10 victory over defending title-holder Griffiths. It was considered a shock of major proportions because Griffiths had made his mark on the game in a stupendous year and had endeared himself to an ever-growing TV audience. Could Davis do the same to Higgins? The answer was an emphatic 'No, not this time.'

As hard as he tried to break him down, Davis did not quite have the tactical nous to topple the man who was to be a bitter rival for the next decade. Yet he fired a warning shot across the Higgins bows with a 136 total clearance in the first session to earn a share of the £1,000 high-break prize. Not to be outdone, Higgins proceeded to sink 15 reds and 15 blacks in the last frame. The magical maximum was on for the first time in world championship history, but Alex ran out of position on the 15th black and, though potting the final yellow, was left with a nigh-impossible double on the green – which he missed.

Nevertheless, Higgins led 9–7 overnight. As the pressure began to tell on Davis in the final session, he swept past him to win 13–9. And even as Cliff Thorburn was threading his way through the other half of the draw, Alex toppled Kirk Stevens 16–13 to set up a final showdown which had all the makings of a cracker. Again I was ecstatic. Higgy was in the world final and, after he had lost to Reardon in 1976, it was surely his turn to take possession of the crown jewels again.

Alas, it was not to be. Alex, mixing caution with his usual flair, set off like an express train to negate the deliberate play of the Canadian, a loser in 1977 against Spencer. He led 5–1 and 9–5 but Higgy just couldn't help himself. He loved playing to the gallery too much and it was to cost him dearly as Thorburn kept him in his sights, then beat him into submission. At 16–16 it was still anybody's game; but a 116 from the Canadian and a final 51 gave him an 18–16 unbeatable lead and the thrill of being crowned the first overseas world champion.

Only the Republic of Ireland's Ken Doherty – who grew up idolising Higgins and arranged a fund-raising testimonial night for him in Belfast in the late '90s – has matched that feat, winning in 1997. Higgins, who poured his heart and soul into it on what was the biggest stage he had ever appeared on, was almost in tears as he attempted to explain his demise. 'Cliff is so tough to beat,' he said, picking his words carefully. 'I call him the Grinder because he puts you through the mincer. But I've had disappointments before and I've always bounced back.'

Unfortunately, there was considerable embarrassment backstage. Lynn Higgins, convinced her new husband would be crowned world champion, had arrived that afternoon with a magnificent cake baked in the shape of a snooker table right down to the last detail and bearing the legend, 'Alex Higgins, 1980 World Champion'. Nevertheless – and despite the dreadful animosity which had built up over the years between the players – Alex and Lynn posed with the cake alongside Cliff and his new wife, Barbara.

There were only a few hints of controversy throughout a gripping final. Higgins complained, unfairly it has to be said, that his rival was impeding his line of vision (where have we heard that one before?), then he countered in schoolboy fashion. Twice Thorburn was interrupted while cueing up a shot: once when Alex swished the ice around his glass, and again after he made a noise when dropping ice cubes into the drink. Childish, really, but enough to disturb the Toronto man's concentration momentarily.

A much-needed summer break beckoned for Higgins and his new bride, Lynn. But there was yet more snooker for both players before then, in the form of the Pontin's holiday camp festival at Camber Sands in Sussex. Higgins beat Dennis Taylor 9–7 to win the Professional title, while Dennis won the Open event with a 7–5 victory against Geoff Foulds (the English amateur international who would go on to be WPBSA vice-chairman and then chairman for a spell in the '90s).

And still Higgins could not pack his cue away for the summer because Barry Hearn had other ideas. Even as the Steve Davis bandwagon was gaining momentum, albeit at a slowish pace, Hearn was already in the fast lane as far as money-making went. On 12 June 1980 he announced a series of London dinner shows, the first of which would feature Steve and Alex. Hearn could see that Steve would be burnt out in a flash if he were forced to drive the length and breadth of the country in search of pay-days between tournaments. Endorsements and sponsorships were top of his priority list – plus these fancy-dan dinner shows at London's top hotels, which used to be featured in earlier times. Higgins was the ideal opponent for Hearn to launch his first series at the Grosvenor House Hotel. Barry, ever the opportunist, invited the press for a run-down of events there one lunchtime.

Higgins turned up half an hour late, accompanied by a cabbie and wearing a safari jacket – stashed full of £20 notes. Bundles of them were literally hanging from every pocket and my eyes popped out of my head. I'd never seen so much money and I said, 'You're mad, Alex. You'll get mugged walking around like that.' Higgy laughed and said, 'I had it off in Belfast yesterday, babes – three grand at the races, and this gentleman [the cabbie] is acting as my minder today.'

Higgins kept going on about a red-hot tip he'd been given for a race that afternoon and advised anyone who would listen to get his money on. Once the press conference finished, Higgins bundled me, long-standing journalist pal John Dee and a couple of others into a taxi and we were whisked off to the Eccentric Club – a wonderful establishment in the West End frequented by the likes of Joe Davis and other great names, and from where Noel Miller-Cheevers launched his International Snooker League. There, on a memorable occasion mentioned earlier, he had conned Alex into giving him a 40-point start and took him to the cleaners.

Not this time, though. Higgins persuaded the doorman to let us all in – though it was strictly a members-only club – bought a bottle of wine for starters, then said, 'Give us your money. Hennessey's coming with me to place the bets, so have six bottles of Chablis ready for when we return with the winnings.' I gave him a fiver, Dee coughed up a tenner and the others also chipped in.

It all happened in a flash and why he picked on me I'll never know, because I knew nothing about horseracing. It was about 3 p.m. by this time and the race was due to start in 15 minutes. We found a betting shop and Alex said, 'Write out the bet and I'll square it with them.' I asked: 'What do I put, Alex?' He looked at me oddly and said, 'Just write £1,000 to win Sunny Smile in the 3.15 at Beverley.'

I nearly collapsed. I just couldn't believe anyone could bet that sort of money because I'd been used to my Mum and Dad having 'a bob each way' if they had a flutter when I was a kid. I don't suppose I'd ever been in a bookmakers in my life – and I was 35 then. 'Just write it,' Alex demanded and, with shaking hand, I did, only for the clerk to reject the bet. We ran out of the bookies and Higgy was getting desperate because the clock was ticking on. We found another bookmaker two minutes later and this time, after some complicated wrangling, they agreed to give us a 7–2 starting price.

We still weren't finished and what happened next has been embedded in my memory all these years. Alex was desperate to make a phone call but the clerk said it was not permitted, so he dragged me out of the shop and pleaded, 'Quick, find a phone – any phone.' We must have run for a couple of minutes before I spotted a carpet shop and rushed in. With Higgy in tow, I ran the length of the shop balancing on top of rolls of the stuff lying the length of the shop. I gabbled breathlessly to a wonderful woman wearing Dame Edna-style spectacles, 'This is Alex Higgins and he's a famous snooker star and we need to use your phone urgently.'

Without batting an eyelid, she replied in the poshest of voices, 'Young man, I have never heard of Mr Higgins but you are most welcome to use my telephone.' I murmured our thanks and Higgins handed me a scrap of paper with a phone number. 'Ask for Steady Eddie,' he said. 'Tell him you're calling for me and that you want to put £200 on the nose on Sunny Smile.' I made the call (to Belfast, it transpired), got Steady Eddie first go and he just said, 'You've got it.'

With that, Higgy said, 'C'mon, we've got to get back to the bookies to hear the race.' I'd hardly got my breath back when we were belting through the streets again, searching for the bookies. We found it just as the horses came under starting orders for what was probably a six-furlong race. After about three furlongs, hearing no mention of our horse and getting worried sick about my fiver – never mind his £1,000 – I asked Alex, 'Are you sure, Higgy?'

He just replied, 'Don't worry, babes, have faith.' He'd hardly finished speaking when the commentator said, 'And we're coming into the last furlong and Sunny Smile is making up ground on the outside . . . Sunny Smile has moved into third . . . and it's Sunny Smile all the way.'

I honestly couldn't believe it and to this day I sometimes wonder if I dreamed the whole thing up. Back we went to the Eccentric Club and there were the boys, Chablis at the ready. Dee just said, 'Well?' Higgins laughed and said, 'Get pouring, babes, we're in the money.' To my deepest regret, I had to leave the party in full swing and get to work at the *Daily Mail* where, feeling heady from the day and from the effects of the Chablis, I recounted the extraordinary tale to all and sundry.

I called John Dee in Wolverhampton a week or so later to chat about the affair and he told me: 'Alex carried on betting and won another fourteen hundred quid. He mislaid the betting slip for the big one and they refused to pay out at first, but he got round them in the end.' John was to become a great friend and ally to me over the years and even now, with a vast knowledge of snooker stored from 30 years in the business, he helps me out with facts and figures from time to time. I always tell him I'll buy him a pint, but I must owe him a brewery by now.

My great adventure aside, the Grosvenor House Hotel event attracted a 400-plus crowd paying £20 a head, with special guests such as Henry Cooper, Eric Morecambe, Des O'Connor and DJ Pete Murray in attendance. They saw Steve, who started and finished with a century, beat Alex 5–2.

Higgins finally got his well-earned summer holiday and took up golf. To his delight, fresh air suited him – after what must have seemed a lifetime of dark snooker halls and artificial lighting. Also, Lynn was expecting their first child in December and he admitted quite freely that the prospect of practising long and hard every day was losing its appeal. But he still had to make a living the only way he knew how. He was soon in action again, competing in Toronto for the Canadian Open crown. Wins over White and Meo counted for nothing when he went down 9–6 in the semi-finals to Griffiths, who in turn lost 17–10 to Thorburn. It was Cliff's third successive win and fourth in all in the Canadian Open.

Another day, another dollar: next came the disastrous Champion of Champions, promoted by Ray Davis at the New London Theatre without TV coverage and watched by me and a handful of others. It was won by Doug Mountjoy, who beat John Virgo in the final after a two-group, round-robin series. Higgins, who had become wrapped up in playing the space invader machines when not performing, finished a lowly third in his five-man group. I felt sorry for Ray Davis, who lost £30,000 on the event, but he had picked the wrong place and the wrong time to launch it. The New London Theatre had been a successful venue for the Benson & Hedges a few years earlier until that event moved to Wembley, but spectators seemed less inclined to bother about this one.

They were a little more interested in the State Express World Cup team event, which followed hard on the heels at the same venue. It was a good-fun tournament with three-man teams from the home countries, plus Canada, Australia and a combined Ireland side featuring Patsy Fagan from the south and Taylor and Higgins from the north. Wales (Reardon, Mountjoy and Griffiths) retained the title with an 8–5 success over Thorburn's Canada. But perhaps the best news of all was that Fagan, who starred for Ireland, appeared to have overcome those terrible problems with the rest, which had surfaced in the same event the previous year.

Higgins seemed more composed on and off the table as the Coral UK loomed large towards the end of the year. Again he reached the final, beating Willie Thorne, Fred Davis and Reardon on the way. The Reardon match was a cracker, Higgins coming from 4–1 down, matching the Welshman's tight play and looking every inch a champion. Again, my hopes were raised. But I suffered a conflict of interest. Facing the Hurricane, in his first major final, was that lad Davis – my local star from Romford, who played just five minutes from my doorstep, and whose manager (Hearn) had welcomed me with open arms a year earlier and had given me a run-down on all the top players and prospects. Why, he'd even given me a lift home to Romford after the 1979 UK Final.

My heart and head said Higgins because of his vast experience. On the eve of the semi-finals I sat with John Pulman, Rex Williams and Alex long into the night and marvelled at their stories about touring Australia and South Africa and the capers they got up to. Alex couldn't have supped more than a couple of pints of lager all night and eventually took to his bed in readiness for his semi-final against Reardon.

Rex and John continued waxing lyrical about their overseas exploits until the conversation turned to Davis. They both agreed he was *the* one to watch among all the youngsters. Hearn had obviously bent my ear whenever he could about how great a player Steve was and I put it down to 'managerspeak'. But Pulman added: 'He's so good already that he will be there or thereabouts for as long as he wants to be.' It was a remarkable statement, considering Steve had never been past a quarter-final before and over the years this cropped up in my stories time and again because it was so prophetical. And old Pully never missed a chance to remind me. 'I should be on royalties for that one,' he'd say with a broad grin in that beautiful, deep-brown voice – matured in good-quality scotch over the years – and then he would add, with a chuckle: 'I'll settle for a Bell's.'

Within hours of Pulman nailing his colours to the Davis mast, Steve beat Griffiths 9–0 to reach the final, having overcome Mike Hallett, Bill Werbeniuk and Tony Meo on the way. The opening paragraphs of one of the legendary chapters in snooker history were about to be penned, even though the writing wasn't quite on the wall for Higgins yet. Davis hammered him 16–6 and, all of a sudden, a star was born. Few outside snooker's close-knit family would have heard of him before his world championship defeat of the Griff. But now, with expansive TV coverage of the UK final, the Ginger Magician or the Plumstead Potter – later to become known simply as the Nugget – was a household name.

He was everything Higgy had rebelled against from his early snooker days. Steve was unassuming, methodical and disciplined. He lacked adventure but employed a great percentage game in which he would run for cover if the odds of scoring weren't firmly in his favour. He was also a prodigious long-potter and break-builder and, with a cool head on his shoulders, the entire package added up to the perfect antidote to the swashbuckling, cavalier style of the Hurricane.

By chance, I bumped into Griffiths as he checked out of his hotel the following morning and didn't really know what to say – and told him so. 'That's all right,' he said. 'Don't worry about it. I always used to say that if you lost, it didn't really matter whether it was 9–8 or 9–0, but I've changed my mind. It's the worst feeling in the world.'

I was given another insight into the world of Higgins midway through the final when Knowles and Meo, then little-known pros, decided on a night on the town in Blackburn with Alex – and me in tow. It was no big deal, just a few drinks at a club once frequented by Higgins when he lived in the area. Despite trailing Davis 10–5 overnight, he'd had us in stitches throughout the journey, telling us how he was exempt from wearing a bow-tie while playing because of the irritable neck-rash it caused him. 'It's called Psychosis Barbie and is derived from the Romans,' he intoned, then led us up the garden path on a side-splitting, make-believe story about Roman Emperor Caligula and co.

There had been no mention of the torrid time he had experienced on the table and by the time we reached Blackburn we were all in jovial mood. Alex made contact with the manager quickly and we were ushered into a side bar away from the heaving masses. But word spread rapidly that Alex was in town and, one by one, former acquaintances stopped by to say hello, wish him well and commiserate on the scoreline. He recognised one or two, but in the main he'd say, politely, 'I'm really sorry but I just don't remember you. I haven't lived here for seven years and I haven't the greatest memory for names and faces.' It didn't matter to most of them – they were just pleased to be able to tell their pals that they knew the great man and had chatted to him at the bar.

EARLY DAYS: HIGGINS
AND SPENCER WITH
THE 1972 WORLD
CROWN – BEFORE
THE START OF THEIR
FINAL.

CENTRE STAGE:
HIGGINS
DOMINATED
THE PARADE
OF KIT KAT
WORLD
CHAMPIONS.

WORLD
CHAMPIONSHIP
LINE-UP: STEVE
DAVIS, LEFT,
TAKES ON TONY
MEO, WHILE
HIGGINS FACES
DANGER MAN
PATSY FAGAN,
RIGHT, AND
LOSES.

A SMILE FROM THE GREAT MAN: BUT ALL WAS NOT WELL AT THE 1990 WORLD CHAMPIONSHIP, WHEN HE ANNOUNCED HIS RETIREMENT.

HAT-TRICK: HIGGINS IN RELAXED MOOD AT THE BENSON AND HEDGES MASTERS IN IRELAND.

HERE'S LOOKING AT
YOU: THE MORE YOU
DRINK, THE BETTER
YOU FEEL, OR SO
THEY SAY.

DAMAGING: BUT HIGGINS RECOVERED FROM HIS FALL AT BLACKPOOL TO BEAT TONY KNOWLES.

REFRESHER: HIGGINS, WATCHED BY ANTRIM, ENJOYS A DRINK DURING THE 1990 PEARL ASSURANCE FINAL.

LEFT: THE BOSS – TOURNAMENT DIRECTOR ANN YATES, WHO LOST COUNT OF HER RUN-INS WITH HIGGINS.

BELOW: CROWNING GLORY – WORLD TITLE NO 2 BECKONS AS HIGGINS CLEARS UP.

DEEP CONCENTRATION:
NOTHING CAN STOP
ALEX CLINCHING HIS
SECOND WORLD TITLE.

TOP: PRIDE AND JOY – HIGGINS WITH HIS WIFE LYNN AND BABY
LAUREN AFTER HIS 1982 WORLD SUCCESS.

ABOVE: MY BABY – LAUREN SHARES THE CRUCIBLE LIMELIGHT WITH
HER DADDY.

PRIDE OF IRELAND: ALEX CELEBRATES THEIR WORLD TEAM SUCCESS ALONGSIDE EUGENE HUGHES, CENTRE, AND DENNIS TAYLOR.

HOWDY PARTNER: NON-PLAYING 'TEX' HIGGINS ENJOYS HIMSELF AT THE IRISH MASTERS.

THAT'S MY GIRL: ALEX AND SIOBHAN KIDD BEFORE
THEIR UNRULY SPLIT.

KISS FOR A QUEEN: HIGGINS GREETS STACEY
HILLYARD BEFORE THEIR MOMENTOUS MEETING.

YOU LITTLE CHARMER: BUT ANTRIM THE LEPRECHAUN WAS BEHEADED UNCEREMONIOUSLY AFTER THE HURRICANE'S 1990 WORLD CHAMPIONSHIP DEFEAT BY STEVE JAMES.

AHOY THERE: ABLE SEAMAN HIGGINS REPORTING FOR DUTY, SIR.

TOP: ALEX AND HIS DAD, SANDY, AT THE IRISH MASTERS.

BOTTOM: MEETING OF KINGS – GEORGE BEST AND ALEX IN DUBAI.

**END OF THE LINE: DAVIS AND HIGGINS BEFORE THEIR
1983 WORLD CHAMPIONSHIP SEMI-FINAL**

Then the mood turned ugly. One guy, slightly the worse for wear, approached and said hello. Alex said he couldn't place him and he replied, 'Oh, we're too big a bloody superstar now to talk to our friends, are we?' It looked as though it could have got out of hand, not that Alex couldn't handle himself. But I was furious. The poor bloke had been put through the hoop by Davis and all he wanted was to relax and unwind. I stuck my oar in, saying angrily, 'Just leave him alone. He doesn't need this aggravation.'

It was sheer bravado on my part, because the guy could probably have flattened me, but he moved off moaning and groaning and I felt quite pleased with myself. Wisely, the two Tonys had stayed out of it, but would obviously have come to his rescue if needed. But when Higgy turned back to the bar and said, dramatically, 'That's what it's like to be Alex Higgins,' they both cracked up. They weren't being disrespectful but it did sound funny and it became a catch-phrase among the three of us for years – although Alex couldn't understand why we were all laughing so much at the time. Incidentally, just about everyone in snooker can imitate the Higgins accent – some better than others – but Meo was able to provide a bonus to his impersonation because he could actually flair his nostrils, à la Higgy, as well.

The following day came the anticipated landslide victory (16–6) and pictures of Davis and new girlfriend Helen, a receptionist at Preston's Crest Hotel where most of us used to stay, appeared in all the national papers the day after that. Beating Griffiths in the world championship first round and whacking him 9–0 at Preston was a big deal. But crushing the self-appointed People's Champion, the best known player of all, and in a major final, was huge news and it put Steve on his way to enormous fame and fortune. In fact, Hearn first upped the stakes with Davis before he had even won the UK title. His fee then for an exhibition was £200 and when a promoter enquired what it would cost to match him with Higgins for a night, Hearn said, 'We'll take what Alex is getting and nothing less.'

Higgins was charging £600 and Hearn, to his amazement, got the nod, but it was a one-off and Davis went back down to £200 until he became UK champion. 'The next morning the phone didn't stop ringing and I was nursing a rotten hangover,' said Barry. 'This bloke was rabbiting on about booking Steve and I was doodling on my blotting pad. He finally got around to talking money and I'd just written a fancy £200 on the pad. I added another zero and said, "Steve's a champion now and he'll cost you two grand." I couldn't believe it when the guy accepted – and the work flooded in.'

Again, though, there was controversy on the table during the final, but not of Alex's making. This time, incredibly, it was referee John Williams, with vast experience behind him, who dropped a clanger. Davis potted the pink and John Willie, as he is known, somehow contrived to lift the cue ball off the table and put it on the pink spot. The blunder was picked up immediately but when Williams then respotted the pink and replaced the cue ball near enough in its original position, Higgins claimed a foul, hoping to get Davis off the table and get himself back in play.

Since referees cannot commit fouls, Higgy was puffing into the wind on this one. Yet he demanded Mike Watterson be involved, only for the promoter to reiterate what Williams had already told the Irishman. Alex was being genuine – of that I had no doubt – but it led to much merriment among the audience and in our Guild Hall pressbox, perched high above the action in a makeshift room built on scaffolding.

A deflated Higgins headed for Farnworth and the Wilson's Classic, but he lost to David Taylor in the first round and Davis prevailed again, this time picking up £5,000 to add to the £6,000 UK cheque he had collected a few days earlier. Higgins then limbered up for the 1981 Benson & Hedges Masters with back-to-back total clearances of 130 and 141 in dead frames, after losing 11–8 to Reardon in a challenge match at Bradford.

He shrugged off all thoughts of a Preston hangover because he hit the jackpot in the Benson's at Wembley after another two years on the fringes. A 5–1 victory over Doug Mountjoy (after waking up just 20 minutes before the off) carried him into a semi-final battle royal against Thorburn. But at 5–1 down and Cliff needing just one to get through, Alex's Wembley dream was looking more than shaky. When Thorburn led 5–3 and 57–0, it was all but over. Yet when Cliff failed to pot what appeared to be a clean red – but which was, in fact, slightly obscured by another – Higgins seized his chance as only he could, to sink an immaculate 85.

Thorburn had other chances, but Higgins, his tail high and the partisan crowd right behind him, came through 6–5 to reach his fourth consecutive Masters final. Then he set about making amends for his Wembley defeat the previous year by bogeyman Griffiths. This time he got it right, winning 9–6 after a tactical battle before a British record major tournament crowd of 2,422. Higgins led 5–3 at the interval and when he won the next three, it looked all over. But Griffiths came back by pulling a 136 total clearance out of thin air, and took the next two as well. But Higgins was too close to the winning line to let go and over he went for a 9–6 success.

He then asked me to give him a lift to Euston the next morning to catch his train home to Manchester. I arrived back at Wembley less than 12 hours later, having battled through the tortuous North Circular rush-hour traffic, excited at the thought of having Higgins all to myself for an hour or so. But things don't always work out the way you plan them and the arrival of John Spencer at the hotel's check-out desk brought a dramatic change. Higgy told Spencer we were going to Euston and, knowing he was heading for Manchester as well, said, 'Why don't you come along for the ride?' Spencer, with a big grin, replied, 'There's no way I could take three hours of you on the train, Alex. Let's go on the shuttle from Heathrow. It takes only an hour and that's plenty.'

Higgins agreed, so back on to the North Circular I drove – into a fearful traffic jam. It was the M25 of its day and not much better these days. But I wasn't worried, because my two superstar passengers hardly noticed their mode of transport (my old VW Fastback banger) as they began discussing Alex's win the night before and snooker in general. I was in my element, though unable to take notes, but I remember Spencer talking about Higgins 'grooving the action' again. Alex agreed, saying it had taken him countless hours on the practice table to regain his natural rhythm. 'It's the only way,' said Spencer. 'You just keep practising and practising until you come through the other end of the tunnel. There is no magical formula.'

Higgins was in a particular hurry to get back to Cheadle because Lynn had been left at home nursing new baby Lauren and he was anxious to show off his Wembley spoils to the two most precious girls in his life. But as usual with Alex, there was drama at the airport, though again not of his making. In fact I instigated it unwittingly, not realising the tension enveloping Heathrow because of the Northern Ireland troubles, which at the time were pretty intense. They missed an hourly flight by a couple of minutes and Higgins, not wanting to wander around the airport with his cue, asked at an information desk where he could store it for half an hour or so while we went for a coffee. The girl, not realising who Alex was, but very much aware of his soft Belfast accent, asked, 'What's in the case?'

And yours truly replied, stupidly, 'He's a snooker player – it's hardly a rifle, is it?'

It was the worst thing I could possible have said because within seconds we were surrounded by security officers. Fortunately, one of them recognised Alex and John and baled us out of a mess in exchange for their autographs. I felt dreadful, but Alex didn't seem fazed. When the time came for them to board the plane, I asked whether it would be possible to have a nice family picture of him and Lynn with baby Lauren, which would have been a real feather in my cap at the *Daily Mail*. Higgins dithered and mumbled something about intrusion of privacy but Spenny, bless him, said, 'Come on Alex, the guy's taken all this trouble to get us to the airport and all he wants is five minutes of your time.'

Alex agreed reluctantly and we said our goodbyes. I telephoned my sports desk and told the news editor of our exclusive story and pictures, then drove back into the office to deliver the words. That done, I crawled away through more horrible traffic and arrived back at my Romford home, shattered, at about 5 p.m. I had hardly sat down when Ken

Haskell, the deputy sports editor, phoned to say Higgins had refused to have the picture taken. I couldn't believe it, so I phoned the house and Lynn answered. 'He hasn't said a word to me about it, but I'll sort it out,' she said. And she did. Next day in the Manchester edition I was given the centre spread with a beautiful picture of the Higgins family in all their splendour and the airport tale (minus my part!). I sent some pictures off to Lynn and it led to a smashing friendship between us.

The new Irish B&H Masters followed hard on the heels of Alex's Wembley success. But though he beat Dennis Taylor 4–2 in the quarters, he was in and out of Goffs, in Kill, Co. Kildare, before he knew it, losing 6–5 to Reardon in a dull semi. Another last-four defeat followed, against Kirk Stevens in the new Lada Classic four-man event in Newcastle (Thorburn beat Stevens in the final) and another niggling result for Alex cropped up when Taylor, who had spurned him as an opponent for his first defence of the Irish title, opted to play Fagan and beat him 22–21 in a thriller at Coleraine to win £2,000.

Higgins then played and lost in another Tolly Cobbold event (no trouble this year, thank goodness) and missed out in the new Yamaha Organs round-robin event at Derby's Assembly Rooms, which was to become a regular venue. Alex drew a fantastic 1,500 crowd – with 200 locked out – for his match with Dennis, who saw him off 3–0. Steve Davis, on a fabulous run, picked up this title as well to sharpen his cue nicely for the fast-approaching world championship. Crucially, he hammered Alex 19–7 in a challenge match at Ulster Hall less than 24 hours after winning the John Courage English pro title, and failed by only four balls to score a maximum against him. Steve also pipped him 5–3 before a mammoth 2,750 audience at Glasgow's Kelvin Hall.

Alex was obviously going to be a major threat to Steve's bid for the 1981 world title and Hearn's old Matchroom psychology of pitching the then amateur star against the best of professionals was working well for him again. Higgins was absolutely determined to go one better at the Crucible than he had done the previous year; alas, the multi-titled Davis, having got his measure on a number of occasions in recent months, had other ideas and avenged his 1980 defeat in the second round by winning 13–8. Alex came back from arrears of 6–2 to be only 9–7 adrift, but Davis stood firm for a great result.

It seemed almost by divine right that Steve would win the first of his six world titles because he had made enormous strides since his last visit to the Crucible Theatre, and so it proved. Jimmy White, making his first appearance there, fell 10–8 to Davis, but only after giving him a huge scare in the opening round. Higgins followed; then Griffiths 13–9; and finally defending champion Cliff Thorburn 16–10 in the semis after an almighty struggle. Thorburn called Davis an 'arrogant bastard' after the penultimate session and accused his followers of gamesmanship – one disciple kept flicking a lighter as Cliff got down on an important blue, which he subsequently missed, and Hearn draped a huge Union Jack over the balcony for that dramatic session. It had the desired effect because the Canadian was unnerved and the next day Davis strode on to the final, thrashing Doug Mountjoy 18–12.

'He is two blacks better than anyone else in the game right now,' was Mountjoy's tribute, although not everyone agreed – especially not a certain little Ulsterman living in Lancashire. But the emergence of Davis as a world force was to end any hopes he had of staying on top of the pile as the tournament circuit began expanding, with regular sponsors for the first time. Curiously, Higgins had long left the Crucible Theatre when there was a major dust-up featuring his old refereeing rival Jim Thorpe, who called Dennis Taylor for a push-shot in his second-round match against Kirk Stevens. Taylor made no protest but promoter Watterson, who watched a recording of the incident that night, decided it was an unfair decision and had Thorpe taken off the match just six minutes before the off the following afternoon.

Senior referee John Williams took over, but the episode left a nasty atmosphere around the Crucible and as a result, the WPBSA voted a few days later to relieve Watterson of the responsibility of selecting referees and decided to appoint all officials from then on. It was no consolation to Thorpe, of course, but he was cheered some time later to read that Dennis had told me, albeit with a huge grin: 'I wouldn't say it was a push-shot – more of a shove.'

Next up on the schedule was the wonderful Guinness Festival of Snooker and Billiards on the Isle of Wight, featuring just about every combination of the game, including singles, doubles, mixed doubles, the women's world championship and an open billiards event featuring the world's finest. The rain tipped down all week and we were literally left squelching around in mud for much of the time, but it was great fun. Alex reached the last 16 of the pro-am, won by Steve Davis, and went one better in the mixed doubles with Sue Johnson.

But Higgy's main interest appeared to be table tennis and Willie Thorne was quite happy to relieve him of a good few fivers throughout the week. One morning Alex asked me for a game. Though nowhere near Tony Meo's standard (he played for London as a junior and was red hot), I was able to handle Alex comfortably over a couple of games. Halfway through the first game he suddenly stopped, walked around the table and said, 'We can take 'em, babes.' I couldn't make out what he was getting at and said so; Alex replied, 'Willie doesn't know you can play a decent game so I'll fix up a match with you and him and I'll lump it all on you.'

Unfortunately for Higgy, I was and still am the biggest coward in the world when it comes to gambling and there was no way I could have taken Willie on with any confidence, even though I could probably have beaten him in a fun game. For once, Alex begged me – he was desperate to get back at the Great WT, as Willie was known to his supporters – but I was terrified of letting him down, so I declined as politely as possible. Willie laughed his head off when I told him.

I had my first taste of late-night money matches during the Festival of Snooker and Billiards and was fascinated to see Kirk Stevens playing hard-nosed, tight-fisted snooker as opposed to the flamboyant style he employed during tournaments. It was a revelation, but he told me he needed the fear factor to play that way, and tournaments simply didn't inspire him. Alex also played a couple of money-matches and lost – he was last seen at about 2.30 a.m. offering a 21-point start to anyone who would take him on.

There were no takers this time, but on a memorable night at Camber Sands during the 1980 Pontin's event, he made the same offer and out from the crowd stepped Big Bill Werbeniuk. 'You can have 28 points,' said Higgins, and was promptly thrashed 3–0 by the Canadian.

There was a welcome break and a nice little earner for the stars when top Maltese tour operator Carm Zerafa set up a Medallion Holidays event in his native country. Mountjoy, Thorburn, Reardon and Higgins were the invited pros but Paul Mifsud, Malta's reigning world amateur champion, lifted the £3,000 top prize. Carm, who still lives in Long Ditton, a mile away from my old family home, was responsible for bringing Tony Drago over to Britain a few years later – thanks to Vic Harris, who spotted the youngster during a London v. Malta match.

Carm was potty about snooker and Tony and was desperate for him to succeed. He even asked me if I would join a management team to look after him, along with Vic plus John and Lesley Carty, who played a major role in amateur tournaments in the south during the '80s (John also edited the popular *Cue World* monthly magazine until it was sold off). But much as I would have loved it, I felt there would have been a clash of interests. As it turned out, Tony and Carm fell out on more than one occasion and it would never have worked. Carm, a lovely bloke, made a big impression on the snooker world for a while; and though he is now retired, I still bump into him from time to time and keep him up to date with all the backstage gossip.

My next encounter with the Hurricane came via my *Daily Mail* sports editor Tom Clarke, the finest journalist I've ever worked for and a great boss. He gave me a start in Fleet Street and allowed me to write about snooker in the first place, opening up a wonderful, colourful world I never knew existed. A couple of months after Davis had won the title, Tom called me into his office and said, 'I've been reading that one or two snooker players enjoy golf, so do you think you could rustle up a few for a game at Wentworth?' I had no idea if it was possible; but, not wanting to lose face, I nodded and began making phone calls.

Ray Reardon, six-times world champion – Yes.

John Spencer, three-times world champion – Yes.

Cliff Thorburn, 1980 world champion – Yes, if he could bring Kirk Stevens along.

Steve Davis, current world champion – Yes, if Barry Hearn could play as well.

Alex Higgins, 1972 world champion – Yes, if I would pay his £69 taxi fare from Northampton, where he was appearing the previous night, and if his manager, Del Simmons, could also play.

It was all arranged in less than a day and I swaggered into Tom's office saying, 'How does five world champs and Kirk Stevens sound?' I loved Tom to bits and felt ten feet tall when they all assembled, as arranged, at Wentworth on a misty October morning.

Even Alex was on time for the *Daily Mail* Challenge: Snooker v. Press. Ian Wooldridge, legendary Fleet Street writer, accompanied Tom, along with Jeff Powell (the paper's No. 1 football writer), racing editor Jack Millan and a few others. Quite a gallery had assembled as Thorburn teed off. The ball sped 275 yards like an arrow straight down the fairway and you could almost see the colour drain from everyone's face when he turned around, spread his arms wide and said, 'OK guys, let's shoot some golf.'

By coincidence, Higgins and Thorburn had the same golf bags, presented to them at a recent pro-celebrity event at Wentworth. One of the regular caddies had looked after Cliff for the day and they got on so well that Cliff booked him for our event. When he arrived and spotted the red-and-white bag outside the clubhouse, he naturally assumed it was the right one. Unfortunately, Cliff arrived a few minutes later and by then it was too late to swap the caddies around. Not that it bothered the Canadian, who played to a pretty low handicap and was two-under at the turn – streets ahead of the field. Alex, who played with Hearn, had a torrid time fending off all the well-intentioned advice from his caddie.

Hearn and Higgins, though on the same side, could not resist having a hole-by-hole bet. Come the approach to the 18th green on a wet, miserable day, Hearn had edged ahead and Higgy needed to win the last to make it all-square. Having paid no heed to the voice of his experienced caddie, he was anxious not to let Hearn rub his face in it and so asked for advice. I'm not a golfer and don't pretend to know which club he told Alex to take. What I do know is that Barry landed smack dab in the middle of the green, while Higgy overshot it by yards. End result: a grinning Hearn put his hand out for the £100 he had taken off the Irishman, who was far too busy rowing with the caddie to worry about paltry matters like that. The pair of them flew at each other, Higgy blaming him for the choice of club and the caddie protesting that he'd played the shot with too much power.

Despite all the shenanigans, I recall clearly that Alex still coughed up his fee, only to discover an hour later, to his fury, that the *Mail* had settled all payments to the caddies. My part in the event was to lure the players there, which I did successfully, then act as chauffeur to Higgins for the rest of the evening. He was playing Steve Davis in an exhibition match at Tolworth, Surrey, just up the road from where I grew up. We arrived back at his Sheraton Hotel by Heathrow in time for him to change into his playing gear, collect his cue and head for the venue. As I walked out of his hotel room he plonked a fat pile of Alex Higgins posters in my hands and said, 'You can sell them for me beforehand while I'm in the dressing-room. Charge £1 a time and we can nick a good few quid.'

So there was Sharon Tokley, Steve's right-hand girl, standing behind the counter of their portable 'shop' selling all sorts of snooker sundries – cues, chalk, cue cases, photos of all the stars, including one of Higgy, and so on. And there was me, standing like a dummy at the side of the table with people queuing three deep and throwing money at me left, right and centre and being promised Alex's autograph during the interval. Meanwhile, Higgy got off the phone to Lynn, strode out to a fabulous reception and proceeded to perform superbly against the world champion. During the interval, Higgy sent me out again to 'nick a few more quid'; looking back it was hilarious, though it certainly wasn't at the time. A queue of fans formed on one side of the table in search of his posters, while at the other side stood at least 100 people awaiting the great man's autograph. 'Tell them I'll do the lot at the end, babes,' he said, interrupting another phone call briefly.

Come the end, Alex was jubilant because he'd put one over Steve and we returned to his dressing-room. 'Come on, Alex,' I said. 'We've got about 200 people out there with your posters for signing.' But he wasn't interested. 'Hearn's mob have got a bloody cheek,' he said. 'They're selling the same poster and expecting me to sign them as well. Fuck 'em all – we're off.' With that, he dashed out through the back-door exit with me in tow and raced to the car.

By now it was about 11.15 p.m. and I was exhausted, but Higgy was full of beans and couldn't stop chatting about how he'd sorted Steve out good and proper. 'You saw it,' he said. 'He's got the world title but I'm the People's Champion.' I didn't know whether to laugh or cry, because I kept thinking about all those people I had virtually conned into buying his posters. About ten minutes later we were passing through a beautiful Surrey village called Thames Ditton, where my roots were and my heart still is. One of the focal points is the picturesque Swan, a typical village pub right beside the River Thames. As we passed by, I mentioned casually to Alex that Jenny Hanley, the children's TV presenter, ran the pub with her husband, Herbie. I didn't know the couple, but my brother Peter owned the boatyard next door and my other brother, Ginger, who worked for him, had befriended them.

'Stop the car,' bellowed Alex, 'we've got to go in.'

The trouble was, the pub was obviously closed and as I was a stranger to the publican, there was no way I could wangle an after-hours drink. 'I just want to say hello to Jenny,' said Higgy. 'I'm a big fan.' I felt so embarrassed but in I went and asked one of the barmaids clearing up if I could talk to Herbie. She pointed him out. I introduced Alex and told him I was Ginger's brother and he was fine about it.

I said Alex wanted to meet Jenny, but Herbie replied, 'We had a really late one last night and Jenny crept upstairs about two hours ago.' He then poured us half a lager each and we sat down for a few minutes of small talk. It was awkward, obviously, because we didn't know each other, and he couldn't have been a snooker fan because although he'd heard of Alex, he knew little about him. But Alex leaned over the table and told Herbie: 'I'm a great admirer of your wife.'

Tragically, only weeks earlier, Jenny had lost the twins she had been carrying. To make conversation, I asked Herbie how she was coping. 'Physically, she's fine but mentally she's still struggling,' he replied. With that, I wished the ground could have opened up and swallowed me because Alex promptly dug his hand into the inside pocket of his coat and fished out a huge pile of photographs of his daughter, Lauren, who was about nine months old at the time. 'This is my baby, Herbie,' he said, then talked him through dozens of pictures.

I'm sure Alex didn't realise he was acting so insensitively, but after about five minutes I kicked his ankle under the table and told him we had to go. Herbie jumped in as well, saying he was shattered, so we said our goodbyes and headed for Heathrow . . . and the final surprise of what had been another extraordinary day for me and probably a regular day in the life of the Hurricane. 'Come up for a nightcap,' said Alex, when we arrived, and because he'd been such a good sport, not even asking for his £69 taxi fare from Northampton, I couldn't refuse – even though I was dead on my feet.

There had been no prizes at the golf, but we had had a slap-up meal afterwards and Thorburn, individual winner of the golf, had been given a dozen bottles of champagne. When Alex, at Heathrow, insisted I have a glass of bubbly with him, I was curious. 'Alex, you're not a champers man, surely?' I asked.

'No, no, it's one of Cliff's,' he said.

I thought it was a terrific gesture by Thorburn to give Higgy a bottle, and said so. The Huricane just grinned: 'He didn't, babes – I nicked it.'

*

JOHN SPENCER
Three-times world champion who took Alex under his wing in the early years and has always had a soft spot for him.

The thing about sportsmen like Alex, George Best and John McEnroe is that they all have genius. They don't know how they did it – they just went out and did it. I believe Alex's nerve-strings were plucked too often. It's a question of age and co-ordination. Once it has gone, it never comes back. I had to come to terms with it and it wasn't nice. I could still think my way around a table but I could no longer hit the balls. Alex had the biggest snooker brain ever and you never lose that. But you do lose your nerve. After his main ban, he believed he was going to be as good as he had been, and he had to adopt that attitude in his declining years because, otherwise, he would not have potted another ball.

I saw a lot of him in his early years because we played against each other so much, and I would say he was my most difficult opponent because he was so unpredictable. You'd play a fantastic safety shot, leave him down in baulk and know you'd be straight back on the table. The next thing is, Alex has potted a phenomenal red down the cushion from nowhere and mopped up to win the frame. It was sickening, but when he was in that mood, there was little you could do about it but sit back and admire the show.

I firmly believe Alex was led astray by all the hangers-on who congregated right from the start of his career. They made him out to be a God-like figure and whatever he wanted, they got it for him. Before long, he began believing them, which was why he became so demanding – on and off the table. Mind you, he made me laugh one night. We'd been playing an exhibition and decided to have a few drinks in a nightclub. We were making our way there and all of a sudden Alex stepped out in front of a police panda car. The driver screeched to a halt and Higgy just said, 'Any chance of a lift, please?'

During the 1976 world championship at Wythenshawe, I used to sit and chat with the hospitality girls and I wound them up by warning them to watch out for Higgins. 'He's wild,' I kept telling them, and they believed me. One night, Alex took a fancy to a bracelet Henry West was wearing and they started arguing about it. Next thing, Alex had a go at Henry and we suddenly spotted a policeman at the door. My wife, Margot, was with me and Higgy started slagging her off as well. With that, I went for him, the policeman went for me and the three of us burst into the Embassy girls' room and collapsed in a heap – Higgy on the bottom with me on top of him and the copper completing the sandwich. And I'd been telling them to watch out for Alex.

Another time, when we were due to play at Middlesbrough, Alex told the promoter he would not play. It made headlines in the local evening paper, but I told the promoter – I believe it was Alan Armstrong – not to worry. A bit later, Alan came up and said, 'It's OK, Alex says he'll play now.' I said, 'Good, because I'm not going to.' With that he sent Alex home and I said I'd sort out the crowd. The place was packed and I explained what a pest Alex had been. I said I'd play a frame with seven players in the audience and donate my fee to charity. We had a great night.

In a way, I suppose, I was teaching Alex a lesson, but he never really respected me until I started running him around in my car. He'd stick his feet up on the dashboard straight away and I warned him to stop doing it. In the end I refused to let him ride with me. He would always ask for a lift, knowing I'd refuse, and that was when we struck up a special bond. He would phone me at 3 a.m., sometimes, asking for advice or telling me about his latest problem, but I never minded. I never told anyone, but if ever I were knocked out of a tournament, I'd always want him to win, and I know he felt the same way about me.

Alex didn't always play the devil. He had a caring side to him and when I first developed Myasthenia Gravis, which has affected my eyesight permanently, he was the only one to visit me. He arranged for a pal to drive him over from Manchester and he spent the day with me. Mind you, Margot got him well and truly drunk, but I can't tell you how much I appreciated his concern. Cliff Thorburn sent me a letter and as far as I can recall, no one else bothered to contact me.

Higgy left an indelible mark on snooker because he was the most aggressive player ever to hold a cue. It made for sheer excitement. You ask ten pros whom they'd rather watch, given the choice, and they would go for Alex every time. His long-potting from baulk was his greatest strength; but he could also conjure shots and pots out of thin air.

I remain convinced he would have won so many more honours if he could have found the right man to manage him – to keep him in check when things went awry and give him the necessary encouragement when he needed it. All those hangers-on have a lot to answer for, in my opinion.

JIM WYCH
Former Canadian pro and now a respected TV pool commentator for Eurosport.
I can't tell any funny stories about Alex, but I'll tell you what – he is one of the good guys as far as I'm concerned. My daughter had just been born and I was struggling financially, practising at Paul Medati's

Masters Club in Stockport and wondering where the next buck was going to come from.

Alex used to practise there as well and he walked in one day, had a chat with me and asked how I was doing. I told him things were pretty tight and he just threw me some keys and said, 'Help yourself.' I know he doesn't drive but it was definitely his car – he must have employed a guy to take him around. He said I could have it indefinitely, then said I should stay with him.

We went back to his place, a few miles away, and he took me into this vast bedroom and told me it was mine. I'd never seen anything like it – there was a huge built-in wardrobe covering two walls. He opened it up and I couldn't believe my eyes. Alex was renowned for his snappy suits and there must have been at least a hundred hanging up. He looked me up and down and said, 'We're about the same stamp, James, so help yourself.'

I was just grateful to have a roof over my head, but he was adamant I should have two or three suits and made me try some on. Boy, they were quality suits and he insisted I keep them. I remember that when Jimmy White was in the 1984 world final against Steve Davis, Alex lent him a suit to play in, then cheered him on all night in the pressroom. Apart from being a wizard on the table, the guy's a class act in my opinion and I have never forgotten his kindness.

My only criticism is that he was a nightmare to practise with. Alex wanted to socialise as well as play, so he'd shoot a red, then sit on the edge of the table and have a conversation with someone. Then he'd pot a few more balls and do the same again. It was maddening, but I never said anything because he was such good company.

Nine

THE DOWN SIDE

It must have been galling for Higgins to read that Barry Hearn had secured off-table work worth nearly £200,000 for Steve Davis before a ball had even been potted in the new season, plus several lucrative endorsement contracts. Alex had never seen that kind of money. He'd never written a newspaper column (Steve earned £25,000 a year from the *Daily Star*) and had never been sponsored by Coral Racing and so on. The list seemed endless. Steve's exhibition fees had risen from £200–£300 a night to £1,500 once he had fulfilled all the engagements undertaken before he had hit the big time.

Alex, the greatest crowd-puller of all, was also able to command the same fees, but Steve's incredible earning power served only to deepen the wound between the two players. Hearn was the shrewdest man ever to be involved in that side of snooker, though Ray Reardon could scrap with the best of them when it came to endorsements. As Hearn said, when explaining the huge increase, 'If you want a Ferrari, you don't pay Ford prices.'

But although Higgins was now managed by Del Simmons exclusively following the dissolution of PSA, his bad-boy image precluded him from the big-money deals available. And his season got off to the worst of starts when he lost 9–8 to a weary Davis in the semi-finals of the Jameson International at Derby. Davis had been trawling up and down the country in his new Porsche – a birthday present from Hearn – while Alex stuck religiously to his bus-bike-train routine.

To make matters worse for Davis, he had accepted a booking months earlier for an exhibition in Jersey – along with Tony Meo and Kirk Stevens – before his showdown with Higgins and they were flown there in a six-seater plane. Davis recalls: 'We flew from Castle Donington, played all day, then were up at six the next morning for the return flight. I drove straight back to Derby, had just enough time for a small kip, then took part in one of the most exciting matches I can remember. Not surprisingly, I arrived in the arena walking on my knees and was happy to be 4–4 at the interval.'

Higgins, in fine form having beaten Fagan, Mountjoy and Griffiths in earlier rounds – and with a summer of golf behind him – was relaxed all the way through and fancied his chances of lifting the Jameson crown. But Davis had other ideas and when Higgins went 8–7 in front with a 95 break, he got that adrenaline rush which was to stand him in good stead throughout his career. He took the next frame to draw level, then pulled a sparkling 95 from his top drawer to reach the final, in which he demolished poor Dennis Taylor 9–0. As if defeat weren't bad enough, Davis also nicked the £2,000 high-break prize from Higgy (who was convinced his 118 made against Mountjoy was enough and demanded his prize money before the final had finished; wouldn't you know it, Davis just had to spoil things for him with a total clearance of 135).

The tour was gathering pace by then. It moved up to Glasgow's Kelvin Hall, a great boxing centre, for the Lang's Supreme Scottish Masters, where Higgins became embroiled in more controversy. Having seen off Vic Harris in his opening round, Alex faced Thorburn in the semi-finals and was horrified in frame five to discover there were fewer points on the board than he thought he had scored.

It turned out there wasn't a proper recorder and that a promotions girl putting up the scores had miscounted horribly, giving Alex four fewer points than he had accumulated from one small break. The usual Higgy fireworks ensued, with Thorburn and the referee on the receiving end. But the Canadian won the frame to be 3–2 ahead at the interval, as the row rumbled on, and clinched the next three to see off his rival 6–2. Again, there was a certain degree of sympathy for Higgins, but he didn't help matters by whingeing on. He even accused Thorburn of being a cheat afterwards and demanded – without success – that the match be replayed.

Nothing was going right for Higgins in a season which had promised so much, and a 6–5 defeat by Davis in the Harvey Demmy Classic final in Manchester hardly helped his mood. Next came his worst nightmare – a ten-day Davis–Higgins tour of Scotland as part of Steve's contract with the *Daily Star*. Out came the Davis promotion shop on the first night; and out from the Higgins pram came the toys.

'Alex walked in, saw the stand and scattered our posters of him all over the floor,' said Davis. 'He didn't like the fact that we were selling Alex Higgins posters and he wasted no time informing the crowd that he would sign only those posters bought from him. I kept well away. Having to face him on the table was enough without going out of my way to confront him in the foyer.' Barry Hearn complained and the promoter actually threatened to withdraw Higgy, but eventually the flames died down and the Hurricane was allowed to sell his own posters.

'As expected, Higgins blew his top and continued to be obnoxious throughout the ten days,' recalls Steve Davis in his book, *Frame and Fortune*. 'He gave everyone hell. We stayed in the same hotel but I made sure I kept well away. To be candid, the only time you get a good word from Alex is when he's winning and, although he played fairly well, I won quite comfortably.' Davis found the tour 'devastating', with a 'gruelling' schedule played through the afternoons and evenings: 'And all through, Higgins remained totally obnoxious. There was no other word to describe him, but I was determined not to let his moods get under my skin and spoil my enjoyment.'

Northern Ireland's semi-final loss against holders Wales in the State Express World Team Cup at Reading was another blot on the Higgins landscape, but the worst was to come. First, he lost 5–2 against Davis in front of his own Belfast crowd in the Northern Ireland Classic (Jimmy White beating Davis in the final). Then came disaster: a 9–4 thrashing by Meo in the Coral UK Championship quarter-final at Preston, which left him utterly deflated.

Yet a bright new dawn appeared to rise for Alex during the championship when Harvey Lisberg, who ran showbiz company Kennedy Street in Manchester, announced publicly that he had signed Higgins to join Jimmy White, John Virgo and David Taylor in his new Sportsworld management group. Lisberg, used to dealing with pop singers and such like, also demanded that his stars, especially Jimmy and Alex, be paid appearance money. Needless to say, his request was knocked back immediately by the WPBSA, which convened a special meeting during the event.

So Higgy had a new manager, yet Del Simmons still appeared to hold the reins. This became evident in later months. Higgins scrambled past Dave Martin – a great character from the North-east who was English Amateur Championship runner-up to Jimmy in 1978 and Joe O'Boye two years later. But when it came to Meo in the quarter-finals, Higgins just fell apart. His highest break was 31 and he made countless errors. He just wasn't himself and within days he had checked into a private clinic in Manchester, supposedly because he had reached breaking point mentally. In reality, he was cracking up from booze and, I suspect, the enormous pressure Davis had exerted on the table since beating him at Sheffield. Alex had hit the bottle hard, had lost weight from his already-spindly frame and needed now to dry out and receive some tender loving care away from the hurly-burly of the snooker circuit.

He returned later in December only to get beaten up again by Davis in an exhibition at York. 'I knew he'd just been discharged from hospital and, unfortunately for him, I was in top form and slaughtered him,' recalls Davis. 'Higgins then went up on stage, thanked the crowd for their support and added: "In the words of Muhammad Ali, my greatest hero, I can return. I shall return." People started clapping and I joined in. I couldn't believe what was going on. It was hilarious.'

Davis beat Higgins again in snow-bound Batley the following night after Alex had arrived several minutes late because of the weather, and all these knock-backs must have had a terribly unsettling effect on the little Irishman. And just in case he wasn't feeling bad enough, Davis knocked in TV's first maximum during the Lada Classic at Oldham against John Spencer, whose own 147 at Slough in 1979 was not ratified on two counts: the pockets did not conform and the TV cameramen were taking a meal break at the time.

A frail-looking Higgy beat Dennis Taylor 5–1 in the opening round of the Lada but fell to Griffiths by the same score in the semi-finals. He fared little better in his defence of the B&H Masters at Wembley, a 5–1 win against old enemy Eddie Charlton being followed by a 6–4 semi-final defeat at the hands of Griffiths. It was their third consecutive meeting at the Conference Centre and was punctuated by a Higgins row with referee John Smyth, concerning a jump-shot on the black when he miscued. He argued at length – there's a surprise – without cause and the Welshman stayed cool to prevent Higgins reaching his fifth successive B&H final. The fact that Davis went on to win the title was merely salt in the wound.

There was more agitation for Higgins when he initially declined to take part in the newly sponsored Irish Championship in Coleraine because, for the first time, there were enough pros to form a knockout series rather than the usual one-to-one format. Higgins was still smarting over Taylor's refusal to accept his challenge for the title the previous year; also because the event had been taken away from his native Belfast. 'I have a commitment to play in Jimmy Tarbuck's golf tournament in Spain,' was his watery explanation for dropping out and it did not please his fans.

In the event, Higgy's pride drew him to Coleraine. He came in at the semi-final stage, beat Eugene Hughes, then lost to Taylor 16–13 after a gallant fightback. Hughes, incidentally, has long since retired; but the teetotal, happy-go-lucky Dubliner from Dun Laoghaire has the best Higgins story ever, set in Australia. For one of the few times in his life, Alex was a completely innocent victim. I see Eugene maybe once every couple of years at the snooker hall he runs in his home town: he still induces tears of laughter, cackling away in his own inimitable style as he repeats the tale, which also involves Tony Knowles. But I dare not relate it. To protect the guilty, you understand.

Everything that could go wrong was going wrong for the troubled Irishman and he was involved in another blow-up during the Yamaha Organs Trophy round-robin event at Derby's Assembly Rooms. Higgins, bracketed with David Taylor, Meo and Thorburn, lost to group-winner Taylor after a fearful row. Higgins accused him of a deliberate miss. Referee Len Ganley sided with the Mancunian. Alex, in a rage, told Taylor, one of snooker's gentle folk: 'Don't ever speak to me again. Don't speak to my wife or daughter – don't speak to my cat.'

It sounds ridiculous, I know, but these tantrums were becoming more and more frequent and players were getting fed up with Alex. None more so than Thorburn. This tense, on-table street-fighter could not have been more amiable when relaxing, yet Higgins contrived to make his life a misery whenever possible. Thorburn believed Higgins had the Indian sign over him, despite his magnificent world-title triumph against him in 1980. And so it proved when Alex, cheered on by his mighty following, came from 4–0 down to win 5–4 in the B&H Irish Masters quarter-finals at Goffs.

Cliff had been so miserable during his year of office because he felt he hadn't received the acclaim befitting his status. Snooker, though emerging in Canada, was not big enough there for him to be recognised fully, and in Britain he was seen as the guy who robbed Higgins of his title. In addition, he had spent two horrible years living in England with his wife, Barbara, and neither could settle. Once Davis had relieved him of the world title in 1981 the couple – now with baby Jamie – began househunting back in their native Toronto. In desperation, Cliff had snapped his cue over a knee after one particularly unhappy match and was trying desperately to break in a new one (no pun intended). Not content with tormenting Thorburn on the table, Higgins then rounded on his own fans in the semi-final against Davis. Having bragged that he would 'destroy' the world champion, Higgins trailed 3–1, then complained about the noisy support he was receiving (the same noisy mob that had roared him on against Thorburn). During a lull in the proceedings Higgins told the crowd, 'Keep your traps shut.'

Mystified referee John Smyth, also a target, told Higgins to 'behave like a professional'. The London-based Dubliner said afterwards, 'Alex started by having a go at the crowd and then at me. I warned him and would have disqualified him if he had continued in the same vein.' Higgins calmed down and actually pulled one back after the interval. But there was no stopping Davis, who won 6–2 as he pleased, yet lost 9–5 to Griffiths in the final. Alex's sourness must have cost him some devoted fans that night. They had cheered him through thick and thin over the years and given him the support worthy of a superstar. Yet he chose to bad-mouth them when he was playing poorly.

It was far from the build-up he had hoped for as he sought again the world title and, given the state of his mind and his health, only a fool or the most fervent fan would have put a penny on his chances of regaining the treasure he wanted most of all.

But you never knew with Higgy.

*

CLIFF THORBURN
1980 world champion and one of the most formidable players ever.

Alex and I have never got on. At our initial meeting in 1973, when I flew over from Toronto to London for the first time, he offered to give me 40 points for a fiver a frame. Being a gentleman, I accepted only 28 and won the lot. All I remember about that occasion was me running down some stairs, having not been paid, with Higgins at the top clutching a snooker ball and threatening to throw it at me.

But he was a terrific player, always a danger, although I felt he was just behind Reardon and Spencer. He had a gift for the game and was the best natural potter I'd ever seen until Jimmy White came along. When I first saw Alex in competition, he had the cue ball on a piece of string and could do practically anything with it. He also had tremendous grit and his 69 clearance against Jimmy in the 1982 world semi-final was the best ever in my book.

Our first big off-table clash came later in '73, when I got involved in a card game with him and a few others. Higgins borrowed £50 from me and I took his wedding ring in return (I had him weighed up by that time). Later that night he and his wife, Cara, came looking for it and Alex pretended to fall down in a faint. I attempted to pick him up, then turned my back on him and he went for me with a bottle. I grabbed him, threw the bottle down, got him round the neck and just pounded his head until my fist was sore.

Apart from clinking the ice around his glass during our 1980 world final, he was quite well behaved. But two seasons later, after I'd lost the title, we played in the Lang's Scottish Masters and I beat him after a row in the fifth frame about wrong scores. He was right, but it had nothing to do with me. Higgins tried in vain to get the match replayed as I went up to my hotel room. Up there, the phone rang. It was Higgins, who said, 'I hope your son doesn't grow up to be like you.' Jamie had been born three months earlier. I ran out of the room steaming, determined to get him, but I was waylaid by two fans on my way up to his floor and that cooled me down.

I was having a dreadful year by the time we got to the Irish Benson's the following February and I lost to Alex 5–4 from 4–0 up. I just couldn't beat him and he knew it. I was in the bar later that week and just happened to be sitting beside the girl he was with. He was playing cards and drinking. Suddenly he says, 'Thorburn, you're a Canadian c*** and you can't fucking play, either.' He walked over to me; I was so mad that I smashed him on the side of the face and he went over. People grabbed the pair of us and a drunk said, two or three times, 'Let's all be friends.' Eventually we went to shake hands, but I just couldn't. There were too many hurts from the past.

So as he came towards me I kicked him right in the nuts.

There were other serious incidents in the following years which hurt me very badly, including the 'little white bags of powder' episode [documented elsewhere in this book]. It would be fair to say I once felt sorry for him and now I can't stand him – can't even bear to talk about him in any light.

Ten

BORN AGAIN

Higgins was probably less equipped than at any other time in his turbulent career to tackle the 1982 Embassy World Championship, yet the omens were good right from the start. Defending champion Davis went 8–1 down overnight against Tony Knowles and dropped the first two frames the next morning to lose 10–1 in the greatest shock of all. Before the session got under way, I remember, I phoned Steve's mum, Jean. A former schoolteacher, she was and still is an extremely down-to-earth mum, who dispensed care, love and discipline on Steve and his younger brother Keith in equal doses. (She also gave me a lot of advice about my then-volatile daughter Beth from time to time; it must have helped because she's grown up to be a smasher.) Even as a superstar living at home in the early days, Steve had to take his turn at the kitchen sink washing the dishes.

Jean told me, 'It's not the end of the world, you know. Steve might even come out and win every frame, although it's doubtful. But it's only a game and he'll get over it if he loses.' Advice Alex could well have done with – and heeded – throughout his career.

Second-favourite Terry Griffiths also bowed out, 10–6 against Willie Thorne, and all of a sudden the clouds lifted from above Higgins and he could see a way through. He beat old pal and practice partner Jim Meadowcroft 10–5 for openers. Then he left Doug Mountjoy shaking his head in despair in the next round after he fluked a red out of a snooker in the final frame to win 13–12, the Welshman having come back from 12–10 down.

But there was a bigger news story in the offing. Between matches, Higgins, taking part in a late-night practice session backstage with Kirk Stevens, decided to relieve himself in a plant pot. He was spotted by a backstage lighting man. A struggle ensued and Alex ripped the chap's jumper. At the time, the *Belgrano* had just been sunk with nearly 300 lives lost during the Falklands War – but Higgins dominated the front pages. Meadowcroft, after enjoying a late, late breakfast with his sparring partner from those early Blackburn days, tried to cheer him up in the hotel bar, saying, 'Alex, in your wildest dreams, do you think you could hit that plant 20 feet away?'

Higgins, in no mood for frivolity and realising it could cost him another hefty fine, asked Jim's advice. 'Middlepocket', as he was known, suddenly had an inspiration: 'Just tell them the plant looked as though it were dying and you gave it the piss of life.' It was a great one-liner, though it did nothing to soften Alex's mood. But it was obvious to those around him that the Hurricane was up for the title. The removal of bogeymen Davis and Griffiths provided just the spur he needed and his manager, Del Simmons, gave me a smashing 'exclusive' about Alex vowing to maintain his exhibition fee of £1,500 if he won the title. In fact, everything seemed to be going his way because he had another stroke of fortune in the quarter-finals. The morning it started, the *Sun* carried a story about opponent Thorne's indiscretions with a married woman. True or not, it served to unsettle the Great WT, who had been sure it would be his year.

Thorne, as fluent a break-builder as you could ever see, nearly matched Higgins all the way, despite the adverse publicity, and scored a 143 best-of-championship break to be just 5–3 behind. He added another century and was 9–7 down after the second session. But he couldn't quite close the gap and Higgins went on to a 13–10 success and a semi-final place.

It had been Thorne's dream to get that far, to play in a one-table situation at the Crucible. Sadly, this never happened for him and it is too late now, even though Willie is still competing (well at times, but not right up there with the big boys). Mind you, he has become an accomplished TV commentator, much in demand, and his exhibitions are matched only by those of Dennis Taylor.

While Higgins was coming through his half of the draw, Ray Reardon, the 49-year-old Welsh warrior who had gone back to club snooker and £5-a-frame wagers at his own centre in Stoke to sharpen his game for one final fling, was roaring through his section like a steamroller. He beat John Virgo and Silvino Francisco with ease; then excelled in topping old rival Eddie Charlton 16–11 to reach his first final since his sixth and last world title win in 1978.

Higgins and Jimmy White were to steal his thunder, though, long before the balls had been racked up for the first frame of the final. In a classic confrontation which has gone down in history as one of the finest matches ever staged at the Crucible, Higgins demonstrated against his protégé just how he had made his reputation as the most unbelievable, most unorthodox player of all time.

It was a pleasure to watch master and pupil at work during a first session which ended all-square at 4–4. I said so in my *Daily Mail* report the next morning and was thrilled to be visited in the pressroom by the 'heavy gang' – Mrs Maureen White, Mrs Lynn Higgins and Mrs Helen Lomas, wife of Alex's close friend Geoff. They told me both players had enjoyed the piece. Big-head or what? But seriously, seldom does a reporter in any sport get a pat on the back and I was genuinely taken aback.

What ensued on the table that day topped anything previously in the 1982 championship. White led 8–7 after another exhilarating session, then 11–8 that night before carving out what appeared to be a match-winning lead at 15–13 with one frame needed. But Higgins responded with a 72, which carried him to 15–14, and he followed up with the greatest break ever. Forget the 147s and any other clearance you've admired, because Higgins came back from the brink as never before or since.

When White scored 41 and missed a black off its spot, then added a further 18, only to bodge the red which would almost certainly have given him the match, it still left Higgy 59–0 down and facing almost certain expulsion. But the Ulsterman gritted his teeth to produce the most spellbinding break of his entire career – even today it is acknowledged as such. Somehow, he conjured an opening and then, as we all held our breath, picked his way through the out-of-position balls remarkably to clear up with a 69. White, just a slip of a lad, wilted in his chair and the rest was almost a formality. He was just one pot away from becoming the youngest world finalist until his mentor and pal struck to level the scores. Alex then sank a 59 in the deciding frame to signal the end. Jimmy, with a ghost-like face, trailed out of the Crucible bearpit looking for all the world like a little boy lost. And I am convinced his fate was sealed that day.

Julian Barnes wrote in *The Observer*: 'Shambling and twitching, pockets distended by duck mascots, rabbits' feet and four-leaf clovers, Higgins lurched appealingly around the table like a doomed low-lifer.' Alex, who loved the description, said: 'I'll not forget the sight of Jimmy walking out of the arena. He'd played magnificent snooker, scented victory, tasted it even and had it dashed from his lips at the last moment. I felt so sorry for him. When you see so much talent in such a young player and know that if it hadn't been for one slip, he'd have been on top of the world, your heart goes out to him. But he took defeat well and, apart from being pals, we became soul-mates after that.'

White went on to feature in six world finals and should have won at least two. But no one, not even Jimmy himself, knows what damage Alex caused him that day. Certainly, the mental scars have been evident in all his finals. Now it is almost certainly too late for White to fulfil his lifelong ambition, although he will argue about that assertion.

While White went back to South London, distraught and bewildered,

Higgins revved up for a final showdown against his great adversary. And what a final. I didn't know Reardon that well at the time and as usual, your impartial reporter was rooting for Higgins. The Welsh legend, displaying the skill and cunning which had stood him in good stead throughout the '70s, opened a 5–3 lead – only for Higgins to transform his deficit into a 10–7 lead overnight.

It was still anyone's game, however, and I can vividly recall sitting on my own in the Crucible press seats the next day as play unfolded. Reardon won the opening frame with a 95 and Higgins looked ill at ease. As Ray was clearing up, Alex sidled round to me and whispered, 'Fetch me a vodka from the players' room.' I had no idea what mixer he wanted and said so. He whispered again, 'Just tell the kid it's for me. He'll know what to give you.'

I slipped out as Reardon carried on potting, found the players' room deep in the Crucible dungeon and asked the youngster behind the bar for a Higgins vodka. He poured tons of the stuff into a long glass and added a splash of Coca-Cola. On the way back to the arena I had a sip out of curiosity and nearly gagged because it was so foul (sadly, I've since grown accustomed to the taste).

Play was in progress in the second frame when I sneaked back into the arena. Reardon was causing more damage at the table and Higgins was waiting right by the press seats, which are situated just below the red curtains through which the players make their entrance. Maybe I'm exaggerating, but I swear he whacked the lot down in one go, then said, 'Fetch me another, babes.'

Back I went and this time, when I returned between frames, Ray was only 10–9 down. Alex took the drink and sipped from it for the next half-hour or so in between visits to the table. The interval came with Higgins 13–12 ahead, Reardon still in serious contention and me a gibbering wreck from all the excitement. Heaven knows how much vodka Alex consumed in that session, yet he came back, fit and eager, to continue in the evening and stretch his lead to 15–12. But Reardon wasn't finished and he ran off three frames in a row. Alex took a toilet break. He returned, refreshed and rejuvenated, a few minutes later and never looked back. He took full advantage of two Reardon mistakes to go 17–15 up, then produced the finest stroke of the entire, enthralling match – a 135 clearance to seal his second world title.

With that, a tearful Higgins called for Lynn and baby Lauren to join in the celebrations. 'My baby, my baby,' he cried. Many wept tears of joy with him as he hoisted his daughter aloft, his past misdemeanours forgotten.

Mark Williams earned £240,000 for his millennium victory in 2000; for Higgins the reward was £25,000 which, 20 years ago, was still considered a fortune. I bumped into Ray upstairs at the Crucible afterwards, congratulated him and told him he should be proud of his performance. But Ray just said, 'What's to be proud of? I lost.' And he was genuinely devastated. Years later he confided that had White beaten Higgins in the semi-final, he knew for certain he would have lifted his seventh world crown because although Jimmy had pipped him twice that season, Reardon felt his safety play would have been enough to unhinge the youngster over the championship distance. In fact, he proved a point the following season by beating Jimmy four times in succession.

Later that night at the Grosvenor House Hotel, during the celebrations, I asked John Spencer where he would put Alex in the order of greats. 'He's the best,' replied the three-times champion. 'He's world champion so he has to be the best around now. It's impossible to compare with past performances or players.' Kirk Stevens was far more animated: 'Alex Higgins,' he said, making a huge circular movement with both hands, 'has the biggest balls in the world.'

Still later and I found myself sitting alongside Lynn on a settee. I was nursing a pint of lager when someone crashed down beside me. The entire pint spilled all over the beautiful chiffon dress she had worn in front of millions of TV viewers and I did not know where to put my face. 'Don't worry about it,' she said. 'We're all celebrating tonight because my Alex has done it, just as he promised me he would.'

At about 5 a.m., as the party wound down, Higgins collared me and said, 'Do I look drunk to you?' He looked 100 per cent sober and I told him so, even though I was so intoxicated by the day's proceedings, as well as the booze I had consumed, that I was pretty high myself. 'Lynn says I'm pissed and has stormed off to bed,' he said. 'Well, I'm not finished yet. The night is young.' But I was well and truly finished and my day of retribution came a few hours later when I awoke with a massive hangover, realising I had to be up and about to report on the traditional WPBSA annual board meeting held the day after the final at the Grosvenor.

The only significant detail to emerge was that Higgins had been censured and fined £1,000 for peeing in the plant pot. John Roberts, a roly-poly reporter based in the *Mail*'s Manchester office, had been dispatched to write the Higgins follow-up, which upset me because I was supposed to be the snooker correspondent – though to be fair John was, and still is, a quality writer.

But the following day, when his article appeared, I was upset because instead of praising Alex, John more or less attacked him and said he had reached the crossroads of his career. I was upbeat, naturally, but that article evaluated the downside. John's analysis, in retrospect, was spot-on.

I phoned Alex at his home that night on the pretext of congratulating him again and he said, 'We can be friends but we can never do business together again.' When I protested, he said, 'You're the *Mail*'s snooker man and you should stop this sort of rubbish appearing in your paper.' He had a point, but I could not get through to him that in the general batting order of the office I was No. 11 and had no voice. Higgins just reiterated his point, then went back to his homecoming party.

David Harrison, then sports editor of the *Stockport Express and Advertiser*, who now runs the *Sunday Express* sports section, remembers: 'I called round on the off-chance to their home in Cheadle the day after his homecoming party and was thrilled to be invited inside by Lynn. Alex was sprawled over a chair, looking bleary-eyed and wiped out, which was understandable. It was a real thrill to interview him and he gave a exclusive for the local paper. Lynn made me a cup of coffee while we chatted and he could not have been more helpful. It was a big feather in my cap.'

Higgins was scheduled to play Steve Davis in several exhibitions around the country in the following days and lost the lot. Steve recalls, 'He seemed a lot less obnoxious since winning the title.' Alex also played and beat Jimmy White 19–7 in Dublin in July, with an incredible 2,000 people packing into the National Stadium for every session. There was an early finish but the Irish weren't worried because Alex won 11 frames in a row to see off his mate.

Higgins finally made it to the golf course after his hectic schedule. But come August the new world champion took his roadshow, complete with opponent John Spencer and a giant transporter (with table, tiered seating and accessories on board), around the south of England on a six-day tour. It was a brilliant concept and it worked – although the logistics must have been horrendous, what with all the unloading and reloading every night. It reminded me of the story Dennis Taylor once told about the time he and Higgins arrived for a show in Belfast, to be confronted by a big crowd and asked by the promoter: 'Where's the table?' Well, he said it was true.

My sports editor had no idea of the spat I'd had with Higgy and, after reading in the *Daily Mirror* about the venture, he suggested I go along one night to write a colour piece. I phoned Del Simmons, who was still close to Alex and still managing him despite the furore caused by Harvey Lisberg at Preston months earlier. I explained my dilemma, with Alex not wanting to be interviewed by me. Del, who always growled rather than spoke, said, 'Silly sod, that's just him. Alex doesn't hold grudges, so give him a ring on this number and tell him we've had a chat.' The first thing Higgy demanded was, 'How much is it worth?'

'Alex,' I said, 'you know I cover snooker all in my own time and you've never asked for money before.' (I used to spend my entire holiday allocation on the circuit at the expense of my family because my main job was as a sports sub-editor and the *Daily Mail* would not give me any working time off.) I laughed aloud when he came back at me, pleading,

'I've got my family to think about. I've got to find clothes for Lauren and it's not that easy. Just give me £200.' I'd never paid a penny for interviews and everyone, from Fred Davis to Reardon to Spencer to Steve Davis, had always been amenable – and the same applies today, especially with Hendry, White, Steve and present champion Mark Williams.

In the end, reluctantly, my sports editor agreed I could pay him £100 – which is why, standing by the urinal at Harrow Leisure Centre, away from prying eyes and doing what a man's got to do, I handed Alex the cash in return for being allowed to have a picture of him taken at the side of the huge wagon outside. Even then things didn't go smoothly, because when he won the final game of the nine-frame encounter in front of a 600-plus crowd, I just said, 'Well done, Alex.' I'd been chatting away to various people throughout the evening and had hardly watched a ball potted, so I assumed Higgy had won. Not so.

He was merely playing out the dead frame, as was the custom, and had actually been beaten by Spencer. He had a bit of a go, accusing me of being unprofessional for not watching every ball. But come on! It was a social event for me and a chance to make new friends and contacts.

In fact, that night I came across Doug Perry, who lived in the Barnet area and was more than keen on promoting and managing Alex. He fielded all the flak in later years when the roof fell in on Higgins and was a genuine nice-guy. Tragically, Doug – primarily a showbiz booking agent who played in a jazz band in his spare time – died a few years ago at the age of 50. It was a terrible shock because he led what you might call a sheltered life: didn't drink or smoke or do drugs. It left a huge hole in Alex's heart because Doug had been his crutch for a good while. He was so loyal, so undemanding, and put up with Higgy's mood changes and foibles all the time. He also provided a refuge for him occasionally at his London flat.

So a new season dawned and this time it was going to be different for the People's Champion, now restored to the throne. Or was it? Alex opened his account with a 6–5 defeat of Griffiths in the Lang's Scottish Masters in Glasgow, but lost heavily in the final to a rejuvenated Steve Davis, eager to let him know the crown was out on loan. Defeats by Griffiths in the Jameson International – won by Tony Knowles in an historic event which saw ranking points awarded for the first time outside the world championship – and by eventual winner Reardon in the new, unsponsored Professional Players Tournament, were disheartening for him. And the Northern Ireland team went down early in the World Team Championship at Reading. That took Alex up to the Coral UK Championship at Preston again and this time he almost came good.

He beat Spencer in the quarters, then Reardon in the semis – after a row with referee John Smyth – to clinch a final spot against Griffiths, who was determined to make amends for his previous two wallopings by Davis. Higgins looked back to his best, though, and when he went 15–13 ahead with three to play, the odds were firmly in his favour. John Dee told me, 'Higgy's got it in the bag. He never loses from this position.' But there is always a first time and Terry staged a splendid recovery to claim his only UK Championship success.

There was a touching cameo played out during Alex's semi-final with Reardon, in which he fired in a 135 clearance in the first session. My family had come up to Preston for the closing stages and Alex sat my daughter, Beth, on his lap and talked her through every shot on the TV action-replay. She hadn't a clue what was going on but she took a shine to him, as did my wife, Andrea.

It was Beth's ninth birthday the next day and the Coral promotion girls arranged a birthday cake and party for her in the hospitality lounge. By coincidence, the day after that was Lauren's second birthday, and while her Daddy was fighting like mad to keep Griffiths off his back during the first day of the final, Beth and Andrea were at Alex's beautiful ranch-style home in Cheadle with Lynn, helping to organise the birthday party. Andrea recalls, 'Lynn was so sure Alex was going to win that we went shopping after the party and I helped her choose a dress. Sadly, it wasn't needed.'

Higgins couldn't possibly have known then, but his star was already on the wane and he was to enjoy only a thimbleful more of success before his ultimate decline and fall. The new Hofmeister World Doubles followed before Christmas and, inexplicably, he teamed up with dreaded foe Eddie Charlton. 'He has the perfect game and anyway, we don't actually have to talk to each other,' was his explanation. In fact, the tournament was a sporting disaster because it was played at cold, unfriendly Crystal Palace Sports Centre right next to the Olympic pool. Griffiths led the protests from players, saying, 'The whole tournament is a shambles. It's too noisy, extremely cold and we don't even have adequate changing-rooms.'

The idea was good but the venue and area were wrong and fans avoided it like the plague. And to cap a miserable week for the Hurricane, he and Steady Eddie were beaten 10–7 in the semi-finals by Griffiths and Doug Mountjoy, who crumbled against Romford stablemates Davis and Meo in the final. Not a happy experience for anyone except the winners and their manager, Barry Hearn, who made his usual excursion to the bank the following day.

January 1983 came around and Higgins lost 5–4 to Bill Werbeniuk in the Lada Classic at Warrington – his first defeat by the giant Canadian in tournament play. To compound that setback, Alex lost by the same score against Big Bill a fortnight later in the B&H Masters at Wembley after leading 3–0. Werbeniuk pulled one back before the interval, then had a £200 bet on himself at 5–1 and cleaned up, thanks to a fluked red in the deciding frame. It was a stressful time for Alex, because although Lynn was expecting their second child in a matter of weeks, his marriage was already becoming frayed around the edges and he just couldn't get his game together. He created another rumpus in the Tolly Cobbold Classic at Ipswich (scene of earlier 'crimes') when he labelled the event a 'Mickey Mouse tournament' after defying new snooker regulations by removing his bow-tie while playing Dennis Taylor.

His fellow-Ulsterman went on to win, then lodged an official complaint. 'The TV lighting was pretty hot out there, but no one sweats more than I do and I didn't even have to wipe my hands,' said Taylor, although referee Peter Koniotis sided with Higgins. There were murmurs about Higgins forfeiting his £1,000 money, but he appeased nearly everyone by promising Patrick Cobbold, his friend and managing director of the brewery, that he would donate the money to charity. A week later he was complaining again – this time with good reason after bowing out of the Yamaha Organs event at Derby, where the format comprised four league tables and an inexplicable method of working out the group winners. As Alasdair Ross of *The Sun* said, 'You need a PhD in maths to work it out – this really is a Mickey Mouse tournament.'

Yet Alex found great consolation in the Irish Championship when he regained his title by beating Taylor 16–11 in the final. Hilariously he had cut a record, '147, My Idea of Heaven', shortly before in England; but he then upset his Irish fans by refusing to autograph the sleeve after giving away dozens of copies. Needless to say, the record bombed. But, like his idol Muhammad Ali singing the Drifters' classic 'Stand By Me', years earlier, it still makes for a good quiz question.

Returning to Ireland, a milk-drinking Higgins lost in the B&H semi-finals at Goffs against Reardon after beating White in the opening round. 'I'm getting worried about you drinking that, Alex,' said a laughing Reardon during his 6–3 win. 'Are you trying to poison yourself?' Higgins then provided a rambling, disjointed TV interview, complaining about the table and using his new catch-phrase, 'The ideal thing is . . .' It went like this:

> *Interviewer* [Jim Sherwin]: Alex, neither of you seemed to be on your game today.
>
> *Higgins*: Well, I think one of the things was that . . . I mean, Ray is an exceptionally good player and I regard myself as exactly the same. The ideal thing is that a lot of safety shots should, you know, trust in playing a thin ball so that they will get back into . . . and a lot of your shots often . . . the runaway shot where you want to keep your ball somewhere near the lower colours to start a break going . . . I mean, you couldn't hold

the white. It seems from past the blue spot you are going
downhill. Would you agree with that, Mr Reardon . . . ?

And on it went. Strong milk, that!

Higgins's season as world champion had lurched from one setback to
another, yet by the time the 1983 championship loomed he had
recovered some of his old bounce. A couple of weeks before Sheffield, he
played an exhibition at Ilford, Essex, for one of my Irish pals, Joe Brown
– one of four boxing brothers who had made their mark either at amateur
or professional level. Joe loved watching Higgins and was keen to
promote him. I arranged a meeting between them at Croydon, Surrey,
during one of Alex's exhibitions and he agreed to do the gig for £1,000
cash. He was true to his word. Well almost. The queue stretched around
the block, such was his popularity, and Joe was rubbing his hands
together in anticipation.

The place was heaving and Higgy was in sparkling form on and off
the table, playing at least a dozen frames. He opened against a kid of ten
and, bless him, split the pack open early on to give him a chance. But the
youngster was too nervous and Higgy, after leaving a few reds over
pockets, stepped in and cleared the table. It set the scene for a magical
night – Vic Harris and Eugene Hughes provided the main opposition –
and Joe was only too pleased to hand Alex his money.

'What about the VAT?' he queried. Joe was dumbfounded because
they had agreed cash, but Alex was adamant and, at 10 per cent, it cost
Joe another £100. Oh yes, and a bar bill of £78 for all the champion's
hangers-on. So that was Joe's profit gone up the wall, but we all enjoyed
the evening so much and he dined out on the tale for years.

On to Sheffield. Alex, though still not firing on all cylinders, was really
up for the defence of his world title, especially as a reasonably flattering
BBC TV documentary, *The Hurricane*, was shown on the eve of the
Embassy. It was to become one of the most spectacular world
championships in history for a multitude of reasons. Griffiths and
Thorburn played out the longest match ever, completing their second-
round match at 3.51 a.m. after Cliff had scored the first world
championship maximum early on, kicking off with a fluked first red
(remember him kneeling by the table and shaking his cue two-handed
after the final black went down?). Dennis Taylor's amazing Joe 90 outsize
specs also made their first appearance on British TV, to the amusement of
fans and players alike. And Davis reasserted himself in ruthless fashion.

Higgins wasn't expected to put up much opposition after his patchy
year in office, yet he forged a path through to the semi-finals, where
Steve Davis was lying in wait. But Alex played as though he knew he'd
done well to get that far and crumbled 16–5.

It was disappointing because he had fought so hard to get there, beating Dean Reynolds and Thorne, then avenging those two Werbeniuk defeats in a hard-fought quarter-final. But Alex and Willie weren't exactly bosom friends and the sparks flew between them throughout. The first session was tainted with acid, the players virtually insinuating that each was playing deliberate misses out of snookers. And Higgins told reporters, 'Willie would stab his own grandmother for two bob.' Great story for us, but Thorne was fuming.

Minutes before he began the semi-final, Higgins sought me out in the pressroom and asked me to get him a pot of honey. He'd been filling himself with vitamin pills and honey in the forlorn hope of getting himself extra fit after a decade of non-stop boozing, smoking and gambling and was convinced this new regime was the answer. I dashed out of the backstage door, across the road and down a side alley to the health shop, then belted back just in time to catch him. But Steve, pumped up like never before and utterly determined to regain his title, never gave him a chance. Alex knew it. 'He did me like a kipper,' he said with honesty and humour. 'Steve played strong, solid snooker. I stuck to the honey and vitamins but I was still stuffed. It was my biggest humiliation.'

Davis went on to collect his second world title with a devastating win against Thorburn, but what Alex couldn't possibly have known was that his own greatest triumph, on the back of his biggest heartbreak, was just around the corner – and against his deadliest enemy.

*

RAY REARDON
Legendary six-times world champion, the greatest stumbling-block to Higgins and still playing socially at 68.
Alex was without doubt my most formidable opponent and I enjoyed many of my great battles with him. He was a tremendous player, so inventive that sometimes I just sat in awe and wondered how on earth he'd played a particular shot. His temperament obviously let him down on too many occasions and it always seemed to me and others that he needed conflict to lift his game.

Yet for all his faults, for all the arguments and incidents, I can't ever remember us falling out or exchanging cross words. Early on in his career I told him, 'Alex, I'll back you all the way if you are in trouble or need help, but don't ever upset me or you'll know about it.'

He couldn't ever have coached anyone – or been coached – because he was so unorthodox, a law unto himself, but he should have won at least two more world titles and plenty of others because he was so talented. A great, great player. People always said John Spencer was my toughest opponent because we had seen off the old brigade of Fred Davis, John Pulman, Rex Williams and co. and were the new order, so to speak. John always used to wallop me in exhibitions but I usually did him when it came to the real thing. I always knew where I stood with John, playing-wise, but Alex was a different kettle of fish. You could never be sure which Higgy would turn up; but we had some fabulous matches over the years and those were the ones I enjoyed most.

Alex had a natural snooker brain. He saw a situation and knew what to do in a flash. We could all see it eventually, but he spotted it immediately: screw, deep screw, reverse side, check side, any side but suicide . . . he created a lot of the modern play. Joe Davis pioneered the game, inventing most of the shots for us to follow. Then came Williams, Pulman, Gary Owen, Spencer and me to carry on the tradition. But when Higgins appeared he brought shots which had never been seen before. I used to go giddy just watching the balls running around the table.

He got into golf in a big way in the '80s and I enjoyed facing him. I've been playing more than 30 years, stemming from my days of working the holiday camps in Devon, and even before I retired I moved to Brixham with my second wife, Carol, where we still live. Whenever I was down there I played at the Churston Golf Club, which is regarded as one of the most prestigious in the West Country. And, would you believe it, they elected me captain in 2000. Not bad, eh?

Alex was once booked to appear at St Mellion Golf and Country Club in Cornwall for a series of exhibitions, with some golf thrown in as well. I lived in Stoke at the time and was given the task of delivering him safe and sound. To make sure he didn't disappear, I invited him to stay at home overnight so we could set off bright and early the next morning for the 220-mile drive. I have to say, some refreshments were partaken of the night before, but we set off as planned, Higgy all restless and twitchy and me eager to deliver the goods. Within minutes, Alex had his feet up on the dashboard, which wasn't very nice, but he behaved himself so I said nothing.

We eventually reached our destination and I unloaded my charge and presented him to David Webb, who ran the complex. 'There you are, David,' I said. 'One Alex Higgins, delivered as requested. See you later in the week for a game of golf.' I started to walk away, and David, who looked horrified, said, 'Where on earth are you going?' I said, 'David, I've kept my side of the bargain – he's all yours now,' and drove off. But Alex was in fine fettle all the time he was there and I can still remember our golf day.

As well as our snooker exploits, Alex and I had some memorable adventures on the golf course and two in particular stand out. As everyone must know from watching him on TV, he couldn't stand or sit still for a moment. He had to keep on the move, and it was the same on the golf course.

We played a four-ball at St Mellion and Alex didn't have the patience to walk with the rest of the group, racing on after every shot. Actually, he wasn't a bad player and tried his hardest. We managed to keep apace until the 17th hole, which was a monster par-five. We all teed off, but then Alex went belting up the fairway, desperate to get on with it. By the time we'd reached the green Alex had putted out and was waiting for us to arrive, itching to get at the last hole. It's not golf etiquette, but no one minded because they all knew what he was like.

The other tale tops everything. We were at the Silk Cut Championship at St Pierre, in Chepstow, for the pro-celebrity event. I was coming behind Higgins, who was playing with the professional, Craig Defoy. We went to the short par-three, which was one of those holes where you launch a wedge, sand-iron or nine-iron straight out in front of you because the hole is way down below. You can see the ball dropping and landing on the green if you play it correctly. When we got there, Craig had just teed off and his ball was right behind the pin.

Higgins took his caddie's advice to take a nine-iron. But he hit the shot too hard and the ball finished in the rough, way beyond the green, and the people below waved up to say they couldn't find it. Craig, being a gentleman, said, 'Take another one, Alex.'

Higgy asked, 'What did you take, Craig?' and he said a sand-wedge. Putting it mildly, words were exchanged between the caddie and Higgy, who then said, 'There you are, caddie, give me a sand-wedge.' Alex played the shot and he thinned it, right off the flange. He went just over the lip and we saw the ball run down through the rough. About 100 yards below we then saw the ball go into a bunker, run out of the bunker, get over the lip, run on to the green and finish about a foot from the pin. We were in hysterics and Higgins turned to the poor caddie and said, 'There you are, Mr Caddie, I told you it should have been a sand-wedge in the first place.'

Naturally, I am saddened by Alex's plight now. He should be a wealthy man today, enjoying his life on the golf course. But there is no denying that he enriched snooker, brought grief to quite a few players and pleasure to millions. An incredible character. A complete one-off.

My favourite snooker story about Alex concerns the time he beat me to win the 1982 world championship at Sheffield. It is folklore now that he peed in a pot late one night and that he was dealt with by the WPBSA the morning after the tournament. I was on the board then and had to sit in judgment, never mind that he'd just prevented me from being a seven-times champion the night before. We convened at 11 a.m. and we had hardly settled in our seats at the Grosvenor House Hotel when Alex walked in and promised he'd be a good boy from then on and become a worthy champion. Minutes after he'd left the room and we were deliberating, there was a knock on the door. In walked a waiter pushing a trolley with 12 bottles of champagne and jugs of fresh orange juice 'compliments of new world champion Mr Alex Higgins'.

Well, what a predicament. Naturally, we opened a bottle to toast his success but just as we were about to raise a glass to him, there was another knock on the door and there stood Higgy with his baby Lauren. 'How long is this going to take?' he demanded. He was tired, he was being pressured by the press and he wanted to go home and celebrate. We told him to get off home and that we'd phone him and, bear in mind, we were in a really sympathetic mood. We had another sip and agreed that Alex really had convinced us he'd be a good boy from then on, so a lenient sentence was in the air.

All of a sudden, in burst Alex and said, 'Is there a fucking decision or what?' I'm sure that helped to up the fine to £1,000 when he might have got away with half that.

But I still have the occasional laugh about it because after Alex had departed, we all tucked in and got pie-eyed. In the end we had to abandon the meeting and after that we resolved to impose a booze ban at board meetings.

Eleven

SIMPLY THE BEST

Australia beckoned the stars in August, a time when most would rather be on the beach or golf course, and Higgins was no exception. But win or lose, the Winfield Masters in Sydney afforded him a rare opportunity to see his sister Isobel and niece Julie, who lived on Queensland's Gold Coast. In fact, Higgy was shunted out 4–0 by Bill Werbeniuk – his third victory over him in four attempts – after Alex had beaten John Spencer in the opening round. He gave Aussie journalists a juicy story for starters by failing to attend the first-day press conference. The other 15 players were there, in front of the TV cameras, but Alex had been too busy the previous night – reacquainting himself with various liquid potions. He was definitely shaken, but could not be stirred from his slumber.

He was back home for Glasgow's Lang's Scottish Masters in September, but after beating Jimmy White 5–3, he fell 6–2 against eventual winner Steve Davis in what was a boring encounter. To be fair, his mind must have been in turmoil because Lynn had packed her bags a month earlier, saying she could take no more. In *Alex Through the Looking-Glass*, Lynn says:

> When he won the world title again he changed, as if to say, 'I'm the champion and I can do what I like', and I never knew where he was. He spent much more time in London with new friends when he wasn't playing and seemed to draw himself away from his family. And I knew he was seeing other women – I could sense it. I was disgusted and afraid of catching something from him.

Bear in mind, this was a Higgins-sanctioned book, so he must have acknowledged Lynn's fears to allow her such a strong voice in it. It was not the best preparation for his new season, but who knows what goes on behind other people's closed doors? As Lynn adds: 'There were other reasons for our split-up, which I'm not prepared to go into.' Later, she also discovered a pattern to her errant husband's behaviour. 'It was inevitable we would separate and it happened in late August 1983. The date is significant now because all our subsequent flashpoints coincided with a new season. It seemed that something snapped inside him as the big tournaments drew near.'

Lynn even took out a court injunction forbidding him from seeing Lauren and baby Jordan, such were her worries about his erratic behaviour even at that time – never mind what has since transpired. It was no surprise, therefore, that with all this going on, he hit rock-bottom, even though he managed to get that judgment rescinded.

Dave Martin, a journeyman pro who would never have presumed to be his better, scored one of the finest wins of his career against Higgins in the Jameson International qualifying round at Stockport. But even as Davis was hammering Thorburn in the final a few weeks later in Newcastle, Alex was making plans to see an old pal, Carol Johnson, who lived in that part of the world with her husband Brian (the short-trousered guitarist in AC/DC, one of Britain's most successful heavy metal bands). It was a perfectly innocent encounter. Alex invited me along. And it was a night to remember, because Carol had a few friends around, the wine and other liquid refreshment flowed freely and I was amazed at how millionaires actually lived.

Carol, a redhead who hit the headlines a few years ago by announcing her love for former Newcastle footballing hero Malcolm Macdonald, was a belter. We had such a good night and I can remember staggering out to the kitchen for a top-up and gazing out of a window on to a swimming pool which was being constructed. Most people see their gardens or a wall while in the kitchen, but here there was this huge, concrete hole literally feet from the window – inside the house!

Alex, as good as gold, wept genuine tears while watching a video Carol had put on about him and his family. To watch himself playing with Lauren at home must have cut him to the quick and everyone in the room was hushed and full of sympathy. 'I just want them back,' he told us sincerely. And while Hennessey, full of wine, decided to stay on and continue partying, Alex called a taxi at around 2 a.m. and headed straight back to our hotel. 'Stay if you want, babes,' he said. 'But I've got a big day tomorrow.'

The next thing I remember is Carol shouting into the spare room, where I had collapsed, and bringing me a black coffee. It was midday, I had missed my planned train and I had left my typewriter and bits and pieces at the venue.

Alex's break-up with Lynn hurt him beyond belief. It was reflected in his desperate 5–2 reversal against promoter-cum-manager-cum-player Mike Watterson in the Professional Players' Tournament at Bristol. And the lowest point of his career was followed by more heartache in the State Express World Team Classic at Reading's Hexagon Theatre. It beggars belief that Higgy lost to bread-and-butter Scots Ian Black and

Eddie Sinclair, though he recovered an ounce of pride by beating the latter in a tie-break to secure a semi-final berth for the Irish. He then lost to Wales's Doug Mountjoy 2–0; and that was the end of Northern Ireland's chances, England winning for the second time in three seasons. 'My mind was shot to pieces,' said Higgins. 'There's no way I could think of anything but how to get the family back together. I was living on tea, lager and fags and my weight dropped a stone in one month. But Lynn really helped and made sure I didn't waste away. To her credit, she did not want to see me vegetate, but at the same time she made it clear the break was final.'

In fact, the couple gave it one more shot with a holiday to Majorca, where the whole thing blew up again and Higgins, in desperation, swallowed a bottle of pills he'd been taking for his nerves. 'Even that didn't shake her, so I swilled down the remains of a champagne bottle, then said I was going to a bar 60 yards away,' recalls Higgins. 'Lynn went into the bedroom and I wrote a suicide note, saying, "Now I've ended it all." With that I stormed out and ordered a bottle of San Miguel. Soon I was getting drowsy. I took another swig of beer and that's the last I remember.'

Lynn says:

> The trouble was that Alex wanted to be a married man but live like a bachelor. I was shocked when he swallowed the tablets but thought he was shamming. Eventually, I got some friends to hunt for him and they found him slumped unconscious against the bar. We rushed him to the nearest hospital and I had to try to make the doctor understand he had taken tranquillisers. It got beyond the stage where they could pump out his stomach, so they put him on a drip. It really was touch and go and he was in a coma for 48 hours. I sat praying by his bedside that he'd pull through and, miraculously, he started to recover. He must have had the constitution of an ox.

She then made arrangements to have her husband flown home to receive attention from his own doctor. The only problem was, Higgy had gone missing. Fed up with the drips and all that accompanies them, he pulled out the lot and escaped. 'I had enough pesetas to buy a plane ticket home without returning to the villa,' he recalls. 'I'd taken the overdose to shock my wife into action and she eventually agreed to consider coming back if I had a complete check-up. She thought there was something seriously wrong because I'd lost so much weight.'

Higgins agreed to book into the local Cheadle Royal hospital for a thorough check-up, but soon walked out. 'I was surrounded by a bunch of headcases and I gave it two days,' he said. 'I never even paid the £400 bill because someone tipped off the papers that I was there.'

You would not have put a penny on Higgins salvaging anything but self-respect in the ensuing 1983 Coral UK Championship at Preston. Such was his mental state that his best bet would have been to turn up, lose in the first round, then head for home out of harm's way. But old Higgy was always the most unpredictable star of all and he had great pal Peter Madden at his side. Madden was the jockey aboard 7–2 winner Sunny Smile (which made me richer by £17.50) and, through Alex, we had become mates. Higgins looked desperately haggard as he began his journey at Preston against Murdo Macleod. No disrespect to Murdo, a jovial Scot, but Alex could hardly have asked for better opposition. Yet when Murdo went 4–0 ahead, all the wise pressroom heads – and mine – prepared for a 'Higgins buried' story.

But the picture changed dramatically as Alex won the next three. He then literally bounced into the Guild Hall arena that evening, with estranged wife Lynn watching, and recorded a 9–6 victory. We had a much better story – after all, everyone likes a bit of romance – and there were hints of a reconciliation, despite a firm 'no comment' from the Hurricane.

His next opponent was Paul Medati, a true sparring partner in every sense of the word. Paul ran the Masters Club at Stockport (and still does), where Higgins practised occasionally. And though Higgy won 9–1 with new-found confidence, Medati would go on to make an indelible mark on his pal in the not-too-distant future. Even so, the general feeling was that Higgins was chasing an impossible UK dream, with or without his beautiful wife. Tony Knowles, his quarter-final opponent who was already making a big impression on the game, went 6–0 down and eventually lost 9–6 as Higgins enjoyed every ounce of luck going. Next came revenge for his 1982 defeat by Griffiths. The Welshman, normally so deadly, had little answer to the precision play of his old rival and fell 9–4.

Higgins had reached the final against all the odds, and waiting to greet him was chief tormentor Steve Davis, who had all but cleaned up on the circuit that season. He looked and played with the air of a man who knew he was unbeatable – untouchable, even – and Higgins knew it as well.

The UK has been devalued in recent years. It used to be played over two days and 31 frames, a genuine championship distance all the great players relished. These days it is confined to 19 frames in one day, thus reducing its credibility as the next best event to the Embassy World Championship. But in 1983 it was still the big one and meant such a lot on a player's record. It started on the Saturday and went on until Sunday night, except when Davis was beating up his opponents and finishing with a session to spare.

And that is the way it appeared to be going when Davis opened a 7–0 afternoon lead on Higgins. In those days I did not have to work on

Saturdays and my daughter's birthday always coincided with the UK event. Beth turned ten that day and, being a dutiful dad, I made the five-hour journey home for a surprise entrance at her fancy-dress party in a beachside pub at Westcliff in Essex. The barman was a pal and shook his head when he saw me. 'That's it for your mate Alex,' he said. 'He's losing 7–0 so you might as well stay on. It's not worth your while going all the way back up to Preston.'

I was mortified because Higgins had grown stronger and stronger throughout the championship and I genuinely felt he had a chance. But I caught the last train back to Preston, arriving at about 1 a.m. with foreboding in my heart. The first person I saw in the hotel bar where we always stayed was Peter Madden, wearing the biggest grin in the world. 'Tell me the worst,' I begged, convinced our mutual friend had one foot on the gallows. 'He's 9–7 down, should be 8–8 and he's racing,' said Peter. 'Sit down, have a drink and I'll tell you all about it.'

Dumbfounded was hardly the word as I listened to Peter's summary. Higgins had won the first three frames that evening, was desperately unlucky to go in-off the green in the next frame, then fought back again to win four of the remaining five to stand just 9–7 in arrears overnight. But this wasn't the carefree Higgins of old. He had matched the immaculate safety play of Steve and had sown huge seeds of doubt in the world champion's mind. Of the two, I know who slept the soundest that night – and the Guild Hall was buzzing with anticipation when they kicked off again on the Sunday. Higgy took the opening frame, which meant Steve had won only one of the last nine. But the Romford man composed himself to maintain a two-frame lead, only for Alex to level at 11–11 going into the final, heart-stopping session.

If the 1980 Higgins–Thorburn world final was breathtaking, this was leaving it way behind in terms of drama and Alex finally got his nose in front at 14–12. Came the interval and he wandered into the pressroom to relax, then roared his head off as John Virgo appeared on telly doing his brilliant impression of the Irishman. Lynn was in the players' room downstairs and Alex phoned and said, 'Quick, Lynn, JV's doing me on TV.'

But after that brief respite, back came Davis to win the next three and Alex's supporters must have had hearts in mouths. It really was nerve-tingling as Higgins clawed his way back to level from 15–14 down after Davis had missed a possible matchwinning black. With one frame to play there was only one winner, and the body language from both players said as much. Higgins, walking taller than at any time in his life, had breaks of 26 and 44 to complete the greatest recovery of all time and pay back Steve for all the pain he had inflicted on him over the past three years. It goes down as one of the all-time classics and I believe Alex will be remembered more for this result than any other. Yes, even better than his two world triumphs.

It was to prove the absolute peak of his career, his defining moment. He had beaten the greatest player of all with a mixture of skill, guts and incredible determination, rivalled only by Dennis Taylor two years later against Davis in the 1985 world final, when he came from 8–0 adrift to win 18–17 on the final black.

But Higgins was brought down to earth swiftly. His immediate reward was to be banned from competing in the forthcoming summer's Australian Winfield Masters (it was later rescinded) following unspecified 'complaints' from the sponsors and organiser Eddie Charlton. Higgins had, allegedly, insulted Michael Cleary, Minister for Sport in New South Wales, who threatened to 'dong' him. Charlton described Alex as 'rude, arrogant, ignorant and a real trouble-maker'.

Charlton also rubbed it in during the Hofmeister World Doubles quarter-finals when he and partner Bill Werbeniuk beat Higgins and Kirk Stevens 5–1. Then came a 5–2 defeat for Alex at Warrington in the Lada Classic first round by John Parrott. The young Liverpudlian was to make a huge impression in the next decade, winning the world title in 1991 and going on to star in TV's light-hearted quiz programme *A Question of Sport*. It was an absolute corker of a match to set before an enthusiastic 2,000 crowd, with support being split down the middle. Parrott went on to beat Knowles 5–1 before bowing out 5–4 in the semi-finals to eventual winner Steve Davis.

Alex also got nowhere in the B&H Masters at Wembley, losing 5–1 to Knowles in the last eight, but the event was memorable because of the 147 made by Stevens against White in the semi-finals. Higgins could not seem to get his act together and he bombed in the Yamaha International Masters at Derby, failing to qualify from his group. But things looked up when he avenged his loss against Charlton by beating him in the Irish B&H, only to fall 6–4 to Davis in a tight semi-final. At least he appeared to be coming into form at the right time, with the world championship approaching. Or so he thought. Another promising youngster, Neal Foulds, saw him off 10–9 in the opening round and that was it for the Higgins season, except that he returned to the Crucible Theatre to cheer on best mate Jimmy White through the semis (where he beat Kirk Stevens 18–16 in a brilliant match).

Higgins then commandeered the pressroom for the final and roared White on with all his might, but to no avail. Davis, who led 12–4 overnight, held off Jimmy's thrilling recovery to scrape home 18–16. I had my first minor face-to-face run-in with Alex after these semi-finals. I was having a quiet drink with Kirk, whom I had befriended a few years earlier at Henry West's Surrey club where he had based himself on his arrival from Canada.

We were discussing his match against Jimmy when Higgins lurched over from the bar and berated me. 'Leave the kid alone,' he said. 'He's on the floor and doesn't want you hanging around him.' I'd actually just finished telling Kirk my heart said Jimmy but I felt the Canadian would have been better equipped to tackle Davis in the final, and he agreed. It wasn't the biggest of rows and Kirk soon calmed Alex down, but it gave me a first taste of how the Hurricane could turn nasty.

Alex's new season began with two quick defeats by Davis, in the Lang's Scottish Masters semi-finals in Glasgow and then in the Jameson International at Newcastle. There he let himself down again by slamming the cue ball off the table to signal his 5–1 beating, then complaining bitterly about how lucky the Romford man had been. His behaviour improved in time for the new Rothmans Grand Prix at Reading; his form didn't follow suit, though, and he suffered yet another reversal, beaten by Mike Hallett in the second round. Even more galling for him was the fact that arch-enemy Dennis Taylor – just three weeks after the death of his mother – went on to claim his first major title after 13 years of trying. It was one of the most popular victories ever, and well deserved.

Alex had hardly set the season alight so far, and there was no reason to suspect he would improve in time for the Coral UK at Preston. But, lo and behold, his big-time form returned and he edged his way into the quarter-finals, where he saw off Thorne 9–5 with an exciting display. Again, however, controversy loomed in the semis against Thorburn. Though he was not the instigator, he certainly had one of the final words.

Higgins was losing 5–6 when the Canadian, after snookering himself behind the reds having potted one, nominated green and hit it – only for referee John Smyth to call a foul because he had not heard him. Until then it had been a shock-free, argument-free zone and Cliff had even allowed Alex to use his cue extension. I heard Cliff's call, clearly, as did many spectators, and that should have been enough. When he appealed to Alex, who always watched every ball played by his opponents, Alex said he hadn't heard because he was concentrating so hard; and so the decision stood.

It was spiteful of Higgins and the referee should have taken Thorburn's word anyway. Cliff stormed out of the Guild Hall arena, fuming for a few minutes, having told Higgins, 'In that case, you can't use the extension.' Higgins merely shrugged his shoulders and proceeded to a 9–7 victory and yet another UK final place . . . against Davis. They seemed fated to match up so often and this time Steve more than avenged the previous year's shock defeat with a comprehensive 16–8 success. Yet the Hurricane, trailing 6–1 and 9–5, charged back to 9–8 before one slip enabled the Nugget to regain full control with seven frames on the spin. His relief was evident. 'It is one of my best wins,' he said. 'It would have been easy to panic when Alex got to 9–8 and say, "Here we go again," but I didn't.'

For Thorburn, not reaching the final was a bitter disappointment. Higgy had put one over him again and he could not hide the pain. 'I was surprised Alex didn't take my word, and disappointed with the ref's decision,' he said. 'We have a code. I've played by it all my life and I had called a foul on myself earlier. I've played long enough to know you give your opponent the benefit of the doubt.'

Higgins got his hands on some fresh silverware at last when he excelled alongside Jimmy White to win the Hofmeister World Doubles – beating defending champions Davis and Meo in the semi-final and scoring an easy 10–2 win over Thorburn and Thorne in the final. 'Alex played out of his head,' said delighted White. But Davis took swift revenge, whipping Higgins 5–2 in the Mercantile Credit Classic at Warrington and getting to within sight of his second televised 147 in the seventh frame with 13 reds and blacks before breaking down. But Davis was squeezed out by Thorne, who went on to win his first and only major crown.

Davis and Higgins then featured in one of the greatest matches in Wembley history weeks later, and you had to spare a thought for the Ulsterman. With more than 2,500 fans in attendance – half that figure is considered a bonus these days – and a big-fight atmosphere abounding, Higgins rose to the occasion. Mark Lazarus, once a Wembley winner for QPR, was chief Davis cheerleader, while Higgins had the usual rabble-rousers in his corner.

It all added up to a phenomenal atmosphere, the like of which I have yet to experience again. And when Higgy triumphed 5–4, he thrust a fist in the air and bellowed, 'We're fucking back!' Such was the noise that it would almost certainly have gone undetected except that Tom Docherty, son of the infamous football manager and a BBC producer in his own right, heard it clearly. He reported it to his boss, who listened and told him: 'Put it out.' Tom was upset and told me so because he liked Higgins and didn't think it fair to drop him in it. But out it went and in dropped the ceiling on Alex again.

On TV the next morning, Higgy said with a smile that he 'hated' Davis but admired him, appreciated how good he was and loved playing him. Steve, with a similar smile, responded later that day, saying virtually the same thing. But the entire episode added up to a ludicrous £1,500 fine for Higgins, which really was unfair. We all say the odd rude word at times and he was on such a high because of the occasion and the fact that he had seen off his biggest rival. Honestly, it made for great telly and capped one of the great, great nights in snooker history. Unfortunately for Higgins, he was beaten 5–1 by Griffiths in the quarter-finals, which was a terrible let-down for his fans. But to be fair to him, he must surely have been put off his stroke by all the controversy.

There was far bigger controversy in the air at the Dulux British Open at Derby, where Higgins fell in the semi-finals against Silvino Francisco, who went on to beat Kirk Stevens in the final after an astonishing behind-the-scenes bust-up between the players during the match. The swarthy-looking South African was convinced Stevens was on drugs and accosted him. He later told a reporter he believed the Canadian was 'as high as a kite – out of his mind on dope' and this was splashed all over the *Daily Star* on the first day of the world championship weeks later. Coincidentally, the WPBSA introduced their own drug-testing at Sheffield and every competitor was tested.

Before then, however, Higgins inspired the new all-Ireland team, featuring Dennis Taylor and Dubliner Eugene Hughes to a thrilling victory over holders England (Davis, Knowles, Meo) in the Guinness World Cup at Bournemouth. Forgotten was the fierce rivalry between the two Ulstermen, and Dennis patted Alex on the knee and told TV viewers: 'What can you say about this little fellow? He's absolutely magic.'

Higgins was bang in the mood and he carried this form into the Irish Masters, which began three days later – only to lose 9–5 against White in the final. There was more disappointment for him when Taylor relieved him of his treasured Irish title, yet he opened his world challenge with a confident 10–4 win over Dean Reynolds before bowing out 13–7 against Griffiths in the next round. 'I'm looking over my shoulder all the time,' he complained, in the wake of the drugs scandal. 'There are pressmen everywhere.' In fact, his early departure did him a favour because rumours abounded that one newspaper was trying to set him up by getting a girl to entice him, presumably so that she could spill whatever beans she could harvest.

Oh yes, Dennis Taylor took all the heat out of the situation with the greatest win of his career when he pipped Davis on the black in that momentous final, watched by 18.5 million viewers.

Weeks after Francisco had been fined a record £6,000 and docked two ranking points for his outburst – later reduced to £2,000 with £1,500 costs and the points restored – Stevens actually admitted to the same newspaper that he was a cocaine addict. The episode hastened the end of their careers.

Even Higgins, unhappy with the drug-testing because 'we all have to deliver into those plastic bottles and it is degrading', admits freely in his book that he dabbled with 'soft' drugs and tried a few lines of cocaine – 'it's a pleasant way to relax and nothing more.' However, he adds, 'I would never resort to drugs to improve my performance. I get my "high" from having a fluctuating audience.' And he rubbishes a *News of the World* story about him having a £1,000-a-week coke habit: 'If I'd still been alive, my nose would have been burnt to a cinder, and it is inconceivable I'd spent that kind of money. In spirit, if nothing more, I'm behind the campaign against drugs. I've seen what has happened to Kirk. I've seen the rotten side of life and drugs are the bottom of the abyss.'

Yet a drugs test request at Preston would eventually see Higgins reach the bottom of the barrel with the most outrageous behaviour of his career.

*

STEVE DAVIS
Multi-titled six-times world champion, a snooker legend, Alex's greatest rival and still causing damage to the top players.

Everyone assumed we hated each other, but there wasn't really any animosity. We were competing against each other and you probably couldn't be too friendly with an opponent like that. It would take a strange person to be very good friends with another top-of-the-cream player, but it was never a problem between us.

There were various occasions when we had a go at each other but looking at it now, they were just fun things. We were incident-free and our only clashes were on the snooker table, yet the press coverage over our differences in style caused people to think we hated each other. I told a story for many years about the time Alex saved my life. I left the stage door at one tournament and these three huge blokes set upon me and started beating me up. Fortunately for me, Alex came around the corner and said, 'That should be enough, lads!'

There was a lot of mutual respect between us and although Alex said on telly once after beating me in the Benson's at Wembley that he hated me but appreciated that I was a good player because of my record, I don't think he really meant the hate bit. Just as I didn't mean it when reporters got hold of me that day and I said, 'Of course I hate Higgins, but I love playing him.' I said it with a smile and it was obvious I was only winding him up.

Alex was a tremendous cueist when he was playing well, and even when I was 7–0 up on him in the 1983 UK final, he was still able to play his game and control any situation. I dominated one session but he dominated the next three. When he was banned from snooker it just about spelled the end for him. I took no satisfaction in saying so at the time, although I'm sure a lot of people he had wronged would have done. But he was a truly great opponent – a genius – and I loved playing him.

BARRY HEARN
Entrepreneur extraordinaire who revolutionised the promotional and managerial sides of snooker and whose partnership with Steve Davis, spanning more than two decades, is still going strong.

I had more fun with Alex than any other snooker player, and that includes Steve. He was a nightmare in more ways than one because you always knew you'd have to lend him money whenever he played for you, and soon as he'd done that lot at the bookies, he'd be back for more. But my golden rule was that the last pot you lent him was just enough to ensure he had his train fare home.

I had him up against the wall at Romford once with my hands wrapped around his neck, because he said he wasn't going to play the evening session, and I've lost count of the arguments I had with him. But they always seemed to get resolved. I couldn't possibly have managed him — although I know he wanted me to — because he was so unpredictable. If he'd been a pain all the time, I could probably have handled him, but you never knew where you were with Alex. You never knew what was going to happen, on and off the table, because of his unpredictability. He was major box office on the table, ensuring there were always bums on seats, because no one ever knew what he would do. But he was unmanageable off the table. Certainly by me, anyway.

I could never have coped with what went on away from the snooker. There would have been a lot of ulcers, a lot of late nights, a tremendous amount of bar bills — and a lot of stories. He is one of the great characters and characters make sport.

He could hardly argue about the one-year ban he served, because he'd been in trouble so many times. He'd got away with so much in the past and you couldn't let him escape with everything. He'd have been doing the Great Train Robbery next. But that just about ruined his career and he had little left in the tank when he returned, except bitterness.

Several years ago I was on the WPBSA board and he was up before us on some crime or another. In he walked with half a dozen bottles of champagne under one arm and his cat under the other. God knows why he had it. He said, 'Can't we just sit down and discuss this problem sensibly over a drink?' So there we were, swigging his champagne and watching the cat pee all over the carpet. He showed some quality by dropping out of my Mitre World Masters at Birmingham after Stephen Hendry (who was world champion) and a dozen or so others threatened to withdraw if he played. He was under the WPBSA ban at the time, but this wasn't one of their events and he was perfectly entitled to play. It was a big-hearted gesture by Alex and I almost liked him for five minutes.

Seriously, like everyone else who ever came into contact with Alex, you can only feel sympathy with him now and just hope he pulls through.

ALAN HUGHES
Regular compère on the snooker circuit and a good friend to all.
Like a lot of people, I always got on well with Alex and I know he used

to love the build-ups I gave him and the other stars before they actually entered the arena. I'm still doing it, of course, but sadly Higgy is no longer playing. For years, though, he never let me forget the time I forgot his name. I'm not sure where the incident happened. It definitely wasn't at Sheffield; probably Derby.

I'd given his opponent, say Jimmy White, the full whack. 'Ladies and gentlemen, please put your hands together and welcome the greatest entertainer there has ever been, the greatest player never to have won the world championship, the man with the cheekiest grin, the housewives' choice . . . ladies and gentlemen, please welcome the Whirlwind from London Town . . . Jimmy White.'

The crowd go wild as Jimmy walks into the arena, shakes hands with the referee and takes his appointed seat.

Now it's Higgy's turn. 'Ladies and gentlemen, please give a great big Derby welcome to the man who revolutionised snooker . . . the man who won the Irish Masters on one leg . . . the man who fought back against Steve Davis from 7–0 down to capture the UK championship . . . the man who has been captivating millions of snooker-watchers for the past two decades . . . ladies and gentlemen, please welcome the unforgettable, unmistakable, never-to-be-forgotten two-times world champion and the man who inspired the Whirlwind so much when he was a kid . . .'

And then I lost it. I could not for the life of me remember who the player was, so I started again. 'Ladies and gentlemen, please give a great big Derby welcome to the man who revolutionised snooker . . . the two-times world champion . . . the man who won the Irish Masters on one leg . . . the man who fought back against Steve Davis from 7–0 down to capture the UK championship . . .'

Suddenly, from the back of me, came a voice: 'You've even forgotten me fucking name, Hughesy.' With that I jerked back to the real world and quickly rattled off: 'The two-times world champion and People's Champion . . . the one and only Alex Higgins.'

He bounced into the arena, muttered something in my ear which I didn't catch, then bowed to all parts of the arena before taking his seat. I felt terrible about it because it was and is the only time I've let myself down. In fact, since then I have always carried little prompt cards around with me. But for ages, Higgy would come up to me and say with a grin: 'You couldn't even remember me fucking name, Hughesy.'

Twelve

SIMPLY THE WORST

Higgins made it back to Australia for the 1985 Winfield Masters, his original ban being overturned, but it proved a wasted trip because he lost 4–1 against John Campbell and probably wished he had stayed at home anyway. It was the prelude to a new season and he was whitewashed 5–0 by White in the Lang's Scottish Masters in Glasgow. Then all hell broke loose when Higgins tossed a TV through a bedroom window during a three-hour eruption at home on the eve of his Goya Matchroom Trophy clash with Dennis Taylor at Stoke. Eventually, the police were called and they carted him off to the local station to cool down for a couple of hours.

Not surprisingly, Lynn left home for the last time, taking the kids with her, and Higgins was walloped 5–1 by Taylor. His season had already fallen apart and several early setbacks heralded the start of a horrifying downward spiral by the man who had thrilled millions over the years. Alex somehow reached the Coral UK fifth round, only to be thrashed 9–5 by White. Then a heavy night's boozing with Jimmy, his best pal and soul-mate – a row over cash tossed in for good measure – did nothing to help their chances of retaining the World Doubles title and they slumped out in the qualifying round. Alex also lost against Davis in the Roger Lee-organised Kit Kat Break for World Champions semi-finals. A warrant for his arrest had been issued that morning for the domestic blow-up and he was, by his own admission, 'easy meat'.

But Alex piled troubles on his shoulders in more ways than one when, in the January, he told a ridiculous lie at the Mercantile Credit Classic after arriving in Warrington with a black eye for his fifth-round match with Dennis Taylor (which he won 5–4). He told a cock-and-bull story about falling off a horse called Dreadnought, owned by a solicitor pal, while out riding early that morning. It was far-fetched to say the least and within hours the truth emerged. He'd had a punch-up with Paul Medati at the Masters Club in Stockport. There was always a bit of niggle between them and when Medati told Higgins he was wasting his time trying to get back with Lynn, the Ulsterman snapped, flew at him and received a black eye for his troubles. In the scrap, Medati's wig came off: there was much mirth in the pressroom when we were told.

It wasn't that big a deal, but Higgy got the full Fleet Street treatment and was beaten, surprisingly, by veteran Rex Williams for a place in the semis. The episode also served to hasten his split with manager Del Simmons – now engrossed in his job as contracts negotiator with the WPBSA – because Alex was becoming an embarrassment to him.

Higgins also threatened to 'blow the lid off the game to the highest bidder', demanding £350,000 for an exclusive interview. There were no takers, and nothing in it anyway. But he compounded his latest problems by demanding his £6,750 winnings from the tournament office, being refused and giving the occupants another typical verbal volley. It added up to a £2,000 fine.

The BCE Belgian Classic, a new tournament in Ostend, gave Higgy some brief respite a few days later. He reached the semi-finals after beating Taylor, only to be edged by Stevens, but he admitted, 'I wasn't mental but I was unbalanced for a while because I just couldn't handle all the pressure.'

Yet he found a rare touch of humour when Alexander Clyde, the *London Evening Standard*'s snooker man, cut his hand so badly while stumbling through a glass door one evening, that he needed prompt attention. 'Alex has hurt his hand,' was the message – and understandably, when two ambulancemen rushed in, they made a beeline for Higgins, who was chatting to White and other friends. 'You're coming with me to hospital,' said one of the burly medics.

'I've done nothing wrong,' protested Higgins. 'I'm innocent.'

When they realised their mistake they tended to Clyde, who then apologised to Alex.

'That's OK, babes,' he said. 'I expect I'll get the blame anyway.'

Clyde recalls: 'When I first met Higgins I introduced myself as Alex Clyde and he said, "There's only room for one Alex in snooker, babes. I'll call you Alistair." And he did, throughout our long association.'

Yet Belgium was but a brief respite and there was added pressure when Higgins returned home to discover lurid newspaper allegations of drug addiction and suicide bids. Perhaps of even more significance, he learned that he would have to face a disciplinary tribunal to determine whether he should be banned for life for his outpourings. 'I was in a trough of despair,' he recalled. 'My wife wouldn't have me back, my private life was being stripped to the bone and my colleagues were ganging up on me.' Yet he received a tremendous reception from a huge Wembley crowd when he faced Griffiths in the opening B&H round. He lost 5–4 but was on his best behaviour, saying: 'I'll keep fighting.'

He demonstrated that attitude in the Dulux British Open at Derby by reaching the semi-finals after an unscheduled working holiday in Dubai, where he cracked a 147 and missed another on the final black. It was just the rest-cure he needed, but Davis spoiled it by beating him 9–3 on his way to winning the Dulux event. But at least we saw glimpses of old Higgy – a charmer with a fund of goodwill and tales for everyone – except that he was unable to book into a Derby hotel anywhere because of his 'previous' form and had to settle for a place 15 miles up the road. He was loved again by players and fans alike, and how he wore it well. So well that he again helped Ireland retain the Guinness World Cup at Bournemouth.

In addition, he had parted amicably from Del Simmons, the one man I always believed was able to keep him roughly on the straight and narrow, and signed for Framework. This was a newish agency, run by pop-related Howard Kruger, whose father used to stage those wonderful rock'n'roll shows of the '60s, when you could see the likes of Duane Eddy, the Everly Brothers, Little Richard and Sam Cooke for peanuts on stage at the local cinema.

Simmons was relieved to an extent because Alex had stretched him to the limit on occasions, but he said, 'The worst thing that happened to Alex was splitting up with Lynn. She's a strong woman, stronger than him, and he needed a proper home base. I am godfather to their children and I know how much he loves and needs them. I can forget all the times I would happily have strangled him because deep down, I'm very fond of Alex.'

Kruger had already signed Knowles, who befriended him while on holiday in Marbella, and White. But though Alex loved being driven around in Kruger's maroon Bentley Corniche, the association would end in abject misery for Knowles and Higgins, who were conned out of fortunes.

For now, however, the little leprechaun was a happy bunny again. Unfortunately it couldn't last. Alex's narrow defeat by Meo in the Irish Benson's was followed by a second-round exit in the world championship, beaten 13–12 again by Griffiths. The appearance of Lynn and six-year-old Lauren raised hopes that they might have been reunited, but it was a false dawn. Lynn had merely taken the opportunity of letting Lauren see her Daddy playing; but at least the couple were relatively friendly.

Alex also played a part in recording Dion's 1960 classic 'The Wanderer', along with new Framework stablemates Knowles, White and Stevens to counter 'Snooker Loopy' by Barry Hearn's five-strong band (led by Steve Davis and helped along greatly by Chas and Dave, who wrote it). But while the Matchroom song roared to No. 5 in the hit parade, Alex and co. flopped. It was good fun, though, and at last it appeared that Higgins had a purpose in life again. But it all went wrong when Taylor beat him to keep a grip on his Irish crown, amid tales of more Alex mayhem at the venue and his hotel.

The worst season of Higgy's life approached and a 9–8 defeat by Thorburn in the Lang's Scottish Masters in Glasgow led to his infamous jibe at the Canadian in a Scottish Sunday paper. Higgins was alleged to have been overheard accusing Thorburn of taking 'little bags of white powder'. Cliff was seething, threatening to sue for libel, while his manager, Robert Winsor, said, 'Higgins was his usual loudmouth self and it is rubbish to suggest Cliff takes drugs.'

Higgins made an early exit from the BCE International at Derby and Rex Williams secured a second surprise win over Higgins in the Rothmans Grand Prix at Reading – but perhaps not that surprising because he had chaired the disciplinary meeting which fined Higgins £2,000 following the Warrington incidents. 'I was on a hiding to nothing,' complained Higgins, but at least he was even-tempered throughout. John Parrott ensured that his mood stayed low with a fine 5–2 win in the Mercantile Credit Classic fourth round at its new Blackpool home.

The walls were closing in on Higgins, in more ways than one.

There was nothing in his demeanour to suggest anything was troubling him unduly when Higgins began his challenge for the retitled Tennent's UK Championship at Preston. He came through a cracking first-round match with 17-year-old Stephen Hendry to win 9–8, then praised the youngster to the hilt: 'He's a better player than I was at his age, but it's a potting game now and the pockets are bigger,' he said. 'He's the best player since the Whirlwind [Jimmy White]. I felt so daunted by him because he was so fearless. I couldn't keep him away.'

Higgins beat Dave Martin 9–6 and followed with a 9–7 success against Mike Hallett. Then followed a fascinating press conference, Alex complaining justifiably that the pockets were cut too generously to aid the less-gifted players. Tony Knowles had made the same point days earlier and was laughed at. But Higgins reinforced his belief, saying: 'The pockets are closing the gap between the best players and the others and the game has been devalued – it has lost its magic. It's all down to the WPBSA and I'm disgusted.' When he went down to the players' room on the floor below, he was obviously wound up, yet he had been rational throughout his chat with us. Then all hell broke loose.

I had no idea what had gone on that night. For the first time since then, Ann Yates, in charge of the pressroom at the time, spilled the beans when I went to see her in Co. Cork where she now lives in retirement. She revealed what really happened the night Higgins butted tournament director Paul Hatherell and prompted an enormous cover-up operation by officials to hide the whole truth.

'Alex was foaming at the mouth – he had lost it completely – and he frightened a lot of people that night,' she recalls:

> I've never told the story before because it was so chilling, so unreal, and I was seriously worried there would be repercussions from his side because he knew a lot of people. But I'm out of snooker now and happy

to be so after all the misery he caused me over the years. I'm sorry about his present predicament, of course – anyone would be – but I just want to unburden myself because it has haunted me for so long.

Everyone believes it was a simple case of Higgins nutting Hatherell because he had been asked to supply a urine sample for a random drugs test. But it went much deeper than that and it was, without doubt, the most difficult, most frightening time of my life.

Alex had been a pain all night after beating Hallett. He'd obviously had a good drink and was spoiling for a fight after being asked to take the test by Hatherell. The next thing was that the doctor appeared looking shaken and said he had been threatened physically in the cubicle. Higgins went back to the players' room, complaining to me that he was always being picked on and that he had already taken a test earlier in the tournament. I tried to explain that the tests were pre-determined long before the tournament had begun, but he would not listen. He bleated that his life was a misery because his wife had left him again, taking their two children with her. Alex then demanded a private meeting with David Harrison, the tournament administrator and MC.

As he went to walk out of the players' room he pretended to stumble and tipped a fresh pint of lager over one of our young helpers in order to create a diversion. Higgins hated authority and always threw up a smokescreen when he was in trouble – on or off the table – especially when his career was on the slide. At this stage I told Hatherell to keep out of the way because Alex loathed him and we knew he would go for him, given the chance.

So Harrison took Higgins, complete with a recharged glass, into the makeshift little tournament office across from the players' room to discuss the situation. I feared the worst and, sure enough, after a few minutes and some heated words, there was an almighty crash as Alex shoved David into a filing cabinet against a partition wall. What he didn't expect was that David would react. He pushed Alex off him angrily, sending him across the room, and the office wall swung outwards with Higgins on it, still clutching his pint of lager. At any other time it would have been hilarious, but Higgy was really steaming – and so was Harrison.

Some time had elapsed by now and Hatherell was getting curious, not knowing what had transpired. He wandered back into the office to see what what going on and when Higgins saw him, he dropped the glass, grabbed Paul by the tie and smashed him with his head by the side of his eye, opening a nasty cut. With the blood pouring out and splattering Paul's shirt, Higgins tightened his grip on the tie and started to choke him. By this time, a Guild Hall security guard had arrived on the scene. He grabbed Alex's little finger and started to bend it back, while David, a powerful bloke, clamped a hand on Alex's wrist and said, 'If you want to play snooker again, I suggest you let go'.

It was a dynamite situation because Harrison was clearly in the mood to break his wrist. There was a stand-off for a moment as Higgins hesitated, then stormed back to the players' room, where John Virgo, John Spencer and Del Simmons attempted to calm him down. At this stage we were trying to keep the lid on things because we knew the press were still upstairs, but Higgins wasn't finished. He punched a hole in the wall, and another three in the door as they tried unsuccessfully to restrain him. He stormed out into the corridor, followed by the three men, and grabbed hold of a pile of dinner plates the caterers had left there. With that, he started skimming them at us like flying saucers and we had to duck all over the place to avoid being hit.

He then started taking swings at everyone in sight. Eventually our own security officer, Frank Baker, wrapped his arms around Alex to stop him causing any further damage and said, 'Just calm down, Alex.' But he was way out of control. There was a huge ball of foam in his mouth and I'd never seen anyone like it in my life. Then Higgins started stubbing his cigarette out on Frank's hand. That was it. Virgo told Harrison to call the police because we had no other option. By this time the press had been alerted that there had been a rumpus, but they had no idea of the full sequence of events and never did get a sniff.

Alex was dragged from the building, face up and heels dragging, by two police officers – one a woman – but not before he gave us a urine sample, which tested negative anyway. The police did not even lock him up and they let him go once he had calmed down. Remarkably, while the WPBSA held an emergency board meeting to consider what action to take later that day, Higgins conducted his own press conference outside his Mottram St Andrew home in the evening, wearing a ludicrous, Biggles-type flying hat with a fur trim and an ankle-length coat. He looked dreadful and his lips were covered in cold sores.

Alex addressed the waiting media, offering his apologies, pleading for lenience and asking, 'Would the British public stand for me not being able to play snooker?' His huge mobile phone then rang and Alex joked, 'The business is fine. Send more money.' Curiously, Higgins was allowed to carry on in the event and won one more match, earning £18,000, before Steve Davis stopped him in the semi-finals.

Higgins was subsequently fined £200 for assault by Preston magistrates and £50 for criminal damage to the door. But worse was to come. Four months later a WPBSA disciplinary tribunal, under the sole charge of Gavin Lightman QC, fined him £12,000 and banned him from five specific tournaments for the Preston incidents and various others – including his 'little bags of white powder' accusation about Thorburn, and insulting behaviour to referees at the Dulux event.

Amazingly, the damaged door, though not in use now, has been preserved for posterity by Preston Guild Hall staff – complete with the three holes. General manager Alan Baker, still in charge, said recently: 'Alex was, without doubt, snooker's greatest crowd-puller here. Though he caused plenty of headaches, he always put bums on seats and we remember him fondly.'

Fortunately for Alex the ban did not start until the new season, which enabled him to play in the world championship. He missed only two ranking events in that period and was allowed to play in the Lang's and two others during the suspension, because they were invitation tournaments.

It was generally felt, and I had to agree, that Alex had had a good result from what had been the darkest night in snooker history. So Higgins survived to fight another day – literally, as later events were to prove. He told Terry Wogan on TV after the verdict: 'I've got a very short fuse. But equally, there's a lot that goes on behind the scenes . . . There are a lot of cliques and much bitchiness and if your face doesn't fit, well, that's the way it is. I feel I've been used and exploited. All I wanted to do was play snooker and nobody played it with greater affection.'

*

PAUL HATHERELL
Former WPBSA tournament director who rode the stormy seas with Higgins.

How the Higgins saga at Preston was kept under wraps for years is a miracle, knowing how sharp the press were, but it was a scary night for everyone concerned. As Ann Yates said, he resented me because I was in authority. Yet it was my job to tell him, after he'd played that night, that he was wanted for a drugs test.

Alex was never the easiest of people to get on with, especially when he wasn't winning, and we all used to dread his presence at a tournament. The crowds obviously loved him, but he was just a pain to us. On the night in question, I informed him of the test, then let him conduct his press conference upstairs. We always left it up to the individual player when exactly he produced his sample, as long as it was witnessed by a doctor.

When he came down, Alex took himself off with a pint of lager and a doctor from the local hospital to a cubicle. I went back to the tournament office and within a few minutes the doctor came rushing back, ashen-faced, and said Alex had broken the pint glass and threatened him with it. Higgins followed and I told him of the consequences if he refused the test. 'Alex,' I said, 'if you don't give a sample you know you'll be dropping yourself in it again.'

By this time he was getting really wound up and Ann could see he was spoiling for a fight. Alex went back to the players' room for another pint and Ann suggested I disappear because I was an easy target for him. When I returned to the tournament office some minutes later, hoping everything had been resolved amicably, Alex and David Harrison were squaring up to each other and it was obvious that there had been some trouble. As soon as he saw me, Higgins dropped his pint glass, grabbed my tie, yanked me towards him and butted me. It all happened in a flash; before I could recover my senses, there was blood everywhere and I could feel him squeezing the tie tight around my neck. I knew I was in big trouble because I daren't respond – that's what he wanted me to do. I didn't exactly turn purple, but I felt extremely uncomfortable until the security officer and David stepped in.

The doctor was still there, still waiting anxiously to get a urine sample from Alex, and he examined my eye and said I'd live. It looked nastier than it was and the cut didn't even require a stitch. I didn't see what happened next, because I was taken away from the immediate area.

But there was an unforgettable follow-up several months later during the WPBSA Awards dinner at London's Grosvenor House Hotel. It was a dazzling affair, a celebration of the previous season's achievements by the players and we were all enjoying ourselves. Dancing followed a sumptuous meal, and my wife, Gillian, and I were out strutting our stuff when Alex appeared with his girlfriend, Siobhan. He'd gone up to his hotel room to change out of his dress suit into casual clothes and, for some reason, had blacked up his face with make-up. They made their way towards us on the dance floor and Alex leaned over and apologised to Gillian for what had gone on at Preston. Before she could even acknowledge his apology, he muttered in my ear, 'And you're a dead man.'

Gillian heard him and was shocked, but I told her to take no notice. He was just getting up to his old tricks again, although I could have done without it on such a happy night.

It would be grossly unfair to say that Alex was a monster all the time because he did have a fine sense of humour when things were going well for him. I'll never know whether he was kidding or not after he won the UK Championship in 1983 because he insisted – with a straight face – that he wanted Alexander Gordon Higgins inscribed on the trophy. I protested that it would go all around the pot and that it just wasn't feasible, but he didn't care. The exchange went on for a few minutes and he kept that straight face. But although he didn't get his own way, I'm sure he was chuckling inside at the thought of getting me going again.

Thirteen

PRIDE OF IRELAND

Alex was hardly in the best of shape, mentally or physically, yet he reached the quarter-finals of the Hofmeister World Doubles at Northampton with Jimmy White. He had been dumped from the Mercantile Credit Classic at its new Blackpool home before Christmas, but he watched the final stages on TV and positively drooled over Hendry, beaten 8–3 in the semis by Davis. 'He's got four years to go to beat my record as the youngest world champion of all and I believe he can do it,' said Higgy. 'He's got flair and the public love him. He's a pure, natural-born talent and he's even a bit reckless like me. The kid's special and he loves to dazzle.'

Nice compliments, and at least Higgy had the B&H to look forward to at Wembley in January – only to receive his biggest head-butt of all. He fought his way through to the final tenaciously, as did Dennis Taylor, and at 8–5 up, manager Howard Kruger had the champagne ready in his dressing-room to celebrate their first triumph together. But the best-laid plans always seem to go wrong. Higgins, leading 50–10 with three reds remaining, had only to push one of them to safety and a third Benson's title was his. He underhit the ball slightly, however; Taylor took advantage and, a long time afterwards, the title was his.

The rest of the season almost passed Higgins by. He lost against fellow-Irishman John McLaughlin in the Dulux, but helped Ireland to a hat-trick of World Team Cup triumphs along with Eugene Hughes and Dennis Taylor. 'We've all had colds and we're going to celebrate by cracking open a bottle of cough medicine,' he quipped. But he was beaten by Griffiths in the Irish Benson's (and fined £500 for being rude and abusive to tournament director Kevin Norton). Then, after being accused of being 'drunk as a skunk' in an exhibition at Newmarket, he fell to Griffiths again in the world championship as the ban loomed.

Alex was in action even before the new season started, reaching the

Winfield Masters semi-finals in Australia, then returning for the new season and losing against White in the Lang's opening round at Glasgow after a row with referee John Williams. Nothing changes. Only two days earlier he had been arrested for causing a midnight fracas outside the Stockport home of his wife's parents, Jim and Betty Avison (just a short distance from where Lynn was living in the detached house he had purchased for her and the kids). Neighbours said he 'ranted and raved' before police arrived and locked him up for six hours before releasing him. Days later, he put his mansion up for sale and eventually moved in with new love Siobhan Kidd. 'She's a psychologist and I know I'm probably a perfect case study for her,' he said. 'She will understand the pressures and stress I undergo.'

Higgins even confessed to being devastated at the fine and ban. 'I didn't practise and, for the first time, stopped going into the snooker halls around Manchester hustling for action, which I'd always done. I really considered giving it all up, but mates like Joe Johnson and Tony Knowles took the time and trouble to have a word in my ear and I knew they genuinely wanted me to get stuck in again.'

Higgins, terrified of water and driving, vowed to conquer both fears during his enforced ban but, somehow, he never got round to completing either ambition. Instead, he fulfilled his Lang's commitment and then, after missing the Fidelity and Rothmans through the ban, headed for Blackpool and a 5–0 win over former English amateur champion Tony Jones in the Mercantile qualifiers. That came after an apparent suicide bid by Miss Kidd after Alex had told her their romance was over.

Alex said he found Siobhan unconscious on the floor of her Manchester flat in Didsbury, called for an ambulance then left without realising she had to have her stomach pumped out. Two days later they were back in each other's arms in Blackpool, Siobhan madly in love, planning marriage and babies galore. 'It was all a misunderstanding,' said Higgins. 'As you can see, we're back together and much in love.'

And so, four days later, to Preston's Guild Hall, scene of Higgy's most devastating crime nearly 12 months earlier. He had already dropped eight places in the provisional world rankings to 17th, because of his enforced absence, and points were becoming precious if he wanted to get back in the top 16. Journeyman pro Steve Duggan, then David Taylor, were sent on their way as Higgy relished the big time again. But horrors – Davis ambushed him 9–2 in the fifth round.

Yet Steve had paid Higgins the highest of compliments beforehand, saying, 'He's one of my few greats. I put him in a special bracket of players. Things like his suspension can lift him to greater things and I get spurred on by playing great players. He is a genius as a shot-maker. He played shots the other players didn't know existed, and at his peak in the '70s there was nobody to match his accuracy and cue power. I have no animosity towards Alex. All I have to do is respect him as a snooker player.'

Higgins, now down to No. 21 in the provisional standings, said, 'It was a big occasion and I failed miserably. But, like Muhammad Ali, I shall return.'

Higgins had a new partner in Dubliner Eugene Hughes for the Foster's World Doubles, because White had teamed up with Matchroom stablemate Thorne, and went one step further than his old mate by reaching the fourth round at Northampton. But Davis whitewashed Higgins 5–0 in the fourth round of the year's opening event, the Mercantile Credit Classic at Blackpool. The Benson's at Wembley gave him slight comfort, although he caused three disruptions against Knowles before falling over the line at 5–4 after trailing 3–1.

Higgins complained twice to the referee and once to tournament director Nick Hill that the Bolton player was standing in his line of fire. Knowles, entirely innocent, was seething at the end and accused his opponent of gamesmanship. 'He always pulls something like that when he's losing,' said Knowles. 'I was going really well at one stage and fancied it.'

But Higgins perished 5–2 against Mike Hallett in the next round anyway, and shock defeats by Joe O'Boye in the Irish Championship quarter-finals and Tony Jones in the British Open set him back further. A first-round defeat with Northern Ireland in the World Team Cup didn't help, either, and although two rare successes against Dennis Taylor and Thorburn in the Irish Benson's lifted him slightly, they were to be his last two wins of the season. Davis saw him off 6–2 in the semi-finals, and then came his most humiliating world championship performance – an early 10–2 defeat by rookie pro Tony Drago, the young Maltese sensation I was once asked to co-manage. It ended Alex's run as a top-16 ever-present.

Even worse, the next day brought a huge, personal attack by Lynn Higgins in the *Daily Star*. Furious with the stories Alex had been spouting to the press about how she charged him £40 for sex, and seething that in his book he had described her as a spendthrift, Lynn reacted after being granted her divorce, saying: 'He will never change. Birds, booze and betting will always ruin his life. They were ruining mine and that's why I decided I had to get out and build a new life and a future for me and my children.'

To compound Alex's misery, Siobhan kicked him out of her flat after he had been accused of wrecking it and then spoiling a new romance she had begun. But within weeks it was all back on again, although the woman living below their Manchester home complained bitterly that they were driving her out because of all the high-voltage rows: 'I've heard a woman shouting, "Don't do it, don't do it", and I've heard Mr Higgins talking to himself and moaning,' she said. 'I've met them both and they are a lovely couple. But I've got to get away because of all the noise.'

In that same summer of 1988, Higgins was accused of battering a plasterer in a fish and chip shop and butting a Manchester nightclub assistant manager in front of various celebrities, breaking his nose. But no charges were pressed. In between these incidents, he was dumped by manager Howard Kruger and made to fly solo with new manager Robin Driscoll, though still embraced by the Framework set-up.

Kruger, who vowed two years earlier when he signed Higgins to 'clean up his act', said: 'I don't want him tarnishing anything we might do with other players. No bones about it, certain sponsors have not been keen to be associated with Alex and I don't want his reputation rubbing off on the other seven members of my team.' Days later, Siobhan told the world that she and Alex were deliriously happy and were planning to wed. 'He's the most gentle, caring person I have ever met,' said Siobhan, now described as an art restorer and psychology student. 'I love him very much and he is not the madman he is made out to be.'

That remained to be seen, as events would reveal.

Back on the table, Higgins launched his new season by slumping to an unfathomable 5–2 defeat against Murdo Macleod in the Fidelity International at Stoke. He then landed in deep water again in a satellite tournament for players outside the top 16, held in Glasgow. Alex reached the final, only to be pipped by Gary Wilkinson on the last black. Ian Doyle, Stephen Hendry's manager and WPBSA board member, accused Alex of making abusive remarks about the venue, the tables and even Glasgow itself. Initially, Higgy also refused to give a sample for drugs testing, then relented – but only in a public toilet, with the press in attendance.

He arrived for his first match sporting a black eye and turned up the following day with a matching one. 'According to Alex, he had an accident in a revolving door – twice,' said Doyle, keeping a straight face. 'He may not think much of Glasgow, but it must have the only revolving door to give someone two black eyes in two days.' Needless to say, Alex was reported by Doyle and tournament director Lawrie Annandale but got away lightly with a severe reprimand and a suspended £1,500 fine. Doyle added, 'He definitely needs medical attention if he is to have a future in snooker. He's still one of the world's best players, but he's not doing himself justice. Unless he gets psychiatric treatment, I fear for his future.'

But after failing to qualify for the Canadian Masters and, thanks to Barry Hearn, Steve Davis and co., Higgins redeemed himself in the most amazing style at the Rothmans Grand Prix in Reading after learning that the Inland Revenue were pursuing an unpaid £100,000 tax bill. Hearn was in dispute with the tobacco company over a renewed sponsorship deal for his Matchroom League and had banned his players from talking with the press at any time, even at official conferences. It was a churlish move by Barry. We were never the enemy and had always backed him 100 per cent on any scheme he launched because he was good for the game.

But the ban proved a blessing in disguise for old Higgy, who sailed into the final on a wave of emotion and cheers from every corner of the Hexagon Theatre and the land. Again, he was beaten by Davis in the final, but while the Nugget refused to attend the sumptuous Rothmans celebration party, Alex stood in for him and received a thunderous ovation. 'It's like the Return of the Pink Panther,' he said. 'Someone up there loves me. By the grace of God, I will be back in the top 16. Apart from Stephen Hendry, none of the younger set is capable of frightening me. Just let everyone know the Hurricane is back – though I may not be at Force Ten yet.'

Higgins, fined a total of £17,200 in his career so far, would surely have had a chuckle or two at the subsequent £12,000 penalty imposed on Davis for refusing to deal with press or sponsors during the Rothmans. 'Perhaps I should have head-butted someone,' said an angry Steve, referring to the Higgins incident a year earlier. But Alex could not maintain his revival and fell at the fourth-round stage of the Tennent's UK in Preston to Knowles.

While the world's top 12 were counting their winnings from Hearn's lucrative Everest World Matchplay Championship, just up the road from me in Brentwood, Higgins was pondering his immediate future: would he be behind bars for Christmas after failing to pay Lynn's £14,000 overdue maintenance for months? The judge told him he faced six weeks in jail if he did not cough up, which stunned Higgins. He was aware of the court hearing, but had been reassured by Framework that all the payments had been made. 'I'm trying to get this sordid thing out of the way,' he said.

Within days he had found £1,000 to appease ex-wife Lynn and the judge, and had done a deal with the taxman. And then, because of insufficient evidence, he also beat a charge of dodging a taxi fare . . . and Christmas hadn't even arrived. With three days to go before the sound of 'Jingle Bells', Higgins was without a rooftop to accommodate Santa's reindeer because Siobhan had thrown him out after another bust-up with the 'most gentle, caring person I've ever met'. She found him drunk on the floor and poured tea over him to wake him up. He was in familiar territory soon afterwards, behind bars at the local nick after smashing up her flat and speaking (said the police) in 'an incoherent voice'. Higgins the charmer was bound over to keep the peace; within 48 hours, as the song goes, he was back in his baby's arms.

But nothing ever added up in Alex's life and almost in the same vodka-soaked breath he was transferred, football-style, for £75,000 to the management company of former Scotland star David Hay in Glasgow. Except that he wasn't, because Hay realised he was taking on more than just a handful and turned his back on the deal. In fact, it was probably the best thing for everyone concerned, because the doors suddenly opened for Doug Perry, the quiet Londoner who admired Alex and had wanted to manage him for years. Doug was always brimful of ideas for Higgy and the chalk-and-cheese partnership worked to an extent. But if poor Doug thought he'd cracked it, he had another think coming.

Mind you, Alex had cracked it in more ways than one after doing nothing in the Mercantile Classic at Blackpool. Following a blazing, three-hour row with Siobhan, he tumbled out of the window of her first-floor flat, which accounted for his smashed ankle and head stitches. She later maintained he was drunk and that she'd locked the front door to stop him going to the pub. Higgins, forgetting they were not on the ground floor, effected his great escape – on to a concrete hard-standing. Downstairs neighbour Mrs Pat Hammond, terrified by the commotion going on above, had called the police and was actually making them a pot of tea when she saw Higgins plunge head-first past her window. One officer said, 'Mr Higgins is not seriously hurt – he landed on his head.' In fact, it was no joking matter because Alex had broken 30 bones in his ankle.

Nevertheless, on crutches, he made his way gallantly yet painfully to Deauville in Northern France for the ICI European Open, an ill-fated venture never to be repeated. Yet it will never be forgotten by those who were there. Eugene Hughes, with his white shirt and black bow-tie, was mistaken for a waiter and Higgy hobbled his way to victory against a bemused Les Dodds in the opening round. John Parrott joked, 'He looks so much like Long John Silver that I keep thinking I should ask him if I can jump on his shoulder.' Then Higgins, facing Thorne in the next round, and unable to walk properly, hopped on his good foot and swung the other one back and forth to gain the momentum necessary to get around the table.

Terry Smith, one of the legendary snooker journalists who is not averse to the odd disaster himself, recalls: 'It was absolutely hilarious because Alex had no brakes. At one stage he swung the bad leg so fast that he almost careered through the partition at the end of the room. The whole tournament was a nightmare, but it was worth being there just to see Higgy in action. I've never laughed so much in all my life – we were all in stitches.'

For all the laughs, though, Alex's courage was applauded, and none more so than when he regained his Irish title from Jack McLaughlin, playing to packed houses at Antrim Forum. Davis called a halt to his run with a 5–0 win in the British Open fourth round at Derby, but was full of admiration for his opponent. And that admiration soared even higher at Goffs, where Higgins pulled off the most incredible success of his career. Before then, however, Higgins was ordered by a court to give Lynn half the proceeds of his house and a share of the profits from his other assets – including a 1,000-acre forest in Scotland and two factory units in Salford. He also had to turn out for Northern Ireland against Canada in the World Cup at Bournemouth and lost his only two frames against Thorburn in a 5–1 defeat.

Given his domestic plight and the injury, Higgins appeared to have no hope of getting anywhere in the Irish Benson & Hedges, let alone become the first Irishman to win the tournament. Yet that is just what he did, with an astonishing 9–8 success over Hendry in the final. Having discarded his crutches at last, Higgins stopped the hopping and was able to limp around the table with slightly more comfort. He beat Thorburn 5–4, Neal Foulds 5–2, then Parrott 6–4 to reach the final. But his chances did not look too bright when Hendry, snooker's hottest prospect, opened a 4–0 lead. They shared the next two; Higgins then won five in a row, four after the break, to lead 6–5. Hendry got back on a roll to be 8–6 up with three to play, only to discover, as many had before him, just what a great battler he was up against.

Higgins, roared on by the huge Goffs crowd, drew level, then conjured a 62 to clinch the final victory of his volatile career – although he wasn't to know it at the time. A dazed Hendry said, 'I can't believe how well he's played. A lot of people have bad things to say about Alex, but he's still a great ambassador for the game. When he's playing well, he is great for snooker because he brings in the crowds.'

Higgins, off the booze for ten weeks and drinking non-alcoholic cider, was absolutely elated. 'There are a few good kids out there and this one's the best of all,' he said. 'We'll be seeing a lot more of Stephen, but I want to make a few more people frightened. They won't think Alex Higgins is an easy touch any more. But I'd willingly change places with him because he's got his whole career ahead of him and I'm 40 now. I was the first Irishman to win the English Masters and now I'm the first Irishman to win the Irish Masters, and that makes me feel so proud.'

It was sheer bad luck that Alex was required to be in Preston for the final qualifying round of the world championship against Darren Morgan at 2 p.m. the next day and, having reached his bed at 4 a.m., missed his early flight to Manchester from Dublin. The former world amateur champion, highly-fancied to go places, was hardly the quality of opponent Higgins needed – especially as Alex was utterly drained by the previous night's exertions. Yet he held Morgan to 7–7 before the youngster hammered a 143 clearance, the highest ever made in qualifying then. Back came Higgins to level, only for Morgan to take the next two for a superb success.

Whether he would have fared so well had Higgins not been so shattered is open to debate, but it meant that for the first time since winning the 1972 title, Alex would not be appearing in the latter stages of the championship.

Even worse, a Hurricane was about to blow right through the snooker world.

*

JOHN CARROLL
Operations director of Ian Doyle's Cuemasters stable and agony aunt to world champions including Stephen Hendry, Mark Williams and Ken Doherty.

Alex and I have always got on. I know he has upset a lot of people in his time, including my boss, but he has always shown me the greatest respect and I used to love his story-telling. There must be a million tales about Higgy and I've obviously got a few of my own . . . This is my favourite.

When he played Darren Morgan, in the final qualifying round of the world championship, Alex must have been knackered. Darren set off in great form and Alex was having a tough time just hanging in. But fair play, Alex kept with him all afternoon and early evening until, at 7–7, the balls opened perfectly for Darren and he launched into what had all the makings of a total clearance. He'd made about 80 and until that point Alex had sat quietly, leaning this way and that way as he does, totally absorbed in the play and just watching what was happening. All of a sudden he said, 'Excuse me, Mr Morgan, but could you stop playing for a moment, please?' Darren looked at him in amazement and said, 'Alex, this is the world championship and I'm in the middle of a big break. I can't just stop like that.'

Higgins ignored him and said to a bewildered referee, 'Excuse me, Mr Referee, but could you ensure that I have a big mug of tea in my dressing-room at the interval, please?' He then turned back to Darren and said, 'You can carry on now, babes.' I cracked up, as did everyone else watching. Poor Darren shook his head but went on to make a 143, which was a record.

And at Huddersfield once, Higgy and Stephen Hendry were doing an exhibition during the last stages of the Open golf championship. They are both golf nuts and at the interval they sat, side by side, eyes glued to the telly as the players strode up the 17th fairway. About 20 minutes later, someone banged on their dressing-room door to say they were due out again. But they wouldn't budge. They were determined to see out the match at any expense.

There was a lot of twitching going on in the audience, but Alex and

Stephen finally emerged with big grins, explained what they'd been doing and carried on with the show – and no one really minded. It has been said many times that Stephen was terrified of Higgy when he was a kid, but don't you believe it. Even at 16 he could take care of himself and he always found Alex extremely amusing. I have always felt the same way about him and even though Ian Doyle was steaming over that 'shake hands with the devil' story, Stephen just laughed it off. I'll tell you how upset he was – he went out and slaughtered Alex in that UK Championship session at Preston. That's how shaken and stirred he was.

Another time, in Belgium, Alex had been knocked out of the European Open and was heading home. We had said our goodbyes and I went off to bed. In the morning I found an envelope which had been pushed under the door of my hotel room with a Euro lottery ticket and a note from Higgy, saying, 'I've bought this especially for you and I hope you win a fortune.' I'll never know why he did it, but I still smile at the memory. Most people don't understand him, yet I know he has a lot of decent points about him.

JOE JOHNSON
1986 world champion and still soldiering on despite several heart attacks.

We were playing in the Hong Kong Open and the sponsors invited us out for a boat trip on the South China Sea on a day off. Willie Thorne, Tony Knowles, Alex and all the regular gang were on board. Bear in mind, this was not some little pleasure boat but a large cabin cruiser. They took us about one mile out to sea, then dropped anchor. It was a beautiful day, not a cloud in the sky, and we were all invited to jump overboard for a swim.

Knowlesy and Willie and most of the lads were in like a shot, but Alex couldn't swim – he was terrified of water – and I didn't fancy it one little bit because I was convinced we were in shark-infested waters. Alex was great, shouting all the lads on as they splashed around and desperately wanting to join them. My then manager, Wally Springett, said, 'Joe, I'll give you five grand if you jump in.' But I wasn't having any of it and said, 'Wally, I wouldn't do it for a million.'

Alex was jealous of the guys and he asked one of the crew if he could possibly lower a lifeboat with him in it, so he could join in the fun. The fellow came back a couple of minutes later with this kiddy's rubber dinghy shaped like a swan. He tied a piece of rope around it and dropped it overboard while Alex clambered down the ladder to the water. He climbed into it gingerly, his little lily-white legs dangling like those of a frog over either side. There was about 20 feet of slack rope and Alex paddled like mad to get to everyone.

Considering his great fear he was brilliant, even though he was hanging on to the neck of the swan like a drowning man. All of a sudden, despite the sea being as calm as a millpond, there was some kind of surge, maybe just caused by his excitement or the waves made by Willie and co. The little swan tipped slightly over and spun a bit, wrapping the rope around Higgy's neck. He was absolutely horrified and thought he was about to breathe his last. 'Help, help, I'm drowning,' he shouted.

Wally said, 'For God's sake, Joe, you've got to jump in and save him.' But I had visions of sharks gobbling up the pair of us and was too frightened. So I did the next best thing. I grabbed the rope and started hauling him in. As I tugged away, so the rope got even tighter and Alex's face began turning purple. Finally, I managed to get him to the side of the boat and helped him scramble on board. He had a huge rope burn around his neck as though he'd been hanged, and I thought all hell would break loose. But he put his arms around me and croaked, 'You've saved my life, babes. I'll be in your debt forever.'

And bless him, we have always stayed friends. I know he has upset a lot of people over the years, but he has never, ever bad-mouthed me and I still have a chuckle when I think of that day.

Fourteen

THE ABSOLUTE PITS

Nothing could have prepared snooker for what was to transpire in the next 12 months as Higgins lost the plot – every which way *and* loose! In fairness, he had sought and won a petition to get Framework Management Ltd wound up in the High Court with debts of £460,000 because the company owed him over £50,000 in earnings. It was to be an ongoing saga, during which Kruger was described by Judge David Jackson as 'incompetent, reckless or worse'. Son of a millionaire and seemingly worth a good few quid himself, Kruger emerged successful in a sense because he pleaded 'nervous anxiety' and eventually got away with it, although he was subsequently disqualified from holding any company directorship for five years.

Yes, the same Howard Kruger who had been appointed to the WPBSA board of directors and who had been given the Services to Snooker Award. And Higgins, his fragile temperament almost at breaking point because he had the taxman and Lynn on his back, could not fathom out how this flash, brash, Bentley-owning kid who lived in a huge house in Hove was allowed to cheat him (and Tony Knowles for a lot more).

Within days of the 1989 world final, Higgins was accused of sabotaging the prestigious Monaco Grand Prix in Monte Carlo by arriving late for the introduction and his match; refusing to wear a dress suit or bow-tie; rowing with opponents Mike Hallett and Knowles; and refusing also to attend the prizegiving ceremony. He was being his cantankerous self, dressed in open-neck shirt, red waistcoat and faded blue jeans. And swearing backstage. Organisers Snooker Europe were said to have been horrified, because they were trying to sell the game to Italian TV, and banned him from their future ventures. Or at least, they said they had. 'He'll never play in one of our tournaments again,' said Denis Thompson-Panther, boss of Snooker Europe Ltd. But he did do, several months later in France.

Higgy was off and running again and summer reports came from the Far East that he was on the rampage during the Hong Kong Open. Siobhan accompanied him and the complaints about his behaviour started during the flight. He fluked his first match against Tony Meo, but was then docked a frame by Paul Hatherell (he of head-butt fame) for arriving late for his match against Dene O'Kane, which he lost 5–2. Higgins argued that this was victimisation. 'I've been singled out and treated harshly,' he said. 'If it had been any other player, a blind eye would have been turned.' With that, he went into his usual red-mist mode. Siobhan was said to have been locked out of their hotel room dressed only in underwear after a bust-up, and to have run, screaming, down the corridor.

'They were having a fight and it became a public disturbance,' said a member of the hotel staff. 'He appeared drunk and left the hotel without paying his hotel bill, which amounted to about £1,000. It was settled by the WPBSA.'

Higgins then made his way to Bangkok for the Asian Open, where he lost his opening round to Stephen Hendry. Next was a return trip to Hong Kong for the Hong Kong Cup with Jimmy White and Steve Davis. Siobhan had returned home, for whatever reason – and the fireworks crackled again when Higgy, apparently drunk, turned up two hours late for an interview with top TV hostess Sue Brooks. 'He was supposed to play a few trick shots with White but he didn't even have his cue,' she said. 'Jimmy refused to let him use his, so he walked out. He eventually returned and we managed to get a few words out of him. He also tried it on with me but I knocked him back. He's a pathetic has-been.' Higgins went on to lose against Davis in the final.

Back home, loyal Siobhan said, 'Everything was just fine when I was with him and there are a dozen red roses in my living-room to say there's nothing wrong between us. We are getting wed as quickly as possible and it will be a quiet affair.' Less than a month later, the romance was off. She had kicked Higgins into touch for the final time after alleging Alex had beaten her with a hair dryer.

In Stoke for the season's curtain-raiser, the BCE International, Higgins crashed 5–1 against promising Mark Johnston-Allen in the opening round, then refused to attend the compulsory press conference. He was put on a charge by Ann Yates, the regular press officer, who had tolerated him for the most part. It was Johnston-Allen's best win to date, but he called Higgins a 'great crowd-puller . . . still capable of some magical touches with his cue', and believed he was far from washed up: 'I'd love to see him back to his old best because there's no one quite like him in terms of crowd appeal and general magnetism. He's a total one-off.'

But the Higgins fuse was burning low, and he erupted at Reading after losing against the amiable Joe Johnson in the fourth round. He turned on the Bradford man unfairly, accusing him of chalking his cue and moving while he was down on a shot. He then cornered *Daily Star* reporter Dave Armitage and launched into a four-letter tirade against him and the paper. Armitage told him, 'You are out of order and don't be so bloody rude.'

Higgins went even wilder, shouting, 'Just fuck off, you gutter-press scum.'

Armitage – all 6ft 5in. of him and containing his own anger well – waved a stern finger and replied, 'Don't be so rude, Alex,' and walked away.

Three hours later, at 3 a.m., chaos reigned when Higgins came upon Armitage, Steve Acteson from *Today* newspaper and *The Sun*'s Alasdair Ross (who had acted as his press officer and minder while Alex was with Framework). They were having a quiet drink with Mrs Yates, her niece Julie and boyfriend, and tournament director Nigel Oldfield. Higgins, sitting several feet away at another table with manager Doug Perry, was in a foul mood.

He shouted to Ann: 'And who's this, then? Another freeloader I suppose. Is the WPBSA paying for her room? When she told him Julie's boyfriend was picking up the tab, he then attacked Acteson, attempting to drag him off his stool. Ross also got a volley and the threat of a heavy glass ashtray. Alasdair, a bear of a man, is not the sort you'd pick a fight with and when he said, 'Alex, you've got one chance and one chance only,' Higgins saw sense. Yet it served only to fan the flames even more and he stormed off with a parting shot, saying of the two officials, 'You're the locusts of the earth.' Another quiet night at the office, then!

I wrote in the *Daily Express* the following day:

> The erosion of the talent which has kept Alex Higgins in the limelight for nearly two decades has led to his downfall on and off the table. His 3 a.m. explosion against the very people who have attempted to protect him from himself was just about the last straw for those who have sung his praises throughout his turbulent career.
>
> The once-mercurial Irishman, like an old fighter who knows the ropes but can't get off them, simply cannot come to terms with the fact that his game is no longer sound enough at the highest level. He is still a great player, make no mistake. But the lack of confidence, demonstrated so aptly during his defeat against Joe Johnson, means every frame these days is a struggle for the self-styled People's Champion.
>
> His verbal attacks on two officials and three snooker journalists – not the dirt-diggers he has come to despise over many stormy years – cost him the last ounce of sympathy in snooker's close-knit village.

And, to add to his problems, yesterday fiancée Siobhan Kidd insisted her relationship with the wayward star was over. The 26-year-old blonde had walked out of the couple's country home three weeks earlier.

Higgins befriended me ten years ago when I first came on the circuit. All he's ever asked of me is that I give him the right to defend or answer any criticism. That understanding had always worked well in the past. Yesterday, there was silence. We even discussed one problem over a breakfast which consisted of a large Bailey's poured over huge chunks of ice at 10 a.m. in the London Tara, an Irish hotel.

Ian Doyle, Stephen Hendry's manager and one of the most influential voices in the game, said, 'He's on the wane and cannot accept it. It is a tragedy that such a genius should be wasted, but for his sake and that of the game, I believe Alex should be banned for at least three tournaments, even a year.'

In fact, he was later fined £3,000 and publicly reprimanded for non-attendance at the BCE International press conference and for his disgusting behaviour at the Rothmans. Days later, with little time for things to have cooled down, the circus arrived in Dubai for the first Duty Free Classic – a major breakthrough in the Middle East following Barry Hearn's successful excursions there with his squad. It is a beautiful place, a real eye-opener for those who believe the Middle East comprises only sand, Arabs and camels. The International Hotel was the height of luxury – like a palace – and the press were suitably impressed by posh rooms, posh restaurants, and a swimming pool with a bar situated in the middle of it. There was also a good old-fashioned pub in the grounds and a late-night disco-bar inside the hotel.

The latest round of trouble began on the second night when Higgins became embroiled in a furious row with Cliff Thorburn's manager, was tossed into the pool by him, held by his hair and ducked. Higgins, though terrified of water, would not say sorry and was ducked again. This happened several times before 27-year-old pro Jim Chambers intervened.

But it failed to dampen the Higgins fire, even though he was in dire trouble from his Reading fracas. The following night he espied big Dave Armitage on the stairs leading down to the disco-bar and started an almighty row. Dave said, 'Leave it out, Alex. I've come here to relax and unwind.' Higgins kept ranting, then jabbed a finger in his cheek. With that, Armitage, a genial, gentle giant, snapped and walloped him. Chambers, who just happened to be there, jumped in quickly to prevent a punch-up and dragged Dave off.

'I lifted Alex off the floor and put him in a chair,' said Jim, but the damage had already been done – not only to Alex, but to Chambers himself, because in the throes of his rescue act, he slipped and fell, tearing his ankle ligaments. He was whipped off to hospital immediately and returned in a wheelchair, still in agony with his ankle in plaster. But Higgins had got what he wanted and now, so to speak, the boot was on the other foot. Armitage was in deep trouble for assault, never mind the provocation, and he knew it. There was even a threat of him being imprisoned, so the following morning, tournament director Hatherell and board member John Spencer attempted to smooth things over without repercussions. Several trips between the two men's hotel rooms were made by the peacemakers before Terry Smith was asked by Alex to act as a witness.

Smithy, one of the few snooker journalists Higgins trusted because he always acted fairly and wrote accordingly, said: 'I went to see Alex and there was an Arab in full robes sitting in the corner of the room. I didn't take much notice, but I said to Alex, "Look, if this thing rumbles on, you and Dave could end up in prison." Alex went on and on and this bloke, Mustapha, just sat there saying nothing. Eventually after a lot of pleading on my part, I asked, "Who is this gentleman, Alex?" He replied, "He happens to be the chief of police, babes, and he just happens to be one of my big pals."

'I nearly fell off the chair and, looking back, I suppose it must have been a great points-scoring exercise by him. Anyway, Alex agreed not to take action against Dave on condition he was allowed to hold a press conference in the hotel's main bar. For once, he wasn't in trouble and he positively wallowed in it, saying how the press had mistreated him for years and how he'd always done his best to be co-operative.'

As usual, the buzz that Alex derived from the incident stood him in good stead and he went on to reach the quarter-finals later that day – albeit from an in-off by Malta's Joe Grech in the ninth and final frame – to regain his top–16 place on the provisional rankings. But Doug Mountjoy ended his participation and there were sighs of relief all round when the rest of the tournament passed by peacefully.

Back in England, Higgins learned that Kruger, who had resigned from the WPBSA board shortly before a disciplinary hearing in front of Gavin Lightman QC, was found to have brought snooker into disrepute on two counts. Firstly, he had allowed Framework Management Ltd to go into liquidation, owing Alex an admitted £21,000 (Higgins argued strenuously it was more like £50,000). Secondly, he had tricked Alex into playing in the Kent Cup in Peking by saying the first prize was £35,000, when he knew all along that the players, John Parrott and Tony Knowles included, were simply on low guarantees.

It pained Alex enormously that he was one step away from bankruptcy and in arrears with maintenance payments to Lynn through Kruger's mismanagement and nothing else. And although it was difficult to have any sympathy with him over the previous few months because of his outrageous behaviour, it was possible to understand just why he had tipped himself almost over the edge. Even the WPBSA told him it was a private matter between two individuals when Alex first attempted to level disrepute charges against Kruger.

His mind must have been in absolute turmoil during those traumatic months and it was little wonder that he was beaten 9–3 by Willie Thorne in the Stormseal UK Open fourth round at Preston. Yet he avenged his defeat by Johnston-Allen with a 5–0 whitewash in the Mercantile Classic at Warrington in the new year and played his best snooker in a long while – only to lose 5–4 to Parrott in the fourth round. He also went out of the Benson's at Wembley where, having been invited as a wild card, he was forced to play on a Sunday morning. Needless to say, this did not suit him. He went down 5–2 against Steve James, then complained about the playing conditions, saying: 'I couldn't trust the table. It was a disgrace.' James loved the conditions, by the way.

Yet Alex, surrounded by 'good luck' cards and trinkets, was in fine form for the Pearl Assurance British Open at Derby. There he progressed to the semi-finals, thanks in no small part to the phenomenal support he received from fans – and Antrim, a little soft-toy leprechaun donated by one avid supporter. He appeared to be drinking milk because, he had been told, it had more protein than steak. And when he was offered a bottle of Pils lager, Higgy, straight-faced, said, 'I'm sorry but the WPBSA do not allow us to take pills.'

Not even a row at a local casino which had opened its doors to players and press alike – where he was banned from entering following a disturbance the previous year – could halt his progress or change his good mood. When he learned that one 6ft 5in. investigative reporter (who shall remain nameless) was looking into a story about the row, he summoned Northern Ireland journalist Kevin Hughes – one of the few he still trusted – and me, in order to give us a run-down on what had happened.

We spent a pleasant hour or so sipping beer in a pub courtyard as Alex outlined why people were always picking on him in the hope of getting some publicity. Yes, he agreed, there may have been a problem the previous year, but he'd done nothing this time to upset anyone. 'Why would I?' he argued. 'I've just beaten Martin Clark to reach the semis and I've got a good feeling about this one.'

Sure enough, Higgins beat Steve James 9–3 to reach the final against Bob 'Frenchie' Chaperon, the French-Canadian who had upset the odds to get that far. Bookmakers stood to lose a fortune on Alex winning his first event in Britain for seven years, but he never really got into gear. You just knew he wasn't in the mood when, after Chaperon went 4–1 ahead, Higgins complained about him, then referee Alan Chamberlain, moving while he was on shots.

The Hurricane regrouped and actually won the next four frames, but despite his sound tactical play the old spark was missing and Chaperon held on for a 10–8 win. Yet Higgins picked up £45,000 as runner-up and this was to prove the highest prize of his career. He accepted defeat with grace, saying, 'I didn't really shine and I can understand Bob's joy. He's got £75,000 in the bank, security and ranking points.' So, too, did Alex: if not security, then enough points to ensure his place in the prized top 16 for the 1990–91 season.

Tragically, for all concerned, events soon to unfold would make it impossible for him to take up that appointed position.

My next encounter with Alex came at Lyon airport in France and was so funny. He had been knocked out of the European Open at the first time of asking by Steve James and was seated, draped over his suitcase on an airport trolley, and sipping a glass of lager. I'd bumped into Dave 'Mantis' Armitage at Heathrow on my way out and we travelled over together.

I was rather hampered because I had been commissioned to rewrite a book on film star Jack Nicholson. In the absence of a laptop in those days, I had lugged over my old Amstrad computer and keyboard, plus a big box full of American cuttings on the great man. I'd been given just two weeks to turn around 70,000 words and Lyon gave me an ideal opportunity to watch a bit of snooker and crack on with it. But I never did get to see the city which, Terry Smith assured me, was beautiful.

There we were, big 'Mantis' (whom Alex despised because of all the recent goings-on) and me. Dave wandered off to the toilet when he spotted Higgins, who was Mr Charm himself to me. 'Nice to see you, babes,' he drawled, not having seen Armitage. When Dave returned, his heart must have sunk.

'Armitage, you're a scumbag and I'm taking you and your trashy paper to the High Court,' he ranted. 'You're a disgrace to your profession and your paper's a disgrace as well. I'm not going to let you get away with it.'

The diatribe must have gone on for at least five minutes, but Dave gave as good as he got: 'You do what you like, Alex, but you've been knocked out of the tournament and I'm just coming into it.' I had to fight hard to suppress a chuckle, but it got Alex going again and, pausing only once for breath when he'd finished, he said to me, 'Mr Hennessey, be sure and have a nice day.' Dave and I could barely walk out of the airport for laughter. It really was straight out of a Monty Python sketch.

Unknown to us, Higgins had been moaning like mad about referee Len Ganley, and just about everything else, after his defeat against Steve James. It was, apparently, a tiresome rant and Ganley eventually snapped, warning Higgy for ungentlemanly conduct. But that was merely a shot across the bows for what was to come. And this would be without doubt Alex's most shameful night of all.

Northern Ireland, captained by Dennis Taylor, had reached the final of the World Team Cup at Bournemouth, against Cliff Thorburn's Canada. Higgins, during a furious exchange, threatened to have Dennis shot the next time he was back in Ulster. Higgins, as hyperactive and as eccentric as usual, insisted on holding a team meeting in the women's toilets before the final 'because we might be overheard in the men's'. What third team member Tommy Murphy must have made of it beggars belief. But Taylor, the most easy-going of men, was content to let 'glory-hunter' Alex rule the roost for the sake of peace.

Trouble came early on when Higgins, having drawn 1–1 with Alain Robidoux, insisted on carrying on against the same player when Taylor should have been the opponent. Higgins lost both frames, leaving the Irish 6–2 down at the interval, and a furious row ensued backstage. Taylor was in line for the £6,000 high-break prize with a 71 scored against the Republic of Ireland's Paddy Browne in the semis. He said he intended to keep the prize money himself because Alex had made it clear years earlier when they first played together that 'there's no way we share it'.

The Irish ultimately lost 9–5 to the Canadians. At his press conference Higgins lashed into Taylor, saying, 'In my estimation, Dennis Taylor is not a snooker person. He is a money person. The more he gets, the more he wants. He will never be sated. He puts money before country. He belongs back in Coalisland. He is not fit to wear this badge, the red hand of Ulster.'

It was a shocking outburst against a man who had stepped aside graciously to enable Higgins to command centre stage and Taylor, who was not prepared to go on record at all until he heard what Alex said, reacted furiously. First, he criticised Higgins for his remarks after the semi-final when, in front of others, he told Tommy Murphy he 'played like a cunt'. That, said Taylor, visibly shaking, 'was a good way to get him into shape for the final'.

Taylor then dropped the bombshell that Higgins had threatened him verbally, saying: 'I come from the Shankill and you come from Coalisland. The next time you're in Northern Ireland I'll have you shot.'

Higgins also left Taylor in tatters with the ugliest, most detestable insult ever concerning his late, much-loved mother, Annie. To my knowledge Dennis has never repeated what Alex said and, having heard the words from an onlooker, I don't blame him.

Dennis was so hard hit by his mother's death in 1984 that a year later, when we met one time in the bar at our Stoke hotel during the International at Trentham Gardens, he was absolutely blitzed on brandy. I'd never seen him in that state and I asked him what on earth he was playing at.

'It's my mother's anniversary and I still can't bring myself to talk about it, not even with my Dad,' he said. I had lost my own beloved father a few weeks earlier and was in pieces myself. I was able to sympathise with Dennis because, like his Mum, my Dad had gone right out of the blue and it had cut me to the quick.

'I can now say "sorry" and understand the full meaning of the word because I know exactly what you are going through,' I said, then shared a few glasses of brandy with him.

So, even six years on, when Higgins launched his bile attack, it struck a raw nerve. Dennis, full of emotion, said, 'I've known Alex since 1968. When he came over from Belfast to Blackburn I found a flat for him, had a TV installed and did my best to help him. I was literally shaking when I went out to play tonight. I wanted to win this for Tommy, but everything was shaking. At the height of the troubles in Northern Ireland, I took all the top players over. Two days after I won the world title, I had the best reception of my life in the Shankill Leisure Centre. I've never got involved in the politics.'

Higgins issued a denial, saying, 'I never mentioned the Shankill. What I said was that I'd blow his brains out if I had a gun.' But Taylor countered, 'I only wish I'd had a tape recorder with me.'

Clive Everton, editor of *Snooker Scene*, wrote a moving piece on the episode:

> One of the most distasteful aspects of the whole affair was the unpleasant whiff of religious bigotry which Higgins injected into the situation. Sport has been one of the few elements which has tended to bind the Northern Ireland community together rather than intensify its divisions. Something in the Higgins demeanour for the previous two or three days seemed to suggest that something nasty was brewing.
>
> At the press conference after the semi-final, Higgins mumbled, 'If I'm not captain tomorrow, I'm not playing' – the kind of classic child's threat, uttered so often during his career that it now tends to be ignored by grown-ups. After the Saturday press conference, he tried to persuade the sponsors to provide him with a car to take him to Annabel's, the London nightclub. Meanwhile the Canadian team, robbed of their rightful place in the limelight, stayed with Taylor in the practice room when, after the press conference, he broke down in tears.
>
> Small children can do the most outrageous things and be forgiven when they say they are sorry. It is not quite so simple for adults because they are expected to have more self-control in the first place.

Then not even personally, but through his manager, Doug Perry, came the Higgins apology 'for remarks made to Dennis, said in the heat of the moment':

> I now publicly retract. I very much regret my outburst. In this
> tournament, I was not playing for Alex Higgins or for financial gain.
> My heart was in doing my very best for my country. My final apology
> is to the people of all the 32 counties of Ireland for any hurt or
> embarrassment caused to them.

Taylor was unimpressed. 'I've read his apology,' he responded, 'but I'll still be sending in a complaint. Some of the things he said in the WPBSA room were unprintable.' For some, Higgins will always be a loveable scallywag; but others will share Taylor's view that 'the majority side with him because they don't know the sort of person he is'.

If the head-butt affair was the most damaging episode in snooker history, this was the most shocking by far – forget all the drug-taking scandals – and it left the sport, alongside Higgins, well and truly in the gutter. He was definitely flirting with the edge of insanity. And when, arriving to deliver presents to his kids, he was refused entry into the home by ex-wife Lynn, he tossed a skateboard for Jordan through the window. This earned him a £50 fine from magistrates.

Despite having spread such chaos all around, the Hurricane was able to keep his wits about him just days after the Bournemouth débâcle to keep young Thai hot-shot James Wattana in check at Preston with a 10–6 win in the final qualifying round for the world championship. 'All in all, you're looking at a very happy man,' he said. 'I missed Sheffield last year and I am overjoyed I'll be back there this time.' It was to prove his burial ground. But not quite yet.

If you had scripted it, no one would have believed it, but Taylor won his first-round match against Thorburn to set up a quarter-final spot against Higgins in the Irish Benson's at Goffs in Kildare. It had all the makings of an almighty explosion. It is difficult to speculate whether Dennis would have swapped his world title for this chance – I suspect not, for obvious reasons – but he wanted Higgins with all his heart. Had I been a bookie, I would not have accepted a punt on a Taylor win. Steve Davis described it as 'the grudge match of all time' – and he's known a few, particularly against Alex and Cliff. He couldn't wait for the action to start and neither could the rest of the snooker world. Astonishingly, Higgins had dismissed his dreadful Bournemouth behaviour as trivial, saying on TV, 'I'm not really bothered about what happened last week.'

The horse show-ring at Goffs is by far the most intimidating snooker arena in the world. Not even the Crucible, scary as it is, has the amphitheatre qualities of Goffs, with a huge crowd downstairs in the main ring (Sheffield has only three sides in the round for spectators) and hundreds more bearing down on all three tiers. The noise is deafening because the Irish genuinely love their snooker and their heroes even more. There was tremendous support from neutrals for Dennis for obvious reasons, but Higgins had his fair share and it was under these bear-pit conditions that they squared up to one another. Dennis shook Alex's hand at the start out of courtesy, but it was a cursory gesture and he refused to look him in the eye.

They shared the opening two frames and there was so much tension that the game was riddled with mistakes. Taylor held his composure better, though, and opened a 3–1 interval lead. Higgins sat, stupefied, on his seat for several minutes after Taylor had left the arena (he had partaken, as they say). When Taylor returned to resume the match, Higgins was not in sight. In fact, he had decided that he wanted to relieve himself; but, rather than walk a few extra yards to the toilet, he peed into a drain out in the open – not once but three times – before Taylor walked off with a 5–2 triumph and (dare I say) the most satisfying result of his career.

Of course, Taylor's last-ball success against Davis before 18.5 million TV viewers was obviously the highlight. But for sheer satisfaction, I'll bet this was right up there with it. It was played in a white-hot atmosphere from start to finish, with a drunken Higgins telling the crowd, 'Ladies and gentlemen, this is the Irish Masters. Let's have a bit of decorum.'

Taylor said, 'I've never experienced anything like it – even playing Steve in the world final. We were both psyched up, but I was determined to win, no matter how well he played. I didn't look at Alex all through the match. I just looked at the table and the balls. I won it for my mother, my wife and Ray McAnally [the Irish actor, a close pal of Taylor's and an avid snooker fan, who had died the previous June].'

In contrast, the Higgins press conference depicted a man clinging to his sanity like a drowning man with his fingertips on the side of a lifeboat. As Everton wrote: 'Slurring at times to the point of incoherence, wild-eyed, heavy with drink, he regurgitated slights, real and imagined. He was "disappointed for the people" . . . Losing early would give him time "in Dublin's fair city, where the girls are so pretty", or for some rounds of golf.'

But Alex reacted violently to questions from the snooker press, especially those from Armitage. He made as if to lurch towards Armitage, saying, 'He put one on me in Dubai,' before his so-called minders swept him off to his dressing-room. Quite naturally, Taylor has little to say about Higgins these days. 'I can't kick the fellow when he's down, the way he is,' Dennis told me at the 1999 Benson's at Wembley. 'You have to feel sorry for him.'

Higgins saved the worst for last, however, after bouncing into the Crucible Theatre arena for his Embassy World Championship first-round match with Steve James with – it seemed – the whole weight of the world off his shoulders. My new employers, the *Daily Express*, and in particular sports editor David Emery, were keen for me to set the scene on the first day at the Crucible.

Curiously, the championship began on Good Friday, and the two players conspired to deliver a good afternoon's play. Alex and Steve laughed their way through a light-hearted session in which the Midlander led 5–4 after going ahead 3–0, 4–1 and 5–2, only for Alex to take the last two frames of the day. They shared a towel to wipe down their cues and generally filled the theatre with good-natured banter.

Sadly, it all turned sour the next evening, even though Higgins won the opening game to level at 5–5. James made snooker history in the next frame with a 16-red total clearance of 135 and the match just slipped away from Alex. Steve, a fearless potter from Cannock, went for everything and came home a 10–5 winner. Higgins sat, shattered, for several minutes. He was still there as the table was covered and the lights dimmed. Then, just as he went to leave the arena, he ripped off the head of Antrim, the good-luck leprechaun who hadn't been able to work his Irish magic this time.

Worse was to follow. As Higgins made his way into the interview room, he suddenly turned on new press officer Colin Randle, who could not have harmed a fly, and punched him in the stomach. Then followed a typical rambling speech from the twice world champion. Swaying from side to side in the interview room, he said:

> Well, chaps, the current events over the past few weeks have not been very good, this way or the other, so I would like to announce my retirement from professional snooker. I don't want to be part of a cartel. I don't want to be part of a game where there are slush funds for everybody, where the players are mucked about. I do not want ever again in my lifetime to get less than job satisfaction.
>
> If Derek Jameson, for instance, can leave the *News of the World* and go to Sky TV, then there has got to be a place for me in this life. I'm not playing snooker any more because this game is the most corrupt game in the world. It needs to be brought to the attention of the Department of Trade and Industry. There are an awful lot of people running about this world who put their kids through certain grammar schools and you get absolute tossers doing jobs for exorbitant money.
>
> Well, I don't really want to be part of it, so you can shove your snooker up your jacks. I'm not playing no more and it's not sour grapes. It's the truth. I wish Cecil Parkinson and Maggie Thatcher would do a probe into snooker. Then we would actually find out the real truth. The Hurricane does not want to be part of this tripe any more – no disrespect to the Northern people because I like tripe.

And on he ranted and rambled, adding:

> Let's see how you do without me because I ain't playing no more . . .
> I was supposed to be a stalwart of the game, the guy who took all the
> brunt. The kid who took all the brunt is absolutely sick up to here. I
> don't like the WPBSA – the way they do things. They can throw me
> out, shove me out. I don't give a damn. I can't handle some of the
> untruths. I am going to the law courts. I am going to fight the
> newspapers. I have got plenty on my plate. One of the first papers I
> go for is *The Star*, *The Sun* – and what's the other one . . .?

It was an incredible outburst and he must surely have been drinking
something a little stronger than water while at the table. His poor
manager, Doug Perry, issued a statement the next day to the effect that
Higgins stood by every word regarding the state of snooker:

> This was not a spur-of-the-moment action. It was the build-up to
> five or more years of total frustration and anger on his part about the
> way snooker has been run. He feels frustrated that there appears to
> be one set of rules for some and one set of rules for others. Last night
> was not just a protest by Alex Higgins for Alex Higgins. His concern
> is for the game and for the new young players coming into it.

The statement was almost as ridiculous as the outburst because, plainly,
Higgins was completely out of control. He admitted early on in his career
that he hated authority and, of course, he was much more of a free spirit in
those days because there was no tournament circuit. But once the game
took off and he had to fall in line, he resented every moment. Also, he had
only Reardon and Spencer to contend with seriously in the '70s; but with
Griffiths and Davis forever pushing him out of the limelight in the next
decade, and White hard on his heels, he found the pressure hard to cope
with. He was still a big star, still in demand – but it just wasn't happening
and, as ex-wife Lynn says, he was boozing far too much.

In a calmer, more sober moment, he spoke of 'burn-out', his label for the
alcoholic breakdowns and public humiliations he had experienced. 'Burn-
out means I break down – emotionally, physically,' he said. 'I can't move,
can't eat and don't want anything.' He attributed his behaviour at Sheffield
to a burn-out situation. 'I'd just had enough,' said Alex. 'They were treating
me like a dancing bear. They were putting the heat on.' In fact, Randle, no
longer with snooker, merely said, 'Thanks for coming down, Alex.'

Three months later, Higgins was brought to task for his horrendous
behaviour throughout the season and banned from WPBSA events for a full
year. He lost the 25 ranking points for which he had worked so hard to get
back in the top 16. Gavin Lightman QC even considered a life ban at the
tribunal, but a statement from Higgins – pledging full support to sponsors,
referees and the WPBSA – influenced the final decision, leaving on file other

charges of verbal abuse of sponsors and referees. Higgins accepted the punishment and even thanked the board for the 'fair consideration' of his case. He said later, 'I have been cast out – not worthy, not valuable.'

So, no Higgins for a year: a whole 12 months' peace for players and officials and some pressmen. Well, not quite. Barry Hearn, launching his Sky World Masters, a Wimbledon-style event with roving cameras at Birmingham's National Exhibition Centre the following January, invited Higgins to play as a wild-card entry as it was not a WPBSA tournament. This sparked a huge row with the snooker chiefs and players and led to a threatened boycott by Stephen Hendry and many others. It looked at one stage as though the whole show would have to be called off through lack of player support.

But in the end, Higgins did the decent thing and dropped out. 'I am aware of the controversy which surrounded my invitation,' he said. 'In the interests of the game, I feel it would be right for me to decline the invitation.' But he added, cuttingly, 'This has the effect of increasing my ban beyond that imposed by the board.'

Hearn, the smartest salesman of all, said, 'I would still love Alex to play because he is such a big crowd-puller and would have attracted tremendous publicity. But at least he has come out of it smelling of roses.'

And Barry didn't do too badly out of it, either, publicity-wise.

*

STEVE ACTESON
Former snooker journalist, now with the *Daily Star*, who wrote a superb profile on Higgins for *Total Sport* a few years ago.

Alex Higgins can silence a crowded room by merely entering it. Drunk or sober, you just never know what mood he is in, or whether he will suddenly fly into a tyrannical rage over an imagined slight. At one stage I used to get on with him, but in October 1990 I was suddenly in the eye of the Hurricane. He'd lost to Joe Johnson in the Rothmans at Reading and was sitting in the lounge bar at the Ramada Hotel with his late manager Doug Perry and a couple of Rothmans girls.

I was at another table, some ten feet away, drinking, laughing and joking with some tournament officials, including Nigel Oldfield and Ann Yates. Higgins was in a foul mood and suddenly launched into Ann, whose niece Julie was staying at the hotel, demanding to know if the WPBSA were paying for her room. Ann told Higgins politely that Julie's boyfriend was paying the bill. 'What boyfriend?' demanded Higgins. My great crime was to say: 'Well, if you look, Alex, he's sitting right beside her.'

I was sitting on a low stool with my back towards Higgins, who then lost his rag as usual and rushed over, snarling 'Acteson, fucking Acteson,' whipped a bony forearm around my throat and tried to yank me backwards off the stool. I'm about four inches taller and four stone larger than Higgins and I wasn't going to have it. I shoved his puny body away and warned him: 'Don't start on me, or else.'

Higgins got the message and started on everyone else instead. He hurled vile language at Oldfield and Yates. When Alasdair Ross, then of *The Sun* and an old friend of his, remonstrated, Higgins threatened him with a heavy glass ashtray. When Ross understandably bridled, Higgins then screamed, 'Look at that – call the police.' Nobody did, and anyway, it was Higgins who would have been arrested.

The press hit back in Dubai soon afterwards. I'd been out playing golf and then clubbing it with *The Star*'s Dave Armitage, a 6ft 5in. gentle giant. Well-oiled, we got back to our hotel in the early hours. I went off to bed but Dave headed for the hotel disco and straight into a storm. A very drunken Higgins spotted one of his press enemies and, spitting venom, marched up to Dave and went on the attack. But was he angry about Dave's report about what had gone on at Reading? No. What had Higgins in a fury was that Dave had got the scoreline wrong, by a single frame, in that defeat by Johnson.

Annoyed at having a pleasant night spoiled, Armitage told Higgins to go away. Instead, Alex became more and more persistent and then made the mistake of reaching up and jabbing a finger in his face. [The rest of the tale is chronicled above.] At the following world championship, Higgins, after losing to Steve James, punched the press officer *en route* to the press conference and spotted me in the audience. 'Acteson, when I write my book, I won't forget about your Chinese whore in Hong Kong. What'll your wife say about that?'

'Not a lot,' I said. 'I'm divorced.'

TERRY SMITH
Former *Daily Mirror* and *Daily Telegraph* snooker correspondent and the first journalist to travel to the Far and Middle East with snooker.
We were out in Dubai for the 1991 Duty Free event. Alex, who is extremely popular there, was invited to visit HMS *Scylla*, one of the huge warships detailed to keep an eye on the Middle East situation following the Gulf War, which had ended earlier that year. Alex was a great hero to the ratings on board and they let him know it.

I was asked to chaperone him and we were looked after really well. We started off on the lower deck drinking cans of lager with the ratings and we made our way up the ship, deck by deck – the quality of booze rising the higher we got. On the second-lowest deck we had lager in a glass and so on. By the time we reached the captain's cabin we were drinking large brandies poured from a cut-glass decanter into crystal glasses. Alex was the perfect ambassador and was a huge hit with everyone. He was even persuaded to don a sailor's uniform and pose for photographs on deck for ages.

He was in his element, and so was I because it was a rare day off for me. We were being chauffeur-driven to and from our hotel, which meant I could enjoy a decent drink as well. But despite my alcoholic haze, complete terror set in as I wandered along the deck to see Higgy sitting behind a battery of Cruise missiles. I stumbled forward, shouting: 'Don't touch anything,' convinced tomorrow's headlines would read HIGGINS STARTS NEW GULF WAR. All I could see was Cruise missiles being dispatched all over the Gulf and landing on friendly countries. The sailors were in hysterics because they knew the control panel was computer-controlled and switched off, which of course meant Higgy had no chance of nuking the region. It all added up to a brilliant, mind-boggling day out, but I was quite relieved to reach the sanctuary of the pressroom the next day.

People don't always appreciate there is a sentimental side to Alex and I'll never forget when he and Ray Reardon reached the 1982 world final. Ray had just beaten Eddie Charlton in the semi-final and he strolled into presenter David Vine's studio carrying a glass of champagne. Viney said, 'You're celebrating a bit early, aren't you?' But Ray replied, 'No, I'm raising a glass to Terry Smith and his wife, Eileen, who have just celebrated the birth of their first child, Richard.' It was a lovely touch. Within minutes, Alex appeared in the Crucible pressroom and stuck a fiver in the whip-round organised by Embassy to buy us a present.

But 24 hours later we had a major eyeball-to-eyeball confrontation about nothing in particular. And that just about sums him up.

I'll never forget when he berated me over my report from Deauville after he'd broken his ankle. I reported in the *Daily Telegraph* about his brave decision to play through the pain and what courage it must have taken for him to take 16 hops to circumnavigate the table in his match against Les Dodd, which he won. It was probably the best report I'd ever written about him, yet when all the press cuttings arrived by fax from England that day, he sought me out and said he wanted to make a formal complaint to my sports editor.

I tried to reason with him, but he was adamant my report was desperately incorrect and that he wanted a retraction in the paper. I was flummoxed and asked him, 'What on earth is wrong with it?' Alex said, 'I took only 14 hops to get around the table and you said 16.' I was gobsmacked and told him in the nicest possible way to stop pestering me.

Fifteen

HANGING ON

Higgins kept a relatively low profile during his exile, except for the release of his video, *I'm No Angel*, which revealed that he and his great pal and fellow hell-raiser Oliver Reed had enjoyed a two-week binge at the film star's Guernsey mansion. During the spree, the mighty Ollie enticed him to down in one a special cocktail, which, unknown to Alex, was laced liberally with Mrs Reed's expensive designer-label perfume. Higgins, who said he was sick for two days, said, 'I got my own back a few days later when I topped up his favourite crème de menthe with Fairy Liquid and he was blowing bubbles all over the place.' All good, harmless fun, I suppose, and better than head-butts, foul abuse and punches.

Lynn Higgins once said Alex had the constitution of an ox. So it proved when he turned up on time the morning after his perfume-swallowing feat for a breakfast TV interview with presenter Mike Morris, who asked him how much the ban would cost him. 'About eighty grand,' replied a smiling Higgins. 'It was the most expensive head-butt ever.' And when Morris asked what lessons he had learnt from it, Alex said with a grin, 'I'll have to learn how to butt a bit harder.'

Months earlier, he had been ordered by Manchester County Court to stay away from Holly Haise, who admitted to being a former call-girl and whose home he had shared in Manchester for nine months. The order stipulated that he was forbidden from 'molesting, assaulting or communicating with her, or trying to re-enter her home'. She was the third woman to effect such an order following ex-wife Lynn and ex-lover Siobhan.

Ludicrously, Higgins headed for the nearby registrar's office two hours later and paid £15 to give notice of marriage three weeks thence – and paid an extra £42 to avoid the notice, which named Holly as the bride-to-be, being displayed publicly. Unfortunately, he forgot to tell Holly of his plans and the whole thing came to nothing – except that Siobhan Kidd stood on the steps of the registrar office on the appointed day ready to throw confetti over the 'happy' couple. Needless to say, neither showed up and Siobhan said, 'I was going to wish them the best of luck.'

Then it was back to the real world for Alex, whose income had dropped dramatically from the regular £90,000-plus he had earned from prize-money alone. His comeback, following what amounted to a 15-month ban, came at Stoke during the pre-season qualifiers. It was the toughest school of all for hundreds of aspiring youngsters plus the has-beens and never-had-beens . . . and Higgins, now down to 120 in the rankings having been stripped of all his points, and a million miles from the limelight he had enjoyed for nearly 20 years.

While the top players enjoyed a summer of relaxation, Higgy was cooped up at Trentham Gardens with more than 400 others trying desperately to revive his career almost from scratch. His first match, against 20-year-old rookie pro Adrian Rosa, from Cannock, attracted huge media interest. Rosa had lost all his previous nine pre-qualifying events, yet he walloped Higgins 5–0 in the Rothmans Grand Prix for the one and only result of his career.

Higgins obviously hadn't put in enough time on the practice table, perhaps banking on his natural talent to get him through. And how it showed. 'I haven't conquered the fear factor,' said Alex, whose all-round game looked woeful. 'But my game is still there – I know it is. It will come by the time this two-month endurance test is finished.'

His next test, four days later, was even more daunting because he was drawn against former world women's champion Stacey Hillyard. His nervousness showed. He was on the mother of all hidings to nothing and it reflected in his play. Yet just before the off, he gave Stacey a bunch of flowers and a good luck card saying, 'Congratulations. Play well. Love, Alex.' It was a lovely gesture to a kid who must also have been quaking in her shoes. And he even pecked her on the cheek with a touch of the old Higgins swagger.

To witness Alex's second coming another capacity 300 crowd rolled up, which included former wife Lynn and their children – Lauren, now a pretty ten-year-old, and Jordan, aged eight. In fact, Lauren actually presented Stacey with the bouquet. But what they saw for starters in this Dubai Duty Free Classic first round must have been upsetting because Higgins was nervy, edgy and lacking in confidence.

Stacey, regarded as the Alex Higgins on the women's circuit (but only for her quick-fire potting), won the opening game on the black. But when she lost the next two frames her own confidence began to evaporate. She forced a black-ball re-spot in the fourth and lost that as well. And when Higgins fluked the last blue in frame five and cleared the pink and black, the pressure was off him and he compiled his only half-decent break – a 50 to wrap up a 5–1 win.

Hillyard was inspired to take up snooker after watching Higgins in the 1980 world final against Thorburn. She said, 'He was a gentleman from start to finish. He didn't intimidate me at all, other than by his reputation, and I should have made more of my chances. I try to play like him because no one else does in women's snooker, and I've been dubbed the Female Hurricane.'

Higgins, relieved to climb his first hurdle, said, 'I just had a bit too much experience for her, but Stacey put up a good show and had a lot of determination.'

Higgins then beat Bill Oliver 5–4 and had a walkover to reach the last 64; but his new-look image took a battering shortly before he lost to Andy Hicks, the British Under-19 champion from Plymouth, who toppled him 5–1 in the Strachan Open. Three days earlier, Higgins was arrested at Uttoxeter racecourse for alleged threatening and abusive behaviour. He had gatecrashed the enclosure for trainers and owners and, after an argument with top trainer Gordon Richards, insulted two secretaries. He spent the night in a police cell. There were also reports of him being turfed out of a Stoke nightclub and Reardon's (a snooker club in the same town still part-owned by the great man himself). Hardly the ideal preparation – but then, when did Alex ever prepare properly?

Higgy must have been biting his tongue throughout these early qualifiers, but poor Mick Price, the most innocuous of men, received the first volley of the Hurricane's return after beating him 5–2 in the Asian Open. 'He has atrocious table manners,' fumed Higgins. 'He just didn't know how to sit down and the speed of play was terrible. He was crawling around the table.' Price, visibly shocked at the outburst, said, 'He was one of my heroes . . . I suppose it's a bit like "How are the mighty fallen".'

And how! After scraping past Londoner Roy Connor in the Mercantile Classic, Higgins was dumped by another hell-raiser, Leicester's Joe O'Boye, in the next qualifying round after which he said, 'I can't wait to get out of this shed.' In his next contest, the Regal Welsh Open, he was beaten 5–1 by 1988 English amateur champion Barry Pinches in the second qualifying round. Here he launched into another attack, this time against referee Vic Bartlam, who failed to call a second miss against Pinches in the fourth frame. Higgins lost a game he should have won, to be 3–1 down. It drained him.

Afterwards, he lashed into Bartlam, saying, 'I can't believe the referee can make such a ghastly blunder. I'm trying to keep my head above water and I've got the welfare of my kids to think of. This is affecting my livelihood and we might as well be tossing coins. It's purgatory for me being involved at Stoke for two months – then this kind of thing happens.'

Pinches said, 'It was a really difficult snooker to hit and I was surprised Vic called a miss in the first place. Alex was brilliant in his heyday but right now he's not playing well. There is something on his mind and he seems to think everything and everyone is against him.'

Higgins then lost 5–3 to Alan McManus in the third round of the Pearl British Open. But he earned praise from the young Scot, who said, 'Alex is still a force and his tactical game is a different class.'

Alex slipped again against another Scot, Drew Henry, in the European Open. Yet there was a hint of the old style as he beat top Dubliners Steve Murphy and Ken Doherty to reach the televised stages of the UK Open and earn a meeting with world champion Stephen Hendry at Preston's Guild Hall – 'scene of some of my tumultuous occasions, good and bad,' as Higgins put it.

How prophetical, because he was to cause another scandal there in the near future. But before then, having qualified for only two of the ten main tour events, Higgins found himself playing and arguing his way in and out of the World Seniors Championship, also at Trentham Gardens. First-round opponent Silvino Francisco pipped him 5–4 on the final pink, then got an earful. Higgins turned on his usual long-playing record to complain about Francisco's 'unacceptable table etiquette'. He added, 'Every time I got down to play a shot I had a guy in the corner moving around. I was trying to entertain and he was playing at a snail's pace.'

The Ulsterman's moans were overheard by the tough South African, who denied his complaints face to face. Higgins later said Francisco had threatened to fight him in the ring and added, 'I am going to complain to the WPBSA.' Francisco hit back, saying, 'He said he would play me at snooker for £100,000 and I told him we could do it in the ring with gloves on.'

It was another tacky episode by Higgins, but he found himself on the plane to Dubai for the Duty Free Classic three weeks later and excelled in beating Willie Thorne and Terry Griffiths before bowing out to Steve James in the quarter-finals. That earned him two vital ranking points, yet the past penalties still weighed heavily on his mind and he threatened to take the WPBSA to the European Court of Human Rights to contest his loss of 25 points. It was to become a familiar bleat over the next nine years.

'I'm determined to get back into the top 32 and I know there are a lot of sacrifices to be made,' he said. 'But at 42 years of age, I'm prepared to make them. It's an Everest to climb but I know it's achievable.' Higgins spent most of his days in Dubai around the hotel poolside under an umbrella reading newspapers, keeping very much to himself.

With his Preston date against Hendry looming, Higgins took himself off to Glasgow for a B&H satellite event, only to be thrashed 5–0 by Ken Doherty. Again, he vented his spleen on the tables, saying the pockets were like buckets. 'I'm not taking anything away from Ken, but they were like pool table pockets,' he whinged. The pattern was so predictable by now: *Win and I'm reasonably happy; lose and I'll moan about everything and everyone.* The older players had been used to it for years, but the youngsters, while still respectful, were getting fed up with it because it detracted from their own good performances and took the gloss off them.

Having been beaten in Dubai, Higgins knew it was all or nothing against Hendry in the UK, for defeat meant he was back in the wilderness until the world championship qualifiers. He practised hard behind closed doors, but when it came to the crunch he was crunched by the world champion and refused to take defeat graciously. For all his pledges to love, honour and obey snooker's rules and its officials and sponsors, he snapped again – Hendry, the young Scot's manager Ian Doyle, referee John Street and tournament director Ann Yates felt the full blast. He was off and running even as the players waited backstage to be introduced at Preston's Guild Hall. And when Hendry opened a 6–2 lead, it was more than Higgins could bear. He helped empty the players' room with his cussing during the interval, then attacked Hendry with a foul-mouthed tirade just before the resumption, saying, 'Hello, I'm the devil.'

In print, it sounds fairly innocuous, but it appeared to be a deliberate attempt to intimidate his young opponent who went on to clinch a 9–4 win and then suffered another verbal battering. Higgins claimed he said to Hendry, 'Well done, Stephen, you were a bit lucky.' Hendry, never one to complain about anything usually, said Alex was 'obscene and abusive'.

Mrs Yates also came in for her share of bad-mouthing and, according to Hendry, Alex had been 'needling' John Street all day. Doyle raged about his behaviour: 'God only knows how I didn't whack him. This man is a menace. Sooner or later, someone is going to get hurt and Higgins must be removed from the game. Nothing would please me more than to see him kicked out. He's so far down the road now that it's beyond a joke. He appeared absolutely sodden with drink and Stephen was mortified with everything that went on. He simply cannot be allowed to abuse players, officials and sponsors in this outrageous manner. He's a demented, raving lunatic.'

Three days later, Higgins was at it again. He had been invited to Leicester City Football Club's centenary celebrations at the Grand Hotel, where he enjoyed meeting up with George Best, Gary Lineker and other celebrities. But when George took himself off to bed, Higgins punched a resident businessman on the nose after he had offered to buy Alex a drink. 'I'm not having that scumbag buying me a drink,' he said. 'I've got two heavies upstairs and I'll bring them down to sort him out.' Again, Higgins was arrested and spent the night in a cell, but no charges were pressed.

He was also reprieved when his hearing into the Preston fracas was postponed beyond the world championship qualifiers, thus enabling him to take part. But after two early wins he was put out by Alan McManus, having acquitted himself well and behaving himself.

Surprisingly, despite the axe hovering over his head, and his previous abuse of Irish Masters tournament director Kevin Norton, Higgins was invited to play in the event again. He drew a sizzling, packed house to Goffs for his opening match with Doherty – North v. South, a magical night in prospect – and the crowd absolutely whooped it up. Alex, given the greatest of receptions (as was Ken), played superbly in the opening two frames. But Dubliner Doherty, who once sold programmes there as a kid and dreamed of being part of the main show, conquered his nerves and sheer excitement to forge a 5–3 win. Higgins was his great idol and in later years he would repay Alex handsomely for enticing him into snooker. For now, though, Doherty said, 'It was a dream to play Alex in front of my home crowd. I'm grateful to have played in a match to cherish. I've never been under so much pressure and the crowd were intimidating but brilliant.'

I sat in the arena enthralled, watching every ball potted, and I remember writing: 'They raised the roof for Alex Higgins at Goffs last night . . . only for Ken Doherty to lower it on him.' It was reminiscent of the wonderful, tension-packed match between Higgins and Steve Davis at Wembley years earlier.

That was the end of Alex's season, but he was invited to take tea at Buckingham Palace – along with several other famous sporting heroes, including England's 1966 World Cup-winning squad and the 1953 England Ashes team – to celebrate 40 years of British sporting achievement since the Queen's accession. In keeping with his eccentricity, Alex turned up, stayed on his very best behaviour . . . and supped tea all afternoon. He even joined Steve and Judy Davis for a cuppa at one point and sat exchanging pleasantries.

Higgins was finally brought to task for the Preston affair nearly nine months later at London's Law Courts; without Doyle or Hendry present to testify, he escaped with two £500 fines for the verbal abuse of Mrs Yates and failing to show Street proper 'dignity and respect'. It was rather surprising that the two Scots were unavailable, in view of the fuss they had kicked up at the time of the trouble. Higgins had actually laid a charge against Doyle about the comments the 'Laird of Stirling' made about him after the incidents, but it was dismissed.

Higgins was back in action at Blackpool for the dreaded summer qualifiers and though he won through in eight of the nine ranking events, he came through to only two of the televised stages – the UK Championship and British Open. Again, the regular grizzles surfaced, about table manners, referees and playing conditions. But he saved the worst for last and, after negotiating the eighth and ninth qualifying rounds of the world championship, he was blown away 10–1 by Brian Morgan and promptly accused the young Essex pro from Benfleet of taking drugs.

It may just have been Higgy's way of making a back-handed compliment after the heaviest defeat of his 21-year career, but it certainly didn't come across like that. In fact, he demanded they both take a drugs test, saying, 'I don't believe that result. On that form, Davis, Hendry or White would not have stood a chance. It was surreal snooker and I'll never believe that result. I've put on my match sheet that I would like both players to be drug-tested. I've never seen anyone play like a machine before.'

Bewildered Morgan, who practised for years at my local snooker centre in Leigh-on-Sea under the watchful eye of Vic Harris, could not believe it. 'I'm a teetotaller,' he protested. 'I don't drink or smoke and they can do any test on me – they won't even find an aspirin. It's a great shame Alex couldn't just accept the result. I've been playing well in practice and it has happened to come through in a match.' Morgan then demanded a urine test with the official WPBSA-appointed doctor.

The test proved negative, obviously, and eventually Higgins issued an abject apology: 'I made a remark which might have been construed as being derogatory towards Brian Morgan. If it was taken in this way I apologise fully and unreservedly to Brian. I have the highest regard for his ability and professionalism and I wish him every success for the future.' You had to wonder whether another player less well-intentioned than Morgan might have taken the issue further. All the way to court for slander, for example.

Alex's first of only two chances to improve his ranking came at Preston, which had become a blind spot for him as far as rationale was concerned. Sure enough, he was trounced 9–3 by Thailand's James Wattana in his opening round and then pointed the finger at just about everyone but himself. Despite the huge crowds he continued to attract, Higgins simply could not reproduce his old spark and, as was his wont, he fell back on the crying game. His main excuse? – 'I was disorientated for most of the time because the tables were slow at Blackpool and here it was like playing on glass and those who qualify are at a disadvantage.' If only he had been able to have a quiet word with himself, work out why he kept complaining, and do something about it.

His next and only ranking tournament outing came in the British Open at Derby, where John Parrott (despite a heavy cold) thumped him 5–0. It is barely worth recording that Higgins carped again, about this, that, and everything. 'I've been a snooker player for 23 years, so I know what I'm talking about,' he announced. And his hate for the qualifiers surfaced when he added, 'I'm not sure I'll go through all that Blackpool rigmarole again.'

Rigmarole or not, he let slip during an overnight stop with Jimmy White that his South London pal was a *This Is Your Life* subject. 'Jimmy didn't take much notice and put it down to Alex babbling on as usual,' said a friend. 'But sure enough, Michael Aspel collared him the next day during an exhibition he was playing in West London.'

Even when Alex *did* play ball, things tended to go wrong for him. A fascinating Hurricane v. Whirlwind national tour was curtailed following the fifth of the dozen planned shows, when the promoters did a bunk with the takings – leaving the two stars with empty pockets and thousands of fans up in arms.

Higgins opened his account at the Blackpool qualifiers by losing his first match, then capturing a Skoda Grand Prix place at Reading against Tony Knowles. He also secured a UK Championship slot against, believe it or not, Dennis Taylor at Preston. After beating John Giles in the final UK qualifier, Higgins complained of feeling somewhat shaky after spending six hours with ten-year-old Jordan at the nearby Pleasure Beach the previous day. 'We went on all those white-knuckle rides and I had a load of bumps and knocks,' he said. 'When I woke up this morning I thought I was going to get a chill because I volunteered to sit in the front seat when we went on the Water Splash and I got wet.'

By coincidence, I had arranged to interview Ronnie O'Sullivan, the Chigwell kid who was making an enormous splash of his own at Blackpool. (He went on to win 76 of his 78 matches – a phenomenal feat which can never be overtaken because the qualifying system has since been revamped.) Ronnie arrived in Blackpool shortly after Alex had won through. I was sitting in the pressroom with *Snooker Scene*'s Phil Yates, picking his brains about my interviewee, when in walked Alex, relaxed and happy to chat after qualifying for the UK final stages.

'Alex, what on earth persuaded you to go on those white-knuckle rides?' I asked. 'It must have been scary.' He said, 'I had to. Jordan wanted to try everything and it was terrifying.' We chewed the fat for a few more minutes then, musing, I asked: 'Where did Lynn get the name Jordan – was it from the River Jordan?'

We could hardly stop laughing when Higgins replied, 'That bitch wouldn't know the River Jordan from the Manchester Ship Canal.' Our laughter was no reflection on long-suffering Lynn, who was a gentle soul. But the way it came out left Phil and me in pieces.

When he arrived at Reading, Knowles, who owed Higgy one from their Wembley encounter a few years earlier, won 5–1, then reached for the ear-plugs as Alex let rip at an impromptu press conference. Every journalist at Reading knew what was in store and declined the opportunity of quizzing him. But Alex took it upon himself to conduct a conference.

'With the grey walls and the cold it was like being in a prison cell,' he moaned. And he should know, having frequented a number of them in recent times. 'I was the one who brought snooker out of the billiard halls and into these upmarket venues. I'm the one who puts bums on seats and it breaks my heart to see the game degraded.'

He also hit on referees again, but someone should have shut him up. The only consolation, I suppose, was that he was drawing near to the end of his tortuous career and perhaps we were all guilty of thinking, 'Let him bang on because he won't be playing for much longer.' Yet there was still some mileage to be squeezed out Higgins.

Dennis Taylor, who had not spoken with Alex since their Bournemouth bust-up, could not have been more motivated when they squared up at Preston's Guild Hall in the Royal Liver UK Championship first round. Higgins had always held him in contempt since their teenage, amateur days together at Blackburn. But Taylor had improved very much over the years and his popularity had rivalled that of the People's Champion because of his easy-going manner and ability to poke fun at himself, even when the going was getting tough.

On this occasion, however, there was a steely determination about him and, despite losing all five of his previous matches that season, it was almost written in tablets of stone that this was the one he would win. And so it proved. Higgins, still roared on by the majority of the crowd, must have known he had stepped beyond the bounds of decency with his verbal assault at Bournemouth more than three years earlier, and he played as though he knew he would be beaten. Gone was the fluency of his break-building and supreme safety play – replaced with jerky movements on the important shots. Taylor, after a hesitant start, sensed it and took a 6–2 lead going into the evening session. He also won three of the next four frames when play resumed to clinch a satisfying 9–3 result.

Higgins was expected to raise a song and dance. However, he took defeat well, saying, 'I've lost quite well and I'm disappointed, but there will be other tournaments.' But it was a big, big win for Dennis, who said, 'It was like old times. I was really keyed up and it is the best I've played for a long while. Facing Alex really helped me and although it was only a last-64 match, it was almost like a final with the atmosphere out there.'

Maybe Taylor intimidated him, maybe it was guilt. Who knows? But Higgins was able to pull himself up by the shoelaces to confound fans and critics alike in reaching the 1994 world championship final stages. He arrived after a London exhibition the night before, without a tip on his cue, to face Liverpudlian Colin Kelly in the first of the three 19-framers that he had to win to get to the Crucible.

Higgins re-tipped his cue (they really need banging-in on the practice table to bed-in properly), then mixed sensible tactics and safety play with bursts of his old self. He looked a certain winner when he led 8–6, but Kelly won three of the next four to take it to a tense, final-frame decider. Alex won this to scrape in 10–9. Amazingly, he turned the clock right back to his glory days in seeing off young prospect Andrew Cairns 10–5 in his next match with a 'purple patch'; then squeezed past old rival Tony

Knowles 10–9 under the most bizarre circumstances in the final qualifier.

Higgins, feasting steadily on a ready supply of Guinness, trailed 6–3 at the interval against Knowles, then went seeking solace at a pub adjacent to the Norbreck Castle venue. Unfortunately, he forgot about the 18-inch wall surrounding it and toppled over, cutting his left arm badly. It was obvious the gash needed stitches, but Higgy wrapped a makeshift bandage around it, opened the evening session with a 99 and fought back to 8–8 with blood seeping on to the table. Knowles won the next; but Higgins, at his gutsiest, took the next two to reach his goal.

'Those people who say I've got no heart should see this,' said an elated Alex, displaying the injury afterwards. 'I didn't realise I'd done so much damage at the time and I was surprised to see a few spots of blood drip on the table. I was lucky because my cue broke the fall and, apart from my arm, I only grazed my stomach. I'm just thrilled to be back at the Crucible for the Lord Mayor's Show and I'm looking forward to it.'

I was torn because Knowlesy had become a great mate over the years and I always wanted him to do well. But Alex deserved all the credit for coming through although, as with his entire career, bad things were just around the corner. With hindsight, perhaps, he might well have settled for losing.

Curiously, before his triumph at Blackpool, Alex was linked romantically with the late Diana, Princess of Wales's astrologer, Penny Thornton. She told the *News of the World* that she had helped put his career back on track by persuading him the Royal family had far bigger problems. 'There's nothing like the love of a good woman,' she was quoted as saying. 'We're happy together and Alex is putting his past behind him – he's a changed man. He's not a tearaway now and I wouldn't be with him now if he were.'

Penny also claimed Higgins saw himself in a new light after she had spelled out the difficulties experienced by Prince Charles and Princess Di. The following day, however, Penny denied she and the Hurricane were lovers, saying: 'We are friends, but it is a friendship born out of astrological interest and rumours of a romance are grossly exaggerated. I have given Alex in-depth astrological advice. How much of this has contributed to him turning the corner and how much has to do with his own determination is impossible to evaluate.'

So that was that. But Alex was soon in the news again, storming out of a BBC TV studio in Belfast after a row with top Belfast presenter Jackie Fullerton, who asked him about his drinking and his sex life. Higgins was adamant they had agreed to talk only about him getting back to the Crucible for the first time in four years.

Fullerton said, 'I've known Alex for a number of years and he is a larger-than-life character whom people always like to hear from. I was obviously going to discuss his world championship chances, but I felt I had to tackle him about his lifestyle because he is always in the news.' Puzzled viewers saw only an empty chair in the studio, then film of Alex remonstrating angrily.

Three weeks later he was back in trouble, starring in an exhibition with Jimmy White 38 miles from Kildare, where the Irish Masters was being held. There is a 50-mile distance rule during major tournaments, but I personally cannot believe it detracted from the televised Benson & Hedges event.

Soon after that, Alex was barred from London's trendy Tramp nightclub because he was not accompanied by a girlfriend. He eventually gatecrashed his way in – only to emerge minutes later carrying two heavy glass ashtrays, which he smashed, and a pink tablecloth. He then disappeared quietly in a car.

And Chas and Di thought they had problems.

*

JASON FERGUSON
Professional player and a member of the WPBSA Board of Directors.

I was invited to play on John Virgo's *Big Break* show along with Alex and another player and he turned up looking a bit the worse for wear without a cue. Us players are funny about lending our cues to anyone, because they are obviously so important to us, so there was a big panic: find Higgy a cue – any cue! Eventually, someone uncovered this old relic which had a loose, screw-in ferrule and no tip. We were all laughing our heads off, but Alex was quite happy to use it and blow me if he didn't pot seven reds in a row with it. We couldn't believe it, but that's Higgy for you.

Another time, Alex had been booked to play me in an exhibition at Rothwell Social Club in Mansfield, where I grew up. With ten minutes to go and a crowded room, there was no sign of Alex and we were all panicking. Suddenly the phone rings and it's him.

'Could you possibly pick me up at Leeds-Bradford airport please, babes?' I was so relieved that I jumped in my car and raced off to get him. When I arrived, there he was without a care in the world, holding his cue and nothing else – not even a toothbrush.

The exhibition obviously started late and there were a few grumbles. But once he got cracking, all was sweetness and light and he really turned it on that night.

There was another, incredible occasion which had no direct bearing on Higgy and yet his presence was there. My fiancée Helen and I decided to get married in a United Reformed Church in Jersey, just to be a bit different. We love the island anyway and it just seemed appropriate that we tie the knot there.

We went to see the vicar, Revd Fred Nodin, and he was taking us through the ceremony, step by step, when he suddenly stopped and asked what I did for a living. When I told him I was a snooker player, his eyes lit up and he pulled out literally dozens and dozens of pictures of Alex. They'd befriended each other some time before, when Higgy did a show on the island, and had kept in touch with each other ever since. In fact, Fred told us that Alex used to phone him from time to time for advice whenever he got into a scrape.

So, instead of discussing our wedding plans, we ended up swapping stories about old Higgy. We all know about his troubles, past and present, but he was one hell of a player and I'm sorry I never got to play him for real in a competition.

Sixteen

THE END IS NIGH

The biggest test of Alex's return came at Sheffield with an all-Ireland clash against one of his own biggest fans. Ken Doherty, born and bred in the Dublin suburb of Ranelagh, was among snooker's emerging breed of clean-cut, clean-living, hard-practising professionals. (Well, almost hard-practising. Mum Rose had occasion to phone his manager, Ian Doyle, in 1997 before the world championship to say she could not shift her bone-idle son from his bed, even at midday. Doyle acted accordingly with a major rollicking and young Ken went on to lift the Embassy trophy a few weeks later. But that's another tale.)

This time Ken put himself under great pressure, as he had done in Kildare, because he knew how important it was for himself and Alex to get a result. It had the makings of a fine contest, but when Ken went 4–0 up with his usual blend of percentage snooker and fine break-building, it looked as though Higgins was set for an early bath. But, fuelled by Guinness, he fought back from 63–0 down in the next frame to stop the rot. The cheers bounced off the Crucible ceiling and he won the next as well to raise his supporters' hopes. They shared the next two to leave Higgy only 5–3 down; but Doherty was composed enough to win the final frame of the session.

The Hurricane entered the arena wearing a bright-red fedora hat and a cheeky grin when the match resumed that evening. But he appeared to be talking to himself as Doherty extended his lead to 8–4. And then came the anticipated explosion.

Higgins, who had no love for referee John Williams – or any other match official for that matter – requested he move out of his line of vision. Williams refused, saying: 'Alex, I'm staying here. I've been standing here all day and I'm standing here now.' When Higgins told him (to cheers from his vociferous fans), 'It's not an unreasonable request,' Williams replied: 'I'm not going to move. You play. If you don't play, Alex, I will award the frame to your opponent.'

Higgins continued his fruitless protest, appealing to the crowd for support. When Williams asked them to calm down, one fan shouted, 'Shut up.' Eventually Higgins, muttering under his breath and clearly unsettled, carried on, lost the frame and walked off for the interval. Doherty, who remained impassive in his seat throughout the altercation, went on to seal a 10–6 win. It was to be the last appearance of Higgins at the home of snooker and I'm sure that possibility must have been going through his mind when he created his usual diversion.

What happened next has burnt in my mind forever. Sometimes I wish I could just keep my trap shut, because it gets me into so much trouble at snooker – especially when I have been admonished for asking too many questions at press conferences. Mind you, Ann Yates once told me to put a zip in it and I went straight to a haberdashery store in Sheffield city centre and bought one.

Jimmy White bounced into the press conference room after a good win and sat for a full minute in anticipation of questions. None was forthcoming. Ann looked at me and made a circular movement with her hand, telling me to get cracking. I merely put the zip up against my mouth and smiled broadly. Another minute went by and Jimmy said, 'That it then, chaps?' and walked out. I daren't repeat what Ann called me afterwards, but it started with a 'B'.

Next, however, I really put my foot in it with Higgins. But someone had to ask the question. 'Alex, was there any point in pursuing the argument with John Williams when he had made it quite obvious he wasn't going to budge?' I queried. With that, he launched into a tirade against me.

'Alex, you've even lost your manners now,' I countered. 'I've known you 15 years and we've never had an argument. Yet I saw you yesterday in the hospitality room and you never even had the courtesy to say hello.' With that, he went for me again, saying: 'The only Hennessey I talk to these days is cognac – three star.'

I retaliated and we virtually wrecked the press conference. He did go on to say, 'What you have to realise is that, like golfers on the tee, snooker players can be distracted or caught out by the slightest thing. What happened out there didn't help me, and the problem is that some referees just won't take a step back – and that's the truth.'

But the real truth was that he'd used the same argument for two decades, whenever he was not getting his own way on the table. I can't ever recall other players complaining about opponents distracting them. Snooker has always been played to the highest standards of grace and good manners, at every level. Racing is said to be the sport of kings; we have the league of gentlemen.

Alex rambled on and on but I left the room with a tear in my eye because I didn't feel I deserved that treatment. All the same, I had to smile as well, because the cognac jibe was another of his brilliant one-liners. I went on to suffer my colleagues saying: 'The only Hennessey I talk to . . .' for the rest of the tournament. But it was a mere drop in the ocean compared with what then transpired backstage when Higgins was asked to take a routine drugs test.

At first he refused, then launched into a verbal assault against Dr David Forster, the WPBSA's medical officer responsible for tests. He eventually agreed to give a sample, then was alleged to have smashed one of the two sample bottles against a wall. It seemed inevitable that another ban would follow; yet, several months on, he was given a 12-month sentence and £5,000 fine, both suspended for two years. But not for that so-called offence.

The WPBSA were forced to concede by Robin Falvey, Alex's sharp-as-a-tack solicitor, that there had been no suggestion from Dr Forster that Higgins had actually thrown the bottle – only that it had been broken (an exclusive in the *Daily Star* had him smashing it). Falvey also proved that Alex had not broken drug-testing rules because the first sample tested negative anyway. But snooker chiefs seemed determined to get him one way or another and he was found guilty of being in breach of the Rules of Discipline, which states that members of the WPBSA 'must conduct themselves in a proper manner consistent with their status as professional sportsmen'.

Higgins had held up a packet of Marlboro cigarettes at his Embassy Press conference, presumably in defiance of the sponsors, and this later constituted the basis of a charge – but only several months later. The punishments led to a huge legal row between the WPBSA and Falvey, who said at the time: 'Mr Higgins accepts the decision but, as a lawyer, I am confused by the board's decision because, in my opinion, having been absolved of the allegations which were the subject matter of the complaint, he was found in breach by virtue of matters which had not formed the basis of the original complaint.'

I'd left my tape recorder running throughout and retrieved it after Higgins had departed for his drugs test. That night, back at my hotel, I played the tape back and came to the conclusion that he was off his rocker. The following morning I saw the *Daily Star*'s Kevin Francis and, trying to justify my side of the argument, said: 'Kevin, I've listened to every word of that press conference and it was the ramblings of an incoherent drunkard.' He shot back: 'And how did Mr Higgins sound?' Stuffed again, although Jimmy White said the packed players' room, watching the press conference on the Crucible monitors, had enjoyed every moment of our little debate. 'Thanks mate,' he added. 'Great entertainment. We loved it.'

I laughed along with him, but it didn't make me feel any better. The day after Alex's defeat, the *Daily Star* went to town on him again. They paid ex-girlfriend Holly Haise to give the low-down on their torrid time together, and she told the world that she had had to go out whoring to keep him:

> He spent the money I earned on exotic holidays, wine and drugs . . . He told people he was living out of a suitcase and earning peanuts, when all the time I was financing him . . . While I was with Alex, I used to see a millionaire two or three times a week and I reckon I must have had £1.5 million out of him before he died and most of it was spent on Alex. I got involved with him in the first place because he was a big name and it was flash to be seen with him. But I soon discovered he was a skinflint and he even used to nick the money I'd earned from punters – up to £400 a time.

It made for sordid reading. Then immediately afterwards came accusations that, far from living rough for the past two years, Higgins had been staying in style at a Mansfield hotel owned by the wealthy uncle of David Singh, an aspiring professional who hoped to enhance his game by practising with Alex. John Singh said, 'He has had £50,000 of hospitality from me and all I ever asked was that he mention it after his world championship appearance this year. But he couldn't be bothered. He was a wreck when I offered him a home and I even had a snooker room, complete with bar, built for him to practise in with David. But he had no respect for people.'

I am convinced that trouble never followed Alex, or that he walked in its shadows, as the sayings go. I believe he pushed it in front of him like a supermarket trolley full of aggravation and bitterness, and pursued it to the bitter end. Only days after his Crucible demise, Alex clashed in a Manchester pub with a 20-year-old fan who asked for an autograph for his snooker-mad grandmother. Higgins flew into a rage, leaving the kid speechless with a foul-mouthed assault, saying: 'If I fucking signed autographs for every fucking granny in the world, I'd be fucking here all night. Now fuck off.' Then, to the bewilderment of other drinkers in the bar, he returned to his pint of Guinness and newspaper as though nothing had happened.

The 20-year-old object of this abuse, stunned insurance clerk Rick Ashton, said, 'I thought it was a stroke of luck when he came in the bar because my granny's a big fan and she loves snooker. But I couldn't believe it when he just swore at me. I was so upset that someone so famous could be so rude.'

Yet years earlier, when I asked him for a signed photograph for my Mum, Alex could not have been more pleasant, even though he'd been knocked out of the world championship the night before. He wrote a lovely message on the picture – 'To Cathleen with all my love' – and Mum treasured it.

I always found the bad stories about Alex and his fans hard to understand because he always helped me out, not just with my family but whenever fans wrote in to my newspaper asking for photographs and autographs. When my dad, Jim, lost an argument on his push-bike with a motorist and smashed his ankle in the early '80s, Alex was only too pleased to write out a get-well card. I sent it to Kingston Hospital, where Dad was detained for several days, and he was thrilled, showing all the nurses and his visitors. And for all Alex's foibles, he was still regarded as a major celebrity, always in big demand at parties and gatherings. When Marianne Faithfull launched her autobiography she invited dozens of stars – yet Higgy was the one pictured with her in some morning papers.

A new season brought more soul-searching for Higgins because he qualified for only one of the six events on offer to him – the Royal Liver UK Championship at Preston – after being beaten by a succession of kids who would not have been anything better than practice partners for him in the old days. That is not to denigrate them, but merely to demonstrate how far the man himself had fallen. Apart from the losses, Alex was showing increasingly how he had crept into a deep shell, no longer able to see off frames and no longer able to find the fluency which was always part of his best game. A prime example came in his Skoda Grand Prix match against Mark Flowerdew, a useful but hardly frightening opponent from Basingstoke.

Alex led 3–0 and should have won 5–3, but he missed an easy red and went down 5–4. The time he took over nine frames was nearly five hours, which said it all. Win or lose, that would have been a two-hour game in the old days. But at least he reached his favourite UK Championship again and appeared to have found a spark when he won his first two rounds. He beat world No. 15 Nigel Bond 9–5, taking five black-ball games and one on the blue; then Scot Drew Hendry 9–7 with some vintage snooker, including a 119 break and a grandstand 94 finale, to reach the last 16 of a ranking event for the first time since 1991. I was bubbling with excitement because he was showing the world what he could still do. I even started composing a piece for the *Daily Express* in anticipation of him winning his third-round match against Dave Harold, saying how delighted I was that the Hurricane was right back in business.

But I was forced to scrap the idea because he lost to the Stoke potter, no mean player himself. Instead of accepting defeat after a good run, Higgins lashed out in every direction again. He said that 'incompetent' referee John Street needed an eye test, remarked that he would rather have a man off the street refereeing him and added: 'It's soul-destroying if you know the referee wants you to get beaten.' Yet he was not even reprimanded by the WPBSA who, instead of protecting Street – or

Williams, for that matter (the two referees Higgins had it in for most over the years) – decided, on hearing a transcript of the tape, that it showed 'no *prima facie* breach' of their rules.

I cannot recall a single question being asked at his press conference because no one could get a word in as he went on the attack against officialdom again instead of acknowledging that he'd had a good run. I wrote in the *Daily Express*:

> If Alex Higgins had walked away from the snooker table, put his hands up and surrendered, he would have earned so many plaudits from even his fiercest detractors. Instead, having been beaten comfortably by Dave Harold, he chose to knock another nail in his coffin. Higgins played his best snooker in years to reach the third round of the UK Championship but failed to sustain it against Harold . . . then launched into his now-familiar tirade of abuse. Ask a simple question, then sit back and listen to ten minutes of pure, undiluted rubbish – and slander – from a man called the People's Champion and still worshipped by his army of followers. If they, too, could hear his ramblings, they would surely change their tune. Against all the odds, Higgins and his snooker cue appeared to be back in harmony over the last week or so. If only he would let his cue do all the talking.

Meanwhile, the qualifying school beckoned for Higgins again at Blackpool and he went out to youngster Nick Walker in the Thailand Open after a dreadful display. He then scraped in 5–4 against Darren Clarke to go through to the last 64 at Plymouth three months hence. Then followed yet another incredible chapter in the Higgins story. He was pitched against Thailand's Tai Pitchit in his opening world championship qualifier and had scored a century in the 11th frame to be certain of pulling back to 4–7. He was still on the break, having potted the last red and going for the black, when he asked referee Williams to move from his line of fire. Williams, standing behind Alex, refused. Williams pointed out correctly that he couldn't possibly be in his sights and Higgins replied, 'No, but you're in my line of thought.'

Higgins promptly began to sob uncontrollably, and the tears continued to flow as he cleared the colours to record a 137 total clearance, his highest break in 23 years of world championship competition. 'I'll be suing him or the WPBSA or whoever's responsible,' said Higgins after going on to lose the match 10–5. 'The man is incompetent and negligent and doesn't know the rules laid down by the Referees' Association. It's the first time I've been brought to tears by a referee. I asked him politely to move but he was adamant he wouldn't and treated me like a schoolboy. I have table etiquette – but I wasn't getting any space.'

Higgy's hatred of referees had manifested itself again, but this time for absolutely no reason. The frame had long been won and a bewildered Pitchit, who had spent a fortnight the previous year living as a novice monk at a Buddhist retreat, said, 'I couldn't believe what was going on. I've never seen anything like it before. Why did he cry?'

The only other outing for Higgins in his worst-ever season came at Plymouth in the Castella British Open. But it was a short-lived venture because he lost 5–3 after being called for a miss in frame seven and blaming referee Paul Harrison for costing him the match. 'I was happy with the referee but not that call,' he said. 'I was out there playing for my livelihood.'

And that was that for another season, except that he made what can only be described as a 'guest' appearance at the 1995 world championship. Doors and hatches were battened down at the Crucible in anticipation of his rumoured arrival, but for poor Manchester-based Danny Bratt, who represented Barry Hearn's interests in the north, it turned into a nightmare.

Never mind the play – all the talk one evening in the hospitality lounge was of Alex's impending appearance. And then the internal telephone rang. Frank Baker, head of security, called up to say Higgy was in the reception area, demanding to see Danny, who turned pale.

'Why on earth would Alex want to see me?' Danny asked Frank.

'I don't know but he's in a steaming mood, so you'd better get yourself down here right now,' replied Frank. 'You can hear him raving and we don't want any trouble.' Poor Danny didn't know what to do, except creep round to the bar area, out of sight.

'Come on, Danny, you'll have to see him some time so you might as well do it now,' said Ann Yates. He blanched and with that we could all hear the sound of Higgins rowing like mad with big Frank right outside the room.

'I wanna see Mr Bratt urgently,' we heard, along with various scuffling noises. In the end, Danny steeled himself and said, 'Right, that settles it. I'm going to front him up.' And so he did, marching to the door to be confronted by journalist Steve Acteson, master impressionist, in fits of laughter. We had all been in on the wind-up and how no one gave the game away was a mystery.

In fact, the only part Higgins played in the championship was to tell the *News of the World* halfway through the event:

> The people who run snooker have banished me to the wilderness. They have stolen my dignity and the chance to earn the kind of living my game deserves. Lauren is now 12 and Jordan 10 and they've had to leave their private school because I'm no longer earning the money. It gets me down, but they won't sweep me away from the game.

> Maybe I'm too outspoken, too honest or just too stupid, but they see
> me as a threat. They don't like the adulation I get from the public. I'm
> stuck in the quagmire at the moment, but I won't sink. I promise you
> that.

And while Hendry was going on to claim his fifth world title, Higgins was having his clothes burnt by ex-lover Holly Haise after being thrown out again from her Greater Manchester home. He was then arrested for being drunk and disorderly after going on a bender to drown his sorrows. His driver was stopped by police under suspicion of being under the influence and Higgins let them have it with the verbals – both barrels. He was hauled off to the police station in handcuffs and left to sober up for six hours before they could make sense of what he was saying.

Inspector Peter Hulse told magistrates in Northwich, Cheshire, 'We couldn't explain anything to him because he was abusive and always interrupting.' Alex was said to have waggled his mobile phone under an officer's nose and shouted, 'You're not having my fucking keys.' He was fined £150 with £114 costs, while it cost his Manchester chauffeur Cedric Ullet £250 and a year's ban for drink-driving.

Three weeks later, Higgins said he had been mugged at a cashpoint machine in Manchester city centre at 5 a.m. after withdrawing £175. He flagged down a passing police car but was so sozzled that he could not make himself understood clearly. A police spokesman said, 'Alex was legless and it was obvious he'd been on a bender. He was having trouble standing up and it wouldn't have been too difficult to take his money. The officers were surprised he could see clearly enough to punch in his PIN number.'

A friend said, 'Alex can hardly remember what happened. He has a few bruises but doesn't know how he got them.'

Alex, broadening his horizons two months later, gatecrashed a Rolling Stones concert at Brixton Academy and draped himself over a line of seats left empty for safety reasons. He was ushered away swiftly by security men, never to be seen there again. But, as he reminded anyone who would listen, he was attempting to rebuild his career, trying to earn a living – which is why he arrived in Blackpool for the new season's qualifiers having climbed to 44, then dropped to 51 in the world rankings. Sadly, he was hardly even a shadow of his former self and lost all five qualifiers to opponents battle-hardened from playing several matches already. To compound his problems, he had been banned from staying at the Norbreck Castle because of previous trouble there.

His attempt at the B&H Championship for players outside the top 16 ended in dismal defeat as well. Higgins desperately needed a decent run, when the January set of qualifiers took place at Blackpool, to remain in the top 64, which would have excused him two early rounds the following season. But his play went from bad to worse and culminated in a 10–7 defeat by Surinder Gill in the world championship eighth qualifying round. Losing 11 of his 12 matches meant that, for the first time in his career, Alex had failed to get through to the final stages of any tournament. Worse still, he staggered from the tiny chicken-run arena at the Norbreck Castle to be confronted by several reporters.

He was wearing a beret and stank of alcohol, but soon warmed to his usual theme of attacking officials. 'I have 17 charges against the WPBSA and I'll see them in the High Court if they don't answer them,' he said. 'My livelihood has been taken by the association and I expect damages. There's going to be an awful lot of people who'll never grace snooker again. I hope to disgrace the people who run this game.' It was all too familiar and did not mask the fact that Alex could no longer play snooker to any kind of professional standard. He also faced another official rap for remarks made to Lawrie Annandale, who was off-duty, and Alan Chamberlain, from an earlier match.

Cliff Thorburn, Higgy's old adversary whose own star had fallen dramatically, put into words what Alex had been trying to say but was unable to because of all the hatred in his heart for the WPBSA. Both players had been subjected to the cramped qualifying conditions at Blackpool and both had bombed drastically. For youngsters making their way, it was not that difficult to accept the conditions because they knew no different.

But for Alex and Cliff, former world champions who had lived the high life in the best arenas, it was a terrible comedown. 'I just can't play here,' said Cliff. 'This place is so demoralising and I don't like the way it makes me feel. Four days before I left home I played an exhibition in front of 1,000 people. Then I get here, there's one or two people in the audience and it's so tough to deal with mentally. You need to have rocks in your head. It's such an abrupt change, like a slap in the face. I'm not saying I'm too good a player for the qualifiers. I'm just trying to explain how hard it is for the top players to adjust to life here.' No ranting or raving – just a glum acceptance that the good times had gone, probably forever.

As tournament director Ann Yates said, 'Alex could not accept that he was just one of hundreds of rank-and-file players trying to battle through. He expected, no demanded, to be treated like the superstar he'd been and that just couldn't happen.'

Two months later Higgins hit the skids again, and this time it concerned an attack on Jordan's 14-year-old pal. Higgins was at Lynn's home in Heald Green, Stockport, discussing with her the fact that their son had undergone surgery without his knowledge. The friend is said to have interrupted them and Higgins lashed out with his foot. Fortunately, he failed to connect, but the police were called and Higgins spent the night in a cell. He appeared, handcuffed, the following day in court and denied causing bodily harm. Higgins was released on bail on condition that he stay away from Stockport and his ex-wife's home.

A week later he failed to turn up for the court hearing, saying he was too sick after enduring an unspecified operation. In fact, he was in sunny Spain, playing golf and living it up. When he finally appeared in court three months down the line, Higgins admitted assaulting the youngster and was conditionally discharged for a year by Stockport magistrates. At this time it became clear that Higgins did indeed have major health problems and that he'd had an operation to remove a growth from the roof of his mouth which suggested cancer.

'He is not the man he was in snooker,' said his solicitor, Robin Falvey. 'His position in the rankings is going down and his ability to earn is not what it was. He is at the crossroads of his life and his illness is a very great difficulty for anyone to face. He is a very caring, sensitive man, despite what you read in newspapers. He has been denied access to his children, but he has never fought the question of custody because he has never had enough money for a fight.'

Higgins said, 'The whole thing was a farce which should never have come to court in the first place. But it is dealt with and I am happy.'

Lynn certainly wasn't happy. 'What would he want custody for, anyway?' she asked. 'I don't know what he's going on about – he can go to Spain for holidays and all over the place. He plays on sympathies. I notice he wasn't so poorly off that he didn't go to the Derby' (Higgins was dragged out of an Epsom racecourse bar after boozing all day – just days before the hearing).

Just three weeks later, Higgins was involved in more legal action, this time of his own making when he issued a High Court writ for damages against the WPBSA. He wanted compensation for 'stress, distress and mental anguish' and accused snooker chiefs of costing him hundreds of thousands of pounds from tournaments, exhibitions and sponsorship. He also charged them with failing to deal with the 17 complaints he had previously made against them.

Meanwhile, another new season and Blackpool beckoned again. But the results for Alex were, sadly, all too predictable. While Stephen Hendry's Scottish stable under Ian Doyle were signing lucrative contracts with Formula One's Jordan team, Higgins was preparing for more misery. Three 5–0 whitewashes, two 5–1 defeats and one of 5–2 spelled out his sorry tale. And then, in the Thailand Open, after winning his first match, Higgins refused point-blank to play under referee Annandale following their spat the season before. He withdrew minutes before the start, then walked out on his fifth-round British Open match against Gareth Chilcott the next day, when 2–1 down, after objecting to referee Williams. Two days later he withdrew from the German Open, claiming illness.

One of the lowest points of Higgins's life came in early December when, tragically, manager Doug Perry collapsed and died at the age of 51. Doug had been his rock for years – the only common denominator he'd had – and Alex was devastated. 'When I heard the news I was shattered,' he said. 'He looked after my career, but he was also such a close friend. Dougie died on stage doing what he enjoyed best.'

Poor, misguided Doug Perry's glasses were even more rose-tinted than mine because he could never understand why the offers never poured in for Alex. 'He was one of the biggest people in any sport and I couldn't, for the life of me, work out why people were refusing his services to advertise things,' he said. 'I mean, even if he is the black sheep, there must be a market for black sheep. I was thinking of drinks advertising – that sort of thing. I knew about his lifestyle and his terrible eating habits when I first took up with Alex and felt, maybe, I could get a fast-food deal or even a chocolate bar contract. And I always thought clothes manufacturers would be interested: he is the ideal shape to model clothes. But I kept hitting a brick wall.' In fact, Alex did secure a contract to model a range of clothes for Burtons. That happened before Doug arrived on the scene, but it was short-lived.

As the disciplinary offences piled up at the WPBSA headquarters over the years and the Higgins reign of terror expanded from officials and referees to players as well, Doug was still at a loss to understand why people within the game steered a wide berth past Alex. 'We feel like black sheep and that people don't really want us here,' he said. 'I always believe they are very pleased and smug when he is beaten.'

Higgins, at his lowest ebb following Doug's death, received a further setback when he was snubbed for a revival of *Pot Black*, the one-frame weekly tournament which helped launch colour television 25 years earlier. Higgins detested playing in it, yet it seemed inconceivable for him not to have been invited as one of the four wild cards, together with the eight winners. It was a golden-oldie show featuring Reardon, Spencer and others from that era. The WPBSA denied ruling him out because he had two outstanding charges against him, PR Jo Lloyd saying there was 'no malice' on their part. But Higgins declared, 'It is an outrage and an insult to snooker fans for them to be so petty-minded, pretending I don't exist. The programme is incomplete without my contribution to the sport.'

The New Year arrived, and so did Blackpool again for Higgins and other would-be qualifiers for the 1997 world championship. In the old days he would have been playing in a top event like the Mercantile Classic. Not now. Two days before he began his futile attempt to reach the Crucible again, he was booted out of the Pymgate Lodge hotel in

Gatley, Cheshire, where he had been staying for the past 11 weeks courtesy of the WPBSA's benevolent fund for players who had fallen on hard times. Hotelier Dave Moorhouse, a former policeman of 30 years and good friend, had taken Alex's Christmas presents for the kids round to Lynn, who lived a mile away.

But a fortnight later he'd had enough of Alex's foul-mouthed antics and instructed staff to pile his belongings, including cues, outside the front door. Police had been called the previous night following a disturbance at the hotel and Higgins, after jumping on to his bed and crying, 'You can't do this – I'm a British spy,' was later bound over to keep the peace. It was the second time Moorhouse had taken pity on him, but this was the end. 'I wouldn't have him back.' he said. 'I feel desperately sorry for Alex, but I can't help him any more. He needs medical aid.

'He's a real Jekyll and Hyde and when he's good he's charming. On Christmas Day and Boxing Day he helped us serve guests and tidy up. I feared it was too good to be true and it was. He just snapped. I am genuinely fond of him and so were the guests. Alex suffers great highs and great lows. He has sung love songs outside my window at 3 a.m. and even knocked on my door and woken me up to ask if I want a sleeping pill. Unbelievable, isn't it?'

Alex also trashed Paul Medati's Master's Club at Stockport, scene of his infamous black-eye incident years earlier after a punch-up between the two players. This time he lost his rag because no one would practise with him. Higgins, full of booze as usual, ripped photographs off the wall and stamped on them, then ran off with Medati's prized picture (one of himself and John Virgo as amateurs, winning the national doubles crown). 'He needs medical attention urgently to preserve what life he has got left,' said a startled Medati.

The following day Higgins rolled up at Blackpool, took an 8–3 lead against unknown Darren Limburg, swigged several pints of booze, then slumped to a 10–9 defeat which consigned him to the following season's new qualifying school at Plymouth. As controversial as ever, Higgins refused point-blank to attend an obligatory press conference. So, at his own instigation, more trouble lay ahead. He'd hit rock bottom on the rankings and would now have to play for a ticket on the main tour.

Rather than face the snooker press, Higgins opened his heart to various news reporters, including the *Daily Star's* John Mahoney. 'People think of me as a loser who has screwed up, but I can't help what has happened,' he said:

> The powers that run this sport have moved heaven and earth to knife me and make sure I never play again at the top level. Well, they're in for a long, hard fight. It is humiliating for me to have to come to Blackpool and play kids on crap tables in a tiny cubicle. I should be

treated better than this, but the people who run the sport are corrupt. After everything I've done for snooker, this is how they've been treating me. It is a national disgrace and they will live to regret it.

He also claimed to have been the Tiger Woods of snooker and said of today's leading players, 'The game is now slap, slap, pot, pot – and all the players are soulless, boring people. None of them is good enough to lace my boots.' Higgins, who rowed with a security officer, then smashed a photographer's costly flash gun after screaming, *'Excuse-moi, excuse-moi,* this is hallowed limits. Everywhere you see here is the WPBSA's hallowed limits.'

He claimed his over-the-top behaviour of the previous few days was triggered off because he had not got over Perry's death. 'If I've been behaving badly, bear in mind I have lost a dear friend,' he said. Having concluded his impromptu press conference, he told *Sunday Express* reporter Sue Blackhall, 'It's a relief to lose tonight. It means I don't have to put up with all the crap I've had over the last 15 years.' She then walked with him to the car park to see him off, then posed the question, 'Where do Hurricanes go when they've blown themselves out?'

The answer was swift in coming: back to the home of former lover Holly Haise, who took pity on Higgins and, while refusing him entry, allowed him to stay in a caravan parked in her garden. But within days she had turfed him out, saying, 'On a nuisance scale of one to ten, Alex rates eleven. He turned up sobbing his heart out and I didn't turn him away. But he was only here to sponge off me. I was probably his last hope and he's blown it.'

Higgins, even more eccentric than ever, plastered newspapers over the windows so no one could see in. But Holly said he cut spy holes and every time he saw her curtains open, he dashed out, banged on the door and pleaded to be let in. 'The last straw was when my 16-year-old daughter Samantha asked to borrow his mobile phone and he would not let her. He didn't even have the decency to pay back some of our generosity.'

Some of Alex's old humour surfaced when he attended the WPBSA's annual meeting in March at Bristol's Hilton Hotel – purely, I suspect, as a mischief-making exercise. When Bill Oliver, a snooker stalwart for many years, was voted off the board and attempted to say farewell, Higgins bellowed, 'Don't cry for me, Argentina' – to which Oliver responded, 'No problem. At least I won't have to deal with arseholes like you any more.'

Even as the world championship began at Sheffield, Higgins, now with a shaven head, was at it again. This time he attacked a *Daily Star* photographer who found him squatting in the Holly Haise caravan. Peter Wilcox claims Alex lashed out with a heavy luggage trolley and walloped him on the back and head. Higgins then ran off, leaving the photographer bleeding and battered on the ground. Holly, who had discovered him that morning and alerted the *Star*, said, 'He's blown it now. The bloke's a real mess.'

Next, as the Higginsless championship progressed, Alex actually raised some salient points with Stewart Weir – former WPBSA press officer and now with the Scottish *Daily Mirror* – accusing officials of operating double standards. 'Last year, Ronnie O'Sullivan urinated in the foyer at Plymouth and was fined £500,' he said. 'I did the same in 1982 at the Crucible into a potted plant backstage late at night where no one could see me and was fined a grand. And at the world championship last year, Ronnie assaulted an official and bit him. He was fined £20,000 and made to pay another £10,000 to charity. But he was allowed to stay in the championship and won £60,000, and he kept all his ranking points. Yet when I punched a press officer in 1994, I was banned for a year and had all my points deducted. And I was fined £12,000 and banned for five events in 1986 after being asked for a drugs test two days after giving one. I blew up because I'd never failed one, yet Kirk Stevens had to have drug rehabilitation. Why was he never caught if he were tested the same as me?'

Higgins also made what appeared to be another valid point when he revealed that he had received a total of £3,500 from the WPBSA's benevolent fund, and was told he could have no more, yet Neal Foulds, once No. 3 in the world, and son of then WPBSA vice-chairman Geoff Foulds, was accused of receiving £30,000. A WPBSA spokesman would not reveal details, saying, 'These details are confidential.'

But there was a happy ending to the Embassy World Championship for Alex when new title-holder Ken Doherty pledged to hold a benefit night for him at the new, imposing Waterfront entertainment centre in Belfast. And for that he had to thank *Sun* reporter Neil Custis, who remembered Ken had idolised Alex as a kid and asked whether he would like to repay him. Ken thought it was a brilliant idea and, true to his word, played Alex before a 2,000 capacity crowd a month or so after lifting the crown.

This raised at least £10,000 for Higgins. We were told it would be kept in trust for him by renowned Dublin tailor Louis Copeland, a close friend and confidante, who helped put the show together. Alex actually played his best snooker for a long time and got to 4–4. When he led by 61 points in the final frame, he looked certain to win. But Ken stretched his charity only so far and, as befitting a world champion, forced his way through to complete a narrow victory. The crowd loved it. They'd had their money's worth and their old hero was on song again – or so they thought.

Louis confessed, 'The ten grand didn't last long. Money never does with Alex when there's a bookmaker in sight.' The final, sorrowful chapter in the Alex Higgins snooker career was just around the corner.

*

ANN YATES
Tournament director of the WPBSA for ten years and the most powerful woman in British sport at the time.

I worked in the WPBSA press office for years and was virtually chief cook and bottle washer in snooker. During that time I got on really well with Alex. But once I became tournament director he made my life a misery. Every time he lost, especially when his career was on the slide, he'd be down to my office like a shot, railing against everything and everyone.

I knew he would blame me in the end. I used to clear the office in anticipation of the onslaught, but I always made sure I had at least one witness because he had a really spiteful side to him. Alex would store things up in the hope of using them for ammunition when he was in trouble.

I came into snooker through Imperial Tobacco, for whom I worked in sponsored events, and showjumping was the biggest one of all. I was only a kid and part of my job was to carry the tray of rosettes for the guys who pinned them on the winning horses. Alex loved horseracing – and anything to do with horses – and he always used to watch showjumping on telly. He first knew me personally through Imperial Tobacco's association with snooker. But apparently he once saw me on TV with the rosettes.

He never said a word about it for years until I was appointed tournament director. All of a sudden I was just a 'bimbo' and a 'sash-girl', and boy, did he let me know it. I thought he was being sectarian, me being an Irish Catholic from the South and him a 'Prod' from the North. I ignored his jibes for a long time on this matter until one year, during one of our many rows at the UK Championship in Preston, he went at me again, going through his bimbo and sash-girl routine, and I snapped. It didn't fit because it was the wrong way round. They wear the sash in the North and not the South and I couldn't understand why he kept throwing it at me.

I asked him what he meant by a sash-girl and he said, 'I saw you pinning rosettes on horses at Hickstead.' I was gobsmacked. All these years later and he had kept it, waiting for the right moment. I'll never forget what he said then. 'I'm like a magpie, babes. I store these things.' All of a sudden it became clear. I never actually wore a sash, but in the main, most of the hospitality girls would wear the promoting company's sash: that was what he was referring to, and he just assumed I wore one as well.

As bad as he was, as wicked as he could be, I still have a soft spot for him because he could make me laugh. But he would not let this 'bimbo' thing go and it got so bad at one stage that I reported him to my bosses and he was fined for that and a few other 'crimes' which had stacked up.

Alex had the most incredible recall. We'd be going hammer and tongs, say, about his allocation of tickets for friends at the world championship at Sheffield and I'd say, 'Alex, you can have three and that's it.' He'd come straight back, saying: 'How come I had six last year, then?' We would carry on rowing and in the end I'd get rid of him. Once he'd gone, I'd check the records out of curiosity and discover he was absolutely correct. He never missed a trick.

I found it very hurtful because we'd been friendly for years before that. He was brilliant at crosswords and I'd be struggling like mad to do the one in the *Daily Telegraph*. All of a sudden, Alex would peep over my shoulder and rattle off several answers. He could also be extremely witty and a great one for one-liners. My favourite was against me and I still have a laugh about it today.

As I said earlier, Alex had been fined for calling me a bimbo and had been threatened with a ban if he persisted in saying it. We were at Blackpool and he was now just one of 500-odd players hoping to get through the qualifying rounds to make the TV stages, which was every kid's dream. But he still saw himself as a major star and expected to be treated accordingly. Again I snapped. He had just been beaten again and I knew an ambush was on its way. So I cleared the decks, leaving only one witness as usual – just in case. Before he could open his big gob, I jumped in and said, 'Alex, have you anything new to say or will it just be the usual rubbish?' Higgins said, 'You speak when I tell you to,' and I saw even more red.

'Now, Alex, is it my fault, the table-fitter's fault, the referee – as it usually is – or could it be God, for once?'

Higgins just stood and stared, hardly believing what he was hearing. I said, 'Alex, you have one more question and one more minute to ask it, and then I'm throwing you out.' He looked at me in amazement because although I'd always stood up to him, unlike some of the other officials, I'd never actually gone for the throat before. He started the usual old claptrap about taking the WPBSA to the European Court of Human Rights and I said, 'Right, your minute is up, so why don't you just do it instead of raving about it all the time? Now get out!'

Higgins left the room somewhat shell-shocked for once and as he passed alongside it, he bellowed through the open hatch, 'I'm going to Uttoxeter races and I'm going to lump every penny in my pocket on a horse in the three-o'-clock race.' With that he snorted and added, 'It's Bimbo Rides Again.'

I cracked up, but in those days the laughs were few and far between; and though I obviously have the utmost concern for his present plight, I will never forget how he tormented me for ten years. I always used to say, after one of his slaggings, that I'd worship the ground coming to him, but that was just a saying. You wouldn't wish what Alex has got on anyone, but that's not to say I'd want to make my peace with him because he was an absolute bastard to me. He did his best to wreck my life and to a large extent he succeeded, since I knew I was never allowed to hit back. He knew it, too, and did his utmost to provoke me, I suppose in the hope that I'd snap and wallop him one day.

It was always murder when he arrived at Blackpool for the qualifiers. I could have sympathised if he'd been decent about it because it was a terrible comedown for all the guys who had always been in the big time. But Alex was obnoxious from the word go. We were all on our guard when he was due to appear and Frank Baker, our head of security, would come rushing into the office saying, 'The eagle has landed.' That was the codeword and we knew we were in for a tempestuous time. All the referees trembled – you could almost see them shaking with fear – in anticipation of having to handle one or more of his matches because they all knew they were in for a torrid time too. He complained when he lost and moaned when he won. Yet the fans always flocked to his matches in the hope, I suppose, of seeing some of the old magic. If only they knew what was going on behind the scenes.

I had a reputation for being a tough lady. I suppose I was, but I had to be because I was in control of so many people – players, officials and press – and there was always something or someone to deal with. Lots of the youngsters couldn't really afford to be at Blackpool for nearly three months because it was so costly. Even a £10-a-night guest house, plus their food, amounted to fortunes, so some took up part-time jobs like waiting and dishwashing. Others became naughty and quite often I'd have visits from the police about this one and that one. They always gave my name if they got in trouble in the hope that I'd get them out of it.

So it was a pretty hectic time for officials and all sorts of criticism was thrown at us. But we all did our best to make things as comfortable as possible for everyone. I like to think most of the kids appreciated what I did for them, but my reputation as an Iron Lady stuck.

Mind you, I did give Prince Naz the boot one day – and not just to flex my muscles. Naseem Hamed, the world featherweight champion, lives in Sheffield and is a mad keen snooker fan. He has his own table at home and wants more than anything to be a good player. Stephen Hendry is his best pal on the circuit, but he also gets on really well with Jimmy White and Ronnie O'Sullivan and he knows top coach Frank Callan. He loves coming into the practice room at the Crucible and scrounging games with them and, of course, they love it because he is such a big name in boxing and a nice lad as well.

But he turned up in shorts one day and I told him he couldn't come in. 'Please, Annie,' he begged, 'I won't do it again.' I made sure the coast was clear, then ushered him in. But he was back the next day, bold as brass, still wearing shorts, and this time all his pleading could not get him in. I told him to go home and put some trousers on and, to be fair, he grinned and did what he was told. That was the first defeat of his career!

JOHN STREET
World-class referee, now retired after years of distinguished service.

The main problem with refereeing Alex was that you never knew which Higgins would turn up. At his best he was magical, so much so that you had to remind yourself sometimes that you had a job to do. He once said I was the best referee in the world and that he was always happy when I was in charge of his games. Then, when he lost to Dave Harold in the UK Championship after making a bit of a comeback, he went for me big time, saying he knew he had no chance when he walked into the arena and saw me standing there – never mind that I'd tossed the coin backstage with the players in attendance to decide who would break off first.

He was a mass of contradictions because, for all his moods, he could be really funny. Years ago I organised a week of exhibitions between Alex and Dennis Taylor in the Exeter area, where I live. To be fair, Alex was on his best behaviour and I used to go back to their hotel after every show for a nightcap. The night porter was Irish and not what you'd call the full 15 reds. Alex asked him on one occasion if it would be OK for him to hold a little party for 200 friends and the poor bloke was gobsmacked. 'We couldn't possibly let you do that, Mr Higgins, because of all the noise,' he said. 'Think how it would disturb all the other guests in the hotel.'

Alex told him he had these super 'waffle-woofers' which he would place in each corner of the dance hall and added: 'They're brilliant because they contain all the noise of the music within the confines of the room.' The porter agreed, tentatively, that it would be OK, providing his boss agreed. Higgy then gave him an order for the booze required for his little party. 'I think we'll need 25 bottles of gin, 50 bottles of vodka, 27 bottles of brandy, 30 bottles of Irish whiskey and gallons of Guinness,' he said. And how he kept a straight face as the porter wrote it all down dutifully, I'll never know.

The following night, once the hotel boss had put the porter straight, Alex tricked him again with a young Spanish student he had befriended after the exhibition. 'I have the ability to hypnotise people,' he told the baffled Irishman. 'I will swing my fob watch in front of her and when I click my fingers, she will wake up and talk fluent Spanish.' The porter looked extremely dubious, but the girl went along with it, pretended to go into a trance, then started gabbling Spanish at the appropriate time. I creased up and so did Alex. He wasn't really being unkind to the porter – just a little bit mischievous.

I just wish he'd concentrated on his wonderful snooker talent more and kept his temper in check. I know some referees were frightened of him, but I always stood my ground, as did John Williams, which probably worked against us at times.

Seventeen

LAST CUT IS THE DEEPEST

Alex had fallen to an all-time low of 156 in the rankings, which must have left him in the depths of despair. Now he had to face four Qualifying School events, with a one-in-eight chance of succeeding each time. Snooker's hierarchy, having decided to scrap the Blackpool scramble for places featuring up to 500 players, decreed there would be these four events with only 128 players involved. And just about every one of these players was young, hungry and eager to grab one of the 32 places available to project them into the big time.

I would challenge any of the top pros – yes, today's world champion Mark Williams, John Higgins, Steve Davis or even Stephen Hendry – to cope with the pressure Higgy must have been under. True, they would have conducted themselves in a more orderly manner. But they have all done it, seen it and got the T-shirts. Mark and John did trawl their way through the Blackpool qualifiers because they were young, gifted and determined to succeed. But today, with all the success they have enjoyed at the highest level, I am convinced the sheer volume of matches and the pressure of being big names would surely weigh heavily against them.

Now take Alex, shot to pieces and not even knowing where his next bed was coming from, never mind his next win. The last person he wanted to face was Neil Mosley, the former World, European and English champion, making his pro début at the Qualifying School. Alex went down 5–1, and it was to be the last complete competitive match of his incredible career. True to character, he bitched and whinged backstage afterwards to such an extent that it spilled over into a public area of the Plymouth Pavilion leisure centre venue.

Such was the commotion that the police were called after Higgins had been asked to leave the building by manager Dave Cottell. Some 12 hours later, at 3.30 a.m., he was found slumped outside a local nightclub with head wounds, plus sprains to his right wrist and ankle. Higgins, who claimed he had been attacked by a man wielding an iron bar – 'an unprovoked assault' – was taken to hospital for treatment. He was discharged after a few hours and left word the next day that he was unable to play his second Qualifying School event. He failed to turn up for the next two, either, and that was the end of the most dazzling but turbulent snooker career of all. It just didn't seem fair to me, but most of his troubles were self-inflicted, and it was widely believed, anyway, that in his sodden state he had fallen down the stairs of the nightclub and hurt himself.

Boxing is littered with characters who became punchy and penniless through age, carelessness or bad management, but I cannot recall any sportsman self-destructing so badly. And still Higgins could not keep himself out of the news because, with few or no options open to him, he again made his way to the house of Holly Haise in Winton, Greater Manchester, for comfort and shelter. It was not to be. Holly telephoned the *Daily Star* – she seemed to have a hotline to the newspaper regarding Alex – and told the news desk Higgins had turned up and had been troublesome. 'He barged in at 5 a.m. and there was a fight,' she said. 'The police broke down my door to get in. I was so scared that I hid under a table, but Alex left while the officers were here. I was terrified.'

It got worse. Alex, full of booze, returned three hours later and got in through the battered door. Neighbours heard screaming before he staggered out of the house, blood seeping from his T-shirt. Holly had stabbed him, not once but three times, to fend him off. A neighbour said, 'We heard a lot of shouting and then Holly yelled at him to get out. She pushed him through the front door and there was blood all over him. His clothes were ripped and he was a mess. He ran down the road with blood pouring down his back and arm.'

Police found Alex hiding in some bushes in a nearby garden and, after sustaining some drunken abuse, helped him into an ambulance for treatment to injuries to his shoulder, arm and stomach. Higgins bellowed that it was a set-up by the press, the Tory government, the police. After being X-rayed, he was involved in angry exchanges with doctors and nurses and discharged himself. He wandered off, bloodstained, and hailed a passing taxi.

The following day, Holly was charged with stabbing the 47-year-old Irishman and was remanded on bail by Salford magistrates. Ten days later she reported to police that she had been beaten up in her flat by two men, who then ransacked it. Months later, she was cleared of wounding Higgins after the prosecution admitted they faced 'evidential difficulties'. Miss Haise said afterwards, 'I've never denied stabbing him. I felt I had to and I admitted it from day one. But I still love him deeply. I want to marry him and put his life back on the rails.'

The picture of Alex, bloodstained and looking absolutely terrible, appeared in all the papers the following day. It provoked a heart-rending appeal in the *Daily Mirror* from his 16-year-old daughter Lauren, who told reporter Paul Byrne:

Dad needs treatment for his drinking. When he gets drunk his personality changes and he gets very aggressive. But he doesn't think he's got a problem. He's made a lot of enemies and I worry that one day he's going to go too far with somebody and wind up dead. He's like Jekyll and Hyde – one minute he's very nice and the next he can say something terrible. You're on edge with him all the time, wondering if he's going to change without warning.

I can't relax with him if he's had a drink. It doesn't scare me when he's aggressive but it upsets me that he can speak to his daughter the way he does. He can also be nasty to Mum. He has no right to speak to her like that. I don't think he realises how good she is to us and to him. Mum has brought us up on her own and has done a good job. Dad should be proud about the way she has coped. Jordan and I could have gone completely off the rails reading all that stuff in the papers about my father. It's thanks to Mum that we are as sane as we are.

The worst thing is that he only ever wants to see me on his terms. If I've made other arrangements, he gets angry and I don't hear from him for ages. He's missed birthdays, and once he didn't even do anything about Christmas. He even swore at me once and we didn't speak for six months. I was talking about going to college but all he did was talk about himself. I said, 'Dad, don't you want to listen to what I've got to say?' and he started getting aggressive. He told me to go and rot in effing hell, so I just put the phone down. He was drunk and I know if he had been sober he would not have said it to me.

I can just about remember when he won the world title in 1982 – all the lights and all the people. I know he was a big star and I'm so proud when I watch old videos of him on TV and see how he used to play. It's a real shame the way he's gone. There he was, walking into snooker halls bursting with charisma and all the fans cheering him. He really had that extra spark. Dad was the best and he threw it all away.

I was staying at a friend's house when Mum phoned to say he'd been stabbed. I was so scared because, for all I knew, he could have been dead. I phoned the hospital and the doctor more or less told me that unless Dad went back for more treatment, his life could be in danger. I was in a total panic because I couldn't get in touch with him. Then, the next morning, Dad phoned as if nothing had happened. I tried to get him to go back to the hospital but he wasn't bothered. Despite all the things he's done, he's still my Dad and I do love him. I don't want any harm to come to him, but I don't know whether he'll ever be able to sort himself out.

Louis Copeland, who has helped Alex financially for a good while, still laughs at the memory of the phone call he made to him after the stabbing. Louis had a reciprocal arrangement with him during his heyday: he supplied Alex's beautifully cut suits and fancy waistcoats (monogrammed 'L.C.') and in return, Alex would give Louis a good plug on TV whenever possible. 'It definitely helped my business to be involved with such a high-profile star,' said Louis, who took to telephoning him at least once a week out of genuine friendship.

'I called Alex two days after the stabbing when I first learned about it to see how he was and if there was anything I could do to help,' said Louis. 'Alex said, "I've been stabbed so many times in the back that I didn't feel a thing, babes." I roared with laughter. That was the thing about Alex. He had such a sharp mind and quick wit and, though not well-educated in the traditional manner, he was certainly schooled in the education of life. When things were to his liking he was terrific company, but he could be really cantankerous if he couldn't get his own way, and you never knew which way he would be.

'But I've given him a few quid now and then to help him out and he still pops in to see me. He looks gaunt, but he appears to be eating regularly and seems much better for it. But like everyone else who has known him a long time, it is heartbreaking to see him in such a state when you remember the good-looking guy captivating the world on TV.' (I understand, in fact, that Louis has been far more generous to Alex than he lets on and has helped him financially on a regular basis with much more than 'a few quid'.)

Higgins was off the snooker tour and worried sick about his health when he received an invitation from Benson & Hedges in Ireland to attend a 1998 champions' dinner at Kildare's much-acclaimed K Club, then a grand parade of all the winners at Goffs to celebrate their 21st year of sponsorship there the following evening. He accepted, happy to be in the spotlight once more, but the euphoria did not last. For some reason, he poured a glass of champagne into the dress suit pocket of Jim Elkins, tournament director of the English Benson's at Wembley. 'It was a silly thing to do, but it didn't worry me,' said Jim, as popular as anyone on the sponsorship side of snooker and as pleasant a fellow as you could ever wish to meet. 'Within an hour, the jacket had been cleaned, pressed and returned.'

Higgins departed from the dinner early after that little to-do and returned to the official tournament hotel, where he really did shame himself. Higgins was chatting to a couple and asked where the woman was from. When she told him Israel, he is alleged to have said, 'Well, Hitler didn't do a very good job, then.' The husband was livid and told Alex: 'I'll give you 20 seconds to retract that.' Higgins cussed and refused – and for his pains he received an almighty thump in the eye. The garda (police) were called to quieten things down at about 6 a.m. and, needless to say, Higgins was absent from the parade of champions that night.

'It's the worst black eye I have seen,' said one journalist observer. 'The woman's husband was absolutely seething over his vile remark and just walloped him – and who could blame him?' Curiously, the story was all over the Irish papers, yet there was not a single word carried in the popular English national press. But that did't prevent B&H from refusing to invite Higgins to the 25th anniversary celebrations at Wembley the following year. The official line from Jim Elkins was, 'He is not well enough to attend.' But it did not take an Einstein to work out the real reason for his absence.

Holly Haise reared her head again, on TV and in print, as the 1998 world championship took off. *Woman's Own* readers learned that Higgins had given her such a bash across the head that 'I had stars in my eyes'. Then she told TV's *The Time, The Place* viewers she thought he was a jockey at first because he was so skinny – and once he had moved in with her, he always arrived home drunk from the pub, showing his aggressive side. 'But love is blind,' she said. 'It overlooks the other necessities of a relationship. He is horrible but I still love him.'

She also said Higgins slapped her around quite often – and once, having decked her, kicked her time and again. These were the actions of a desperate man who, having been informed he needed a throat operation to remove cancerous cells and that he had only a 50–50 chance of surviving, was living each day in a blind panic. In the middle of July 1998 I received a phone call from Jimmy White and there was a note of urgency in his voice. 'Higgy's in deep trouble and he's worried sick about his kids,' said Jimmy. He then told me about Alex's life-or-death operation and how he kept putting it off. 'Is there any chance you can get him a few bob for his story because he's worried about his kids and he wants a holiday before he goes into hospital?'

I called my boss, Mike Allen, at the *Daily Express* and was delighted to learn within minutes that the newspaper would pay Alex £10,000 for an exclusive interview with Anna Pukas, a top feature writer who had covered wars and famines – the worst sights ever. Jimmy was also well pleased and asked me to call Alex on his mobile phone. 'Jimmy,' I said, 'you know how much Alex hates me following that row we had at Sheffield.' White said he had already squared it with him, but when I called, Higgins said, 'I don't want anything to do with you or your paper. I don't know why you're bothering me,' and cut the line.

Back I went to Jimmy, who re-opened negotiations with Alex. This seemed to go on all day, back and forth, but finally Jimmy phoned that evening to say it was back on: 'Tell Anna to make her way to Manchester in the morning and contact him there. There's just one snag – he wants the tax paid on.' I said he wouldn't be paying tax because he had no income, but Higgins stood firm and in the end, I called Jimmy and said,

'Look, if there's any tax, I'll write a promissory note pledging to pay it. It won't be any more than £2,000, if anything, but I feel it's the least I can do because I've had so many good stories from him over the years, so it's a bit of pay-back time.'

I kept the office informed and was told, after much discussion there, that the *Express* would up the offer to £12,000. Not bad for an hour's work, I thought. Anna made contact with Higgins, who told her: 'I have no interest in talking to you or anyone in the press. Why are you ringing me?' Anna assumed, naturally, that the deal was off. The phone lines between Jimmy and me hotted up again over the weekend and by the Monday it was back on.

Poor Anna had never experienced such an assignment and I could hear the bewilderment in her voice as she kept me in touch with events in Manchester. It was real cloak-and-dagger stuff. She arrived on Monday afternoon to be told by Higgins she would have to wait until the following night. But he stressed there were to be no pictures. Anna explained that it was normal procedure to take a few shots, but he was adamant. He then relented, saying, 'If the contract is to my liking and if the cheque is acceptable, I'll give you an option of a picture at a later date.'

I was beginning to wish I'd never got involved because I was the middle-man. Jimmy would only go through me and Alex would only go through him, so I was being shunted all over the place. Anna kept calling to find out what Alex wanted and it was turning into a nightmare. She told me about the photographs and I relayed this to Jimmy, who said; 'Leave it to me.' One hour later he called to say, 'Alex is as sweet as a nut. You can have the pictures.'

Even as I was breathing a deep sigh of relief, Jimmy added, 'All he wants is another grand.' I protested and Jimmy suggested, 'Why don't you just snatch one or two when he comes out of the pub?'

But the *Express* deserved better than that for the money. I phoned Anna and said, 'Do me a favour. Take £1,000 out of your account and give it to Alex on top of the cheque. I've already withdrawn a grand and it's in my top drawer at work. Just help yourself when you get back to the office, and please don't tell anyone there because it will just complicate matters.'

Anna protested, but I'd had enough. I honestly couldn't afford the money (I was broke as usual) but I was desperate to get the issue wrapped up. Anna, ever the professional, felt duty-bound to keep her boss in the picture – as it were – and to my amazement, the *Express* agreed to add another £1,000 to the bill, making a total of £13,000.

Anna was led a merry dance around Manchester for another day. Finally Alex's long-time pal Doug James, who had been escorting Anna – and apologising for his weird behaviour – took her to a café, where

Higgins went off to the men's toilet to peruse the contract. But the café was about to close so he then swept them off to a Chinese restaurant in the heart of Manchester's Chinatown. It was 11.45 p.m. and within five minutes Higgins had ripped up the contract and stormed out.

Loyal Doug phoned Anna the next day to say, 'It wasn't anything you said. It's the illness. He's frightened and he's put off going to hospital for a week. All this interview business is just a ruse to put it off a little longer. He says it's not life-threatening but it is. I was with him when the professor told him. Three doctors have told him it is throat cancer, but he is in complete denial and it's making him unstable. I've been his friend for 25 years but I'm drained after one day with him now.'

That afternoon, Higgins called Anna again and said he would talk about his illness, then reiterated that he wanted 'two grand for the tax and a grand in cash, up front, for photographs'.

So Anna, weary and perplexed by now, met Higgins again in a pub, where he confirmed he had been ill for a year after having a cancerous growth removed from his mouth 12 months before then. Next stop was the Allied Irish Bank, just around the corner, where Higgins made a dramatic entrance, saying, 'I'm Alex Higgins and I need to see the manager about an urgent enquiry – we'll go into this room.' Some 15 minutes later an anxious-looking manager appeared, looked at the cheque and said, 'It's a perfectly ordinary crossed cheque, Alex.'

Higgins demanded: 'How long does it take to cash?' When told it would be seven days because of the approaching weekend, he said, 'I haven't got seven fucking minutes,' and threw the cheque back at Anna. She shook hands with both men and made her way back to the pub to collect her overnight bag, absolutely bewildered. Higgins stormed in a few minutes later as she was buying a farewell round. 'You shouldn't be here,' he screeched, then berated other drinkers for talking with her.

Anna bought Alex a glass of lager but he eyed it, smiled and said, 'Is it from you or the paper?' Anna, who could not believe it, said, 'Alex, it's from me. It's just a drink.' Higgins hesitated for a moment, then said, 'Well, the paper pays your wages,' then poured it down the sink.

I had no idea what had been going on and, not having heard from Anna for more than 24 hours, phoned Jimmy and said, 'The only way we're going to get him to sit down and talk is if we go up to Manchester in the morning.' Jimmy agreed, and my brother Ginger, who had known him for years, borrowed a Mercedes and was all set to run us up there early on the Friday morning. But late on the Thursday night I had a strange feeling that things were not right. Anna's mobile phone had been switched off and the entire affair had a fishy smell about it. At 6 a.m. I walked round to my newsagent for a copy of the *Express* and sure enough, there was Anna's exclusive account of what had transpired – and all for nothing. It hadn't cost the paper a penny. I sat for an hour or so wondering what on earth I was going to say to Jimmy. He had worked virtually non-stop for a full week to broker the deal for his old pal.

At about 7.30, Jimmy phoned and said, 'Right, I'm all set. Tell Ginger he can pick me up straight away.' I can remember spluttering as I attempted to explain what had happened.

'Well, it's his own stupid fault,' he said. 'We couldn't have done any more to help him.' I agreed, but still felt we could do a salvage job by offering Alex's story to another paper. I wasn't being disloyal because the *Express* already had what it wanted. My previous sports editor, Des Kelly, had taken himself off to the *Daily Mirror* a few weeks earlier, so I phoned, explained what had happened and told him, 'You'll get the story for £10,000 now, I'm certain of that.'

Des, full of interest, promised to keep me in touch with developments – and two years on I'm still waiting. The following day, the *Mirror* ran a rehashed story about Alex suffering throat cancer and being terrified of dying. That would have been OK as far as it went, but the last paragraph stated: 'He tried to sell his exclusive story to a newspaper for a reported £10,000 fee.' No prizes for guessing where that information came from because only Anna, Jimmy, myself and the *Express* executives who sanctioned it in the first place were aware of the fee discussed. And Des Kelly.

I was in despair when I called Jimmy to tell him what had happened. 'Just phone Alex – he'll understand,' he told me. So I did and Higgins went mental. 'You're just making money out of me,' he croaked. 'I'll have you shot the next time you appear at a tournament.' I responded, 'Alex, all I've tried to do is raise some funds for you. Are you telling me you will have me killed?' He muttered something about disloyalty, denied he'd ever said it, then ended the call. My girlfriend, Val, was sitting opposite me at home and said I'd literally turned white on the phone. I was horrified that he could even think of doing such a thing and duly reported it to my boss. Others told me he was always issuing death threats and Jimmy laughed it off, saying, 'Take no notice. Neither of us could have done any more to get him the money.'

But Anna's instant description of Alex in her article was spot-on. She wrote: 'He treats strangers like lackeys and friends like slaves. I never once heard him say thank you to anyone.'

Three months later, Higgins plucked up courage to have the operation and was said to be at death's door soon afterwards. Surgeons in his native Belfast carried out the op to remove a cancerous lymph gland in his throat at the city's Royal Victoria Hospital and apparently gave him little hope of survival. Yet Higgins, if nothing else, is one of the world's greatest battlers. I remember saying to Ray Reardon many years ago: 'It would never surprise me to receive a phone call saying Alex has been found dead in a gutter somewhere.' No malice was intended, but Ray summed him up perfectly, saying: 'He's far too cunning for that. He'll live forever.'

The first public appearance by Higgins following the operation was in May 1999 at the funeral of his great hell-raising friend Oliver Reed, who had collapsed and died after a serious drinking binge in Malta where he was filming *Gladiator*. The service was held in St James's Church at Mallow, Co. Cork, where, by coincidence, the Hennessey tribe were born and bred. My cousin, Nuala Cusack, who still lives in Mallow, was among hundreds of locals who turned out to watch the events in the hope of spotting Reed's film-star pals, but all they saw was a tragically gaunt-looking Higgins paying his last respects. 'He seemed like a dead man walking,' Nuala told me, while another observer said, 'He looked like a withered old man.'

Higgins, now 50, living in a bungalow normally reserved for pensioners in Lisburn, Co. Antrim, and existing on State hand-outs, defied doctors' orders – and those of his sisters, Jean and Anne, who keep a careful watch on him – to travel to the West of Ireland to say farewell. 'Ollie and I were great mates and nothing would have stopped me coming today,' said Alex.

Later, after the burial service in Reed's home village of Churchtown, a few miles from Mallow, Higgins raised a glass of Guinness and said, 'The cancer is in remission and doctors say I have to be a good boy. But I couldn't come to Ollie's funeral and not have a few pints. I don't think it will do me any harm.' In fact, Higgins proved to be the star of the show – the only big name, apart from film director Michael Winner, to pay tribute to Reed. And Alex's popularity seemed just as great as ever, judging by the number of drinks bought for him by well-wishers.

Two months later, Higgins was persuaded to join a 200-strong anti-smoking action group, spearheaded by Dublin solicitor Peter McDonnell, which was taking legal action against tobacco firms. Again, viewers were shocked by his gaunt appearance when he was interviewed by the BBC's Michael Buerk in a hard-hitting programme called *Tobacco Wars*. Higgins said he was led 'like a lamb to the slaughter' when tobacco companies such as Embassy and Benson & Hedges made cigarettes freely available to players at the tournaments. 'I feel nothing but disgust for them,' he said. 'The tobacco companies and snooker were as thick as thieves and in the early days I was unaware of the dangers. Cigarettes have ruined my life. If you are around the product you've got to smoke it eventually, especially when there is booze on the premises. And there was always booze available.'

This was an illogical argument because Alex had always smoked, long before either company became involved in snooker. And why is it that Steve Davis, John Parrott, Stephen Hendry and the vast majority of players have never smoked – or resorted to booze at tournaments? I'm not being hypocritical here, because everyone knows I enjoy a good drink. But I certainly would not blame the sponsors.

Despite his dreadful condition, Alex was seen smoking 'long roll-ups' and drinking cider in a backstreet Dublin bar a few weeks after his TV appearance. He was also playing pool for £10 a frame. There were no shortages of takers and Alex cleaned up to the tune of £380. Two days later Higgins, said to be taking 38 tablets each morning to boost his recovery from the operation, failed to show for a planned TV interview with Clive Everton at the RTE studios in Dublin, leaving word that he was confined to bed.

Shortly after that, however, he was discovered dossing in a Manchester billiard hall, using the holdall containing his belongings as a pillow. 'He looked so sick and frail that a gust of wind would knock him over,' said one player at the Crucible, in Derby Street. 'I was so upset that I telephoned the WPBSA at Bristol to tell them the state he was in. He made enemies but gave pleasure to millions. They should take pity on him now.'

Holly Haise read about his latest plight and told the *Daily Star* she wanted to offer Alex a roof over his head 'with no strings attached'. She added: 'I can't let him sleep out on the streets. We've been through too much together for that. I can't stand around and watch him kill himself. It broke my heart when a friend told me Alex was really down and out with nowhere to go. He used to have loads of people to put him up, but he has lost most of them and is desperate.'

Needless to say, Higgins never got in touch.

Brough Scott tracked Higgins down to Lisburn in December 1999 for a *Sunday Telegraph* feature and arranged to meet him in his local pub, the Hertford Arms, where Alex spends a lot of his time watching horseracing broadcasts. Scott, steeped in racing himself, wrote, 'You notice the jeans hanging emptily on bamboo legs and Higgins, who spoke of having 43 treatments for cancer, says, "Yes, I could be a bit heavier", before embarking on his regular tirade against the WPBSA, and the [hoped-for] court case in which he expects to win a lottery-style pay-out.' But Higgins, polite as anything, spoiled the mood for Brough when he turned on the local bookmaker and demanded a 'charity bet'. Brough observed: 'You remember the phrase, "could start a fight in an empty lift".'

Jimmy White told Brough, 'He looks desperately thin. He never seems to eat anything, yet he got himself over to the States for Lennox Lewis's fight last month (where he bumped into Dennis Taylor, of all people) and his health isn't really up to it. Actually, I feel he has got a bit of a case against the WPBSA and, with the new board, I feel they should sit down and see if they can settle something.'

The year 2000 saw Higgins collapsing, apparently with dehydration, after being invited to the Middle East for the Dubai World Cup horseracing event during the first week of the Embassy World Championship. He stayed a while longer hoping to obtain some coaching work; but frankly, he was in no fit state to embark on that exercise, because he was wafer-thin and ill. He said he had run out of medication and was actually being rushed back to England when he collapsed at Dubai airport and was taken to hospital, dehydrated (his condition was also said to have been booze-related). Alex was placed on a saline drip and hooked up to a heart monitor. A few days later he was given the all-clear to travel and quickly dispelled rumours that his demise was imminent.

In fact, he was back in the news only months later in Manchester, allegedly pouring the slops of other people's drinks into his own glass. The mighty had fallen, and how. He had been trading on sympathy for some years. And that sympathy was almost threadbare by this time.

Yet the Ulsterman was able to make another public appearance – sadly at the July funeral of another pal, Paul Young, singer with Sad Café then Mike and the Mechanics, who had a heart attack at just 53. 'I had to come because we'd known each other for 15 years and we used to go out all the time,' said Alex, after the service at Altrincham Crematorium in Greater Manchester. Higgins, who looked even more gaunt and more haggard than ever, added, 'He was a really great fellow and he enjoyed life. I wouldn't have missed his funeral for anything. I was terribly upset by his death and had to pay my last respects. My motto is the same as Paul's – "Live and let die".'

*

LYNN HIGGINS
Married to Alex for six years and mother of his two children.
I wish I'd never had that first drink with him. Deep down, I always knew he was a madman and I can't fathom out why I kept going back to him. But I kept on trying, for the sake of our children. He was a real Jekyll and Hyde – one minute he could be a loving, caring father and husband and the next a drunken wreck. Deep down, I believe he always wanted to be a bachelor because most times he was a lousy lover, husband and father.

Only hours after Jordan was born, I was told in hospital that Alex was out celebrating with a girlfriend, and that was the beginning of the end. I took a long, hard look at my life and realised I wanted something better because his love was for horses and booze and not for us. What sort of father would roll home drunk and sit up all night watching videos of horse races, then sleep all day when the kids wanted to play?

When I had the children I put them first, naturally, and he was pushed into the background a little and couldn't cope with it. I didn't want the children to be brought up in an atmosphere like that because I had a good home life when I was a child, and I wanted the same for my two.

He bought the big house in Prestbury to charm me back, but material things didn't matter to me – it was happiness that counted – and it made no difference. We just seemed to drift far apart and I wasn't happy. So much had happened that I couldn't forgive him, and I kept throwing things back at him. It was just hopeless and he soon became little more than a lodger at home. He thought that I, with two kids, would be happy to stay at home as the innocent housewife and mother. But he was wrong.

It was the drinking that split us up, though. I couldn't cope with it because I don't drink much myself. I just hated it, so he'd hide it from me all the time because he knew it annoyed me. When it became obsessive, he'd say, 'I'm just going for a walk,' but I knew he'd be in the Bull's Head pub just across the road. He drank vodka because he'd been told it didn't leave a smell on the breath, but I knew he'd been drinking and I couldn't cope with it any more because it would turn him really nasty. I could cope with the arguing but I couldn't cope with him smashing things.

Just before Christmas in 1985 we had invited some friends round, but Alex had been watching horseracing on the telly all afternoon and he'd been drinking. There was no way I would let my friends come round and drink all evening and watch him change personality, so I said, 'No, they're not coming.' He stormed out to the pub and got back about 11 p.m. He started saying, 'This is what I think of your gold cutlery,' and began throwing it around; 'this is what I think of your Waterford Crystal.' Everything started going through windows, including a TV set, so I locked Lauren, Jordan, the au pair and myself inside a bedroom.

He was trying to hammer through the really thick door with a golf club and I made the children hide under the bed. It was horrific for three hours until he decided to lock the gate. He went outside and I called my mother and told her to phone the police. My Dad arrived and the police came and it was just awful. Really upsetting. That was when I went back to my Mum and Dad with the kids. There was a court case later and he was bound over to keep the peace.

But he was a brilliant actor, so pitiful, especially in the role of a broken man. He would call round to my parents and cry and plead with me to go back. On reflection, I'm surprised it took me so long to realise I had to get away from Alex. Finally, he agreed to buy me a detached house near where my Mum and Dad lived, but then he would land on my doorstep at all hours, phone me from wherever he was playing and even burst into restaurants where I would be eating with friends.

Even after years of suffering this kind of behaviour, I obviously don't wish him any harm because he is still the father of our children. But after all this time, I'd just like to get on with my life. Once, after we'd split for the final time, he suspected I had a boyfriend and threatened to kill me. He was raging, saying, 'I'll kill you and him if I find out it is true.' He looked wild, like someone possessed. My Mum and Dad could have had him jailed several times in the early years after our split, but I always stopped them from pressing charges. He even attacked my Dad once, but we decided to leave well alone.

Yet Lauren was the real driving force behind him winning the world title back in 1982. If he got really stressed out he'd sit with her and she'd tell him, 'Win Daddy, win Daddy.' It had an amazing effect because he'd get a second wind and start winning again.

For all our problems, and especially his these days, I know he loves the kids and they love him. He's always asking about them and I know he misses them.

KEN DOHERTY
1997 world champion and the first from the Republic of Ireland.

Alex did so much for snooker and it is heartbreaking to see him down and out now. Forget all the bad things about him. He was a genius and I wish his great talent could have been appreciated by today's young snooker audiences. For many fans, especially the Irish, he will always be the No. 1 man.

I keep reading that he's potless, but he should be a multi-millionaire because of what he did for the sport and I believe he should be invited along to the world championship every year in recognition of his achievements. Footballers have testimonials at the end of their playing days and I don't see any reason why we can't make Alex as comfortable as possible, financially, at least.

I feel so sad for him. He is one of the all-time greats and an inspiration to everyone who plays snooker. He's the only reason I took it up and he should be given a pension to keep him afloat. I would love to see our governing body do something. I like to think I did my little bit for him when we staged the testimonial after I won the world title, and I'd be first in the queue to help again. As a kid, I sold programmes at the Benson & Hedges Irish Masters at Goffs and the highlight was always when Alex played. The crowd used to go mad when he appeared and my dream was to play against him there.

That dream came true in 1992 and it was pretty scary at first. Alex came out and played two brilliant frames and my heart began to sink. But I steadied myself and went on to beat him. It was an incredible night and I've never experienced such an atmosphere. I'd already faced him in the first round of the 1990 world championship and although he had an almighty row with the referee, he was as good as gold with me. When a reporter asked me whether it had put me off I just said, 'That's Alex for you and we expect it. But it certainly didn't affect me.'

I just wish he'd had a think about what he was going to say before opening his mouth because a lot of the time he just blurted things out he didn't really mean. But you ask anyone, especially in Ireland – he'll always be our No. I snooker hero. Nearly 300,000 people turned out to welcome me home when I won the world title – even more than the turn-out for Alex Ferguson's homecoming Treble-winning Manchester United two years later. But Alex never, ever experienced anything like that.

I even got to parade the trophy around Old Trafford the Saturday after I won it in front of a 50,000 crowd at half-time, and they gave me a Mexican wave all around the ground. Then, when the Republic were playing a friendly against Liechtenstein at Lansdowne Road, I was invited to take the trophy along. I'd have been going anyway with my mates and it was such a surprise. I couldn't believe it was happening to me, yet I can't help feeling that's exactly how Alex should have been fêted, especially when he won in 1982.

However, a measure of his popularity came when I took part in a benefit match for him at The Waterfront in Belfast. More than 2,000 packed in to watch our nine-frame clash, which turned out to be a mini-classic. Alex lost 5–4, but he played some cracking snooker. It wasn't the Hurricane of old, the one we always pretended to be when we were learning the game. But Alex must have put in some serious practice because he looked the business again and the crowd loved it.

JIMMY WHITE
The Whirlwind, six-times world championship runner-up and never a winner, yet the man who has taken over as People's Champion from Alex and is the Hurricane's closest friend.

Many people are under the impression that I started playing snooker because of Alex, which is not the case. I'd been playing for a few years when he came to London for an exhibition and I had a frame with him. I was only 14 and Alex told my Dad, Tommy, that he liked the way I played.

From that night, although I was a good few years younger, we struck up a kind of friendship and whenever Alex was working down south, he'd phone and ask if I wanted to play a few frames against the locals during the interval. Did I? Alex was huge then and to be asked to play on the same bill was a dream come true. Dad would drive me in his old van to wherever – Southend, Croydon, anywhere – and I'd always win a tenner or so while Alex was relaxing during his hour-or-so break. I was pretty nippy around the table anyway, but I may well have shifted up a gear to get in as many frames as possible.

He never attempted to teach me how to play, but there is no doubt I learned all about technique from watching him in action. He gave me great encouragement in those early days and said I played the game the same way he did – nice and open – which was flattering to say the least. But Alex is a Jekyll-and-Hyde character, probably the most complex in a sport that was full of characters in the '70s and '80s.

I've probably been as close to Alex as anyone, yet I have no idea of the private hell he must have put himself through, the demons which must have tormented him throughout his highly-strung life. As I started making my way through the amateur ranks, our paths seemed destined to intertwine. Once I had won the World Amateur Championship at 18, I turned pro. Yet our first big meeting was in the world championship semi-finals at Sheffield in 1982. I took a 15–14 lead and was almost certain I had made it all the way to the final when I opened a 59–0 gap in the next frame. Even when I missed the shot that would have put me through, the balls were spread so awkwardly that I didn't believe he could dish up.

But Alex pulled off the best clearance of his life to pip me on the black. I might just as well have been at the races in the final-frame decider because my head was in a jamjar and I could only sit and watch dumbstruck as Alex finished me off. It was a terrific comeback, but after accepting the enormous cheers of the crowd, his first thought was for me and he gave me a cuddle as if to say sorry in front of everyone. That night an even stronger bond developed between us and, as he says, we became soul brothers – and have been ever since.

That's not to say we've always seen eye to eye. My daughter Lauren was born about six weeks before Lynn produced their baby and, to my astonishment, they called her Lauren as well. Soon after that, Alex was staying over one night and we were talking about our babies and what a wonderful feeling it was to be a dad. All of a sudden, Alex said, 'James, do you think you could change the name of your baby, please?' I cracked up, but my wife Maureen gave him a piece of her mind, although she saw the funny side of it eventually. Years later, I was telling the story to a reporter and Maureen said I shouldn't because it sounded as though we were having a go at Alex.

But Lauren, who was 11 and had never heard the tale, said, 'Mum, it's really funny and Alex won't mind.'

I've had plenty of heartache in my life over the past few years and poor old Higgy is going through it himself right now. He came to see me at Reading when I was playing for England during the 2000 Nations Cup team event featuring the home countries, which we won. He didn't look too bad.

There was a terrible picture of him in the *Daily Mirror* a few months later and John Hennessey telephoned me to say how shocked he was at Alex's appearance. But I reassured him Higgy looked a lot better than the photograph.

Some weeks later Alex came across with me to Jersey, where I was playing, and he seemed quite perky. Louis Copeland, his tailor pal in Dublin, reckons he has started to eat proper meals, so we are all praying he'll be OK. But I do feel the WPBSA could be doing a bit more to help him when you consider how much he did to popularise snooker.

Eighteen

IF ONLY

If only . . . The two words should be emblazoned on the brain of Alex Higgins. If only he hadn't butted a tournament director in 1986 and been fined £12,000 and banned for five tournaments. If only he had not been seduced, financially, by unscrupulous manager Howard Kruger. If only he hadn't threatened Dennis Taylor so horribly. If only, weeks later, he hadn't punched a harmless press officer . . . He would have been sitting happily in the world rankings at No. 14 with never a hint of the gruelling, tormenting qualifiers at Blackpool. He would almost certainly have been guaranteed at least £30,000 without ever taking his cue out of its case in the 1994–95 season and maybe, just maybe, he would have flourished again and his health would not have collapsed so drastically.

Higgins had everything to gain by behaving himself after losing to Steve James in the 1994 world championship first round. Yes, the defeat was hard to bear, yet he'd achieved his objective by climbing back into the élite bracket, and there were signs that his game was actually coming together again. But booze again played a major part in his downfall. He really needed the heavy hand of Del Simmons to calm him down before he left his dressing-room for the press conference that night, especially as he had already been informed he was wanted for drug-testing.

Sadly Del, never frightened to threaten him with 'a slap' if he got out of hand, had died a few years earlier. And Doug Perry, manager until his own untimely death, simply did not have the strength of will to impose himself on the Hurricane, who was completely out of control, like a runaway train, and refusing to admit he ever had a problem – never considering it might just have been his fault on the odd occasion. No, with Alex, someone else was always to blame. If only he could have approached that vital flaw in his make-up, I am convinced he would have scaled far greater heights.

As it is, he goes down as a genius, albeit flawed, with only six major titles to his credit. Yet he still retains the affection of millions who, like me, remember the sheer excitement and adrenaline he brought to the game. The 17 charges he pressed against former WPBSA officials have been erased, according to association press officer Bruce Beckett, who also confirmed that Alex's two outstanding High Court actions against the WPBSA had expired. He is at liberty to resurrect them, but you get the impression that Alex would rather continue his crusade, railing about the injustice of it all, than accept a pay-off.

Higgins once wrote, 'To the outside world I'm a hell-raiser, a temperamental genius always on the look-out for trouble. Well, that's not the real me. My family think they are reading about a stranger when they pick up the newspapers. Underneath it all, I am a shy placid person, no different from when I was a kid.'

Alex Clyde, former *London Evening Standard* snooker correspondent, summed up in a nutshell exactly what Higgins brought to the sport when he wrote: 'When Alex was around there was always a story – sometimes heart-warming, sometimes bizarre, sometimes outrageous but never dull. There was danger in the air. The press loved it and nobody dozed off.'

Claude Abrams, respected editor of *Boxing News*, the weekly trade paper which is a must for all fighters, pigeon-holed him when he compared Mike Tyson with Higgins. Claude, also a big snooker fan, said, 'Their behaviour towards authority and opponents is so similar and you can see both of them going down the same road . . .' He did not need to spell out the rest of his thought process.

Many people have tried to help Alex over the years – especially Louis Copeland of late. But the one constant factor in his turbulent life has been Jimmy White, the chirpy South Londoner who modelled his game on that of Higgins, then refined it and added his own classy touches. Mind you, Jimmy could well have said 'if only' a good few times throughout his own colourful, mischievous career after a heartbreaking 16–15 defeat by Higgins in the 1982 semi-final. But he has never dwelled publicly on the past. Not even on those six losing world finals.

Even today, having experienced a good few Higgins broadsides in his time, White shows only affection and concern for the Hurricane: 'He was the greatest and people should be taking care of him, whatever his problems and whatever pain he has caused to himself and others.'

Millions of Alex Higgins admirers will surely echo that sentiment.